MEMORIES OF OUR FUTURE

MEMORIES OF OUR FUTURE

SELECTED ESSAYS 1982–1999

Ammiel Alcalay

Introduction by Juan Goytisolo

CITY LIGHTS BOOKS
SAN FRANCISCO

MEMORIES OF OUR FUTURE
Copyright © 1999 by Ammiel Alcalay
Introduction © 1999 by Juan Goytisolo
Translation © 1999 by Peter Bush
All Rights Reserved
10 9 8 7 6 5 4 3 2 1

Cover design by DiJit
Book design by Robert Sharrard
Typography by Harvest Graphics

Some of these texts have appeared in the following publications: *Afterimage, Aperion, Chimera, Discourse and Palestine, al-Fajr, For Palestine, Found Object, Grand Street, In Defense of Mumia, Jerusalem Post Magazine, Jewish Social Studies, Jews and Other Differences, Kol Ha'Ir, al-HaMishmar, Lusitania, Meditteraneans, Middle East Report, The Nation, News From Within, New York Times Book Review, Paper Air, Shofar, Svijet,* and the *Village Voice Literary Supplement.*

Library of Congress Cataloging-in-Publication Data

Alcalay, Ammiel.
    Memories of our future / Ammiel Alcalay.
        p.   cm.
    ISBN 0-87286-360-3 (pbk.   :   alk. paper)
    1. Sephardim—Intellectual life.   2. Middle East—Intellectual life.   3. Arab-Israeli
conflict.   4. Palestinian Arabs—Intellectual life.   5. Sarajevo (Bosnia and
Hercegovina)—History—Siege.
    1992–1996.   I. Title.
    DS134.A66   1999   99-34696
    814'.54—dc21   CIP

City Lights Books are available to bookstores through our primary distributor: Subterranean
Company, P. O. Box 160, 265 S. 5th St., Monroe, OR 97456. 541-847-5274. Toll-free orders
800-274-7826. FAX 541-847-6018. Our books are also available through library jobbers and
regional distributors. For personal orders and catalogs, please write to City Lights Books,
261 Columbus Avenue, San Francisco, CA 94133. Visit our web site: www.citylights.com

CITY LIGHTS BOOKS are edited by Lawrence Ferlinghetti and Nancy J. Peters and
published at the City Lights Bookstore, 261 Columbus Avenue, San Francisco, CA 94133

For months, while we wandered through Sarajevo—putting ourselves up in the empty apartments of strangers—I never stopped silently hoping that what mattered most might somehow be miraculously saved. . . I was kidding myself. I had underestimated the ghastly persistence of that barbaric hatred of memory, of civilization, that had burned down the Vijećnica and murdered the paintings. One day the news arrived: they burned down your library. I believed it, but at the same time I couldn't. I did everything I could to find the whole truth of what had happened. I managed to piece it together, after months of searching out and questioning unrelated and disinterested eyewitnesses. Not only was everything burned, but an entire ritual had been performed for the occasion. Armed men forced people in the neighborhood out of their apartments, like at a performance, to watch . . .

IVAN LOVRENOVIĆ, *Ex Tenebris: Sarajevo Diary*

Somewhere on the middle floor, when my neighbor sees me, he opens the door and starts cleaning his cold gun. . . but the poor man does not know that I, too, have the right to live.

ALI PODRIMJA, *Smile in The Cage*

For a long time now
I have felt ashamed of my freedom
Every day I pull a stake down off your fence
and burn it for warmth.

LULJETA LLESHANAKU, *"Electrolytes"*

Contents

Local Politics: The Background as Foreword

The tensions between poetic or artistic and theoretical discourses are nothing new and have been with us, in one form or another, for a long time. On a very local level, within the current American context, this tension manifests itself in what is essentially a somewhat rarified labor issue: theoretical language, in the guise of an ahistorical and generally monolinguistic rendition of postmodernism, has become the gate-keeper through which entrance into the academic employment office is gained. Poets and artists have, in far too many cases, either succumbed to a simple-minded ignorance of the value of theoretical possibilities or attempted to emulate the worst excesses of that discourse in order to gain entrance. The compartmentalization of roles in American life, and particularly American cultural life, is a phenomenon that not enough writers, in particular, have resisted with sufficient force or imagination.

In general, options are quite circumscribed and movement seems either circular or vertical. In the circular model, writers remain primarily concerned with their own work and that of other writers in a set of circles that diminishes or increases according to narrower or wider acceptance and recognition. In the vertical model, many have sought a safe haven in academia, primarily as a means of sustenance, but also with the desire to create changes in the existing or dominant approaches to things. Many of these efforts have been successful but only within the very limited terms already set by the institutions themselves. "Storming" the MLA convention by being featured within its confines does not represent a model of either intellectual alertness or cultural resistance whose effects might eventually resonate or be felt in a larger context.

In between the circular and the vertical, there remains a sphere within which the too often designated or self-designated "public intellectual" can maneuver. The subjects revolving in this sphere, however, hardly ever meet any objects of resistance in the form of people or realities that might disarm their confidence in the ability to speak or write about things they may know little or next to nothing about. The ability of increasingly ungrounded theories or conjectures to infiltrate and overtake various aspects of the culture industry has a lot to do with the fact that, unlike "us," people under one form of siege or another have the luxury *not* to, in the words of the Slovenian poet and cultural critic Aleš Debeljak, "glamorize the illusion of unfettered subjectivity, released from reason's focus." In places where there is at least some sense of a consciousness of a time of collective historical crisis, "the human ability to perform rational and moral judgements"[1] can play a very different role than it has come to represent in our politically correct environment, where limited allocation too often takes the place of a truer democratic access to power and resources. In most of the rest of the world outside North America, historical conditions have made the stakes of public utterance a bit higher, given that writers can easily become political targets that regimes of one kind or another justifiably feel threatened by. This, naturally, is not to say that cultural figures or even entire cultures have not been targets in North America: one has only to consider our own, in the American Indian scholar Ward Churchill's words, "little matter of genocide."

Many of these impositions and limitations have to do with the generally perceived lack of urgency in a society constantly promoting the assumption of certain levels of comfort, while at the same time obfuscating or isolating the very real urgencies and levels of *dis*comfort that exist in American life, or that have been created elsewhere by the obscenely disproportionate levels of consumption taken to be normal here. Following public discourse closely in Europe, the Balkans, and the Middle East at numerous points of urgency—namely, wars that took place during the period these texts were written (the Israeli invasion of Lebanon, the crisis in Algeria, the Gulf War, and the wars of Yugoslavia against Slovenia, Croatia, Bosnia-Hercegovina, and now Kosovo), has made me acutely aware of just how effective the constantly administered soporific agents have become, as we phase out, resting in the safe reassurance that our voices and actions cannot themselves have either agency or effect. The blissfully uninformed nature of the coverage of Kosova, particularly by the American left, put this awareness into even starker relief as both the European and Balkan press assumed the implications of issues and events that were not even remotely available within American consciousness. Far from simply being an acceptable state of affairs, the insularity of American cultural life presents very real political problems and writers have a crucial role to play in disturbing this deadly slumber.

My primary entrance and connection to writing is through poetry. More specifically, through a deep immersion in what has come to be called the New American poetry, as well as the other art forms it coincides with, most significantly, jazz and painting. The poets and writers—from Pound, Williams, Stein, H. D., and other early figures, to the various movements and clusters of associated writers (Objectivists, the Harlem and San Francisco Renaissances, the Black Mountain and New York Schools, the Beats, the Umbra Arts movement, and so many others)—have certainly made this American century comparable to other great historical periods of poetic and literary innovation and production. Yet, even prior to first attempts at getting my work published in the late 1970s, I felt a certain dissatisfaction with the trajectory I saw many of my contemporaries engaged in. Part of this had to do with my growing familiarity with other languages and cultures, but it also had to do with being caught in a kind of odd, generational limbo. Having grown up, through a variety of circumstances, with personal recollections and encounters with the likes of Charles Olson, Vincent Ferrini, Robert Creeley, Kenneth Patchen, Hugo Weber, Ornette Coleman, Denise Levertov, Douglas Woolf, John Weiners, Steve Jonas, and others, I simply took for granted the fact that the artists who mattered worked outside any official institutional affiliation and for a very small but highly involved audience, consisting primarily of other working artists. However, I also understood that power must be negotiated and taken, not only in response but as initiative, in order to *be* responsible and play some part in altering consciousness, shifting relations, and tilting the balance. I would like to think that much of the work in this book emerges from this impetus, as a kind of public literary activism.

My attempt at addressing these issues has been to move laterally, across a variety of roles, and the work gathered here has accompanied energies that took other forms—poetry, prose, translations, editing, scholarly work, teaching, political activity, and a variety of both public and not so public projects—over the course of the past fifteen-odd years. Each of these roles has brought a different element into play: as a poet, for example, I've understood that the best way for work from other languages to be fully absorbed into this culture is by filtering it through the linguistic sensibility of the most innovative writing available, precisely because of the contradictory fact that poetry largely remains a noncommodity in our culture, or at least not an easily marketable one. All this means is that, because of the initially small audience and lack of commercial viability, enough attention can be paid to making such work meaningful. It is instructive to remember, for example, that the great poet Paul Blackburn's translations of Julio Cortázar preceeded what became known as the Latin American boom, one of the few instances in this century when Americans have had the chance to get somewhat of a handle on a relatively representative range of texts in translation (no matter how exclusive even that selection was), from a particular region. In other instances, when texts were approached through some ulterior motive, the work as a whole did not seem to adhere to the body of American writing or culture but tended to become disposable once its shelf life had run out. The ideological characterization of most Eastern European writing of the 1970s as "dissident," with that becoming the ostensible reason for its translation, is a case in point, and also one of the reasons why it was so difficult to publish work from Bosnia prior to the attention focused upon it by the war.

The reason I dwell on this is that my experience in presenting unknown or marginalized literatures has taught me that an extremely wide net needs to be cast in order to create the conditions through which such work can find a productive space in American culture, a place where poets and writers can get to it and begin relating to distinctly new forms, idioms, sensibilities, and experiences as part of their own vocabulary. Casting such a net has meant turning into a kind of full-service bureau through which I could both help create the conditions for reception of works and then carry those works over in a variety of ways. Within these different roles, my work has spanned a range of cultural, political, and historical concerns. As someone barely born here (in larger historical/chronological terms), much of my work has involved the process of both finding and losing my "self" within the gaps I find in American discourse, gaps primarily having to do with either the lack or the suppression of any tangible global political and historical space or consciousness, however these end up getting defined.

Part of the difficulty of working through such a situation is that I feel as if I have embarked upon an enormous journey only to come back to where I started from: in my case, a distinctly American language and American idiom, only to wonder what happened along the way. Every now and then I wish myself innocent, as if I could simply have gone on writing, from the age that I seriously began to occupy myself with writing, just letting myself work out of and through the language and the circumstances given to me without taking the actual physical and linguistic and cultural and political and experiential steps back and forth to other places that I did take. But when I read work by people who I think should know better, I realize that I *had* to traverse those territories: even if afterwards the words I write remain identical, they would have to, at some level, be marked by knowledge picked up or shed along the way. For me, "coming back" to an American idiom, means opening that idiom up to meanings that have either been stifled or still remain unexpressed. Both the idea of place and particular places play an enormous role in this itinerant work and in my choices as a writer and translator. I have very consciously striven to stretch what might be thought possible in an American context; that is, I look for work that I would like to have seen somebody write here, but they can't, or haven't, or wouldn't be able to because the circumstances for that writing don't exist in quite such a configuration. As "translator" of my own work, I engage in this very process, displacing in order to reconfigure. The essays collected here map this process through a diversity of forms and matters.

Two crucial geographical areas and states of mind on this map have been the Middle East and the Balkans; involvement in these areas has meant confronting deep pockets of resistance to change of any kind, in both expected and unexpected places. And there has been even deeper resistance to changes in discourse that would propose a reconsideration of stillborn icons in favor of fertile memories that could lead to the breaking of barriers and the creation of new relationships among texts, peoples, nations, and regions. The narrative of this book, then, traces the intellectual, cultural, spiritual, political, and physical journey I have embarked on in order to unearth such possibilities and make them real, in whatever limited way I've been capable of.

This kind of political and cultural work has meant that all of the texts included here are strategic interruptions meant to open a space for discourse where precious little had existed before. This has been an effective way to create certain political facts and actualities which then become, not arguments, but positions or road hazards for others, a way of putting people on guard. Thus, much of the work involved in creating such conditions is "pre-work," as I navigated the changing politics of editorial policy in a variety of contexts to publish book reviews, cultural or political commentary mentioning or quoting yet untranslated writers, as well as more personal texts that locate and contextualize unfamiliar times and places within potentially useful terms and parameters. Some of the texts had very specific objectives when they were written, such as demanding that certain books get published by embarrassing enough people into recognition of their importance. Some had consequences even I couldn't anticipate in my wildest dreams, such as when I received a letter from the Moroccan political prisoner Abraham Serfaty, from Kuneitra prison, mentioning that he was glad to see the kind of critical work on Arab Jews I was then doing for *Middle East Report*. Others are essays in the true sense, testing the waters while the larger projects of which they formed only a small part were waiting to be realized.

These larger projects include *After Jews and Arabs: Remaking Levantine Culture* (University of Minnesota Press, 1993), published some four years after it was completed; *Keys to the Garden: New Israeli Writing*, published in 1996, after close to fifteen years of attempting to publish works by individual authors included in that anthology; and the translation of Bosnian texts into English. (*Sarajevo Blues* by Semezdin Mehmedinović, published in 1998, the first complete Bosnian literary text emerging from the war to appear in English, followed unsuccessful attempts before the war and more successful attempts during the war, including translating and editing numerous war-related books and articles.) Many of the essays included here provide the glue through which these larger endeavors have been made to cohere, enabling readers to look behind the scenes, in an attempt to display more openly just how contentious and complex these projects were. Most important, though, all of my efforts have embodied a commitment to creating relationships within the places and cultures I have worked in. This has happened through particular instances, such as helping to get the first account of a Bosnian survivor of a Serb-run camp published, providing materials for a major anthology of contemporary American poetry in Croatian, serving as a founding member of East for Peace (a *mizrahi* social and political non-governmental organization active in the 1980s in Europe and the Middle East), writing transcripts at trials of Palestinian political prisoners in Jerusalem, working on the creation of a set of alternative textbooks of contemporary Israeli literature in Hebrew, and other activities. But it has also meant, perhaps more importantly, allowing these activities, cultures, places, and languages to shape the priorities and forms my own work has taken.

Although it has become a truism that we live in the age of information, or information overload, we have also ceded more and more control over that information. As information has become a commodity to be traded for the best price, even some of the most discriminating thinkers have lost sight of the fact that information is valuable, and should be put to use where it might have best effect. At the same time, it has become easier and easier to acquire the trappings of global knowledge, but at little personal risk or cost, as yet another item placed in the ubiquitous shopping cart. Poetry, and language perceived or filtered through the sensibility of poetry's value, still resists the marketplace, no matter how hard some may try. As Jack Spicer wrote: "A poet is a time mechanic not an embalmer. The words around the immediate shrivel and decay like flesh around the body. No mummy-sheet of tradition can be used to stop the process. Objects, words must be led across time not preserved against it. . . . Words are what sticks to the real. We use them to push the real, to drag the real into the poem. They are what we hold on with, nothing else. They are as valuable in themselves as rope with nothing to be tied to." [2] The connection between words and the world, as well as the consequences of such connections, is something we must never lose sight of; as Adonis, one of this century's greatest poets has written: "The writing of poetry is a reading of the world and the things in it, a reading of things charged with words, and of words tied to things. . . . Language, viewed from this perspective, is not a tool for communicating a detached meaning. It is meaning itself because it is thought. Indeed, it precedes thought and is succeeded by knowledge. . . . Poetry, according to this definition, is more than a means or a tool, like a technology; it is, rather, like language itself, an innate quality. It is not a stage in the history of human consciousness but a constituent of this consciousness." [3] Thus, not only language but individual languages, with their own ties to diverse places and histories, are irreplaceable constituents of human consciousness and knowledge of the world. Given our particular relationship to words, immersing oneself in languages and places other than one's own is a unique privilege that too many poets have given up all too easily. Without losing sight of the possibility of universal desires, claims, and responsibilities, by taking advantage of this privilege, I have been able to maintain a diversity of selves and roles that can act locally in many places at once.

Ammiel Alcalay
May 30th, 1999

Acknowledgments

The work in this collection includes and involves a diversity of people, places, and relationships. Over the years, I have acknowledged many of these in other works while this book, in a sense, navigates through and across all those. The idea behind this book owes a special debt to Lynne Tillman—it was she who first suggested I gather different things I'd written over the years to see what kind of connections might emerge. Here I would simply like to give my heartfelt thanks to those editors, journals, and little and bigger magazines who supported my work by publishing it, as well as to the organizations, collectives, and other bodies that provided a venue by inviting me to speak or participate in some way: *Amnesty International*, for asking me to transcribe the trials of Faisal Husseini in Jerusalem; Martim Avillez, for supporting our work on *For/Za Sarajevo*, the first collection on Bosnia to appear in the United States during the war; Avi Bardugo and Shlomo Elbaz, for our participation in *East for Peace* and the Mizrahi/Palestinian dialogue in Toledo; Jacob Bender and Rabbi Rolando Matalon, for inviting me to speak at an event on Israel in New York; Erez Bitton at *Aperion*, where some of these texts appeared in Hebrew; Alex Berlyne, the book editor at the *Jerusalem Post* to whom I was connected by Nissim Rejwan; Jonathan and Daniel

Boyarin, as editors of *Jews and Other Differences,* published by the University of Minnesota Press; Ken Brown and Hannah Davis at *Mediterraneans;* Zlatko Dizdarević, as editor at *Svijet* in Sarajevo, and for all our work together; Professor James Fernandez, at the King Juan Carlos Center at NYU, for inviting me to participate in a conference on Juan Goytisolo; Martha Gever at *The Independent Film & Video Monthly;* Beth Goldring and Daoud Kuttab at *al-Fajr* in East Jerusalem; Jarrod Hayes, Yasmin Yaldiz, and the editorial collective at *Found Object;* Viktor Ivančić, Heni Erceg, Zoran Erceg, and everyone at *Feral Tribune* in Split, for their relentless humor and courage; the late Edmond Jabès and his widow Arlette, for graciously agreeing to be interviewed; Laura Levitt and Miriam Peskowitz, as editors of *Judaism Since Gender,* published by Routledge, as well as for editing a special issue of *Shofar: An Interdisciplinary Journal of Jewish Studies,* where an earlier version of the same text appeared; Ivan Lovrenović, for his continuing example of intellectual honesty, and as editor of *Forum Bosnae;* Lisa Suheir Majaj, for asking me to write on Etel Adnan; Scott Malcomson, for unflinching support, superb editing, and making a number of the crucial texts here possible as an editor at the *Village Voice Literary Supplement;* Ehud Maltz, at *Kol Ha'Ir* in Jerusalem; Nadine McGann at *Afterimage;* Tony Medina, as one of the editors of *In Defense of Mumia,* published by Writers and Readers; Annelies Moors, Toine van Teeffelen, Sherif Kanaana, and Ilham Abu Ghazaleh, as editors of *Discourse and Palestine: Power, Text and Context,* published in Amsterdam by Het Spinhuis; Jay Murphy, as editor of *For Palestine,* published by Writers and Readers; the *New York Times Book Review;* Gil Ott, for early, essential, and unequivocal support and advice as editor of *Paper Air;* Senad Pečanin and everyone else at *BIH Naših Dana* in Sarajevo, for their exemplary work; Richard Peña at the *Film Society of Lincoln Center;* Aaron Rodrigue and Steve Zipperstein, for inviting me to write for *Jewish Social Studies;* Ilan Scheinfeld, then an editor at *al-HaMishmar;* Anton Shammas, for all kinds of help along the way; Professor Laurence Silberstein, as editor of *Mapping Jewish Identities,* published by New York University Press; *The Southwestern Review;* Jean Stein at *Grand Street;* Joe Stork and Jim Paul, then at *Middle East Report,* where a variety of texts included here first appeared; Michael Warshovsky and Tikva Honig-Parnas at *News From Within* and the *Alternative Information Center* in West Jerusalem, and Art Winslow at *The Nation.* Finally, many thanks to my editor Bob Sharrard, for everything, and to City Lights for enabling me to realize so many different projects over the past few years. For the epigraphs by Ali Podrimja, I thank Dukagini Publishing in Kosova, and Uk Zenel Buçpapa and Henry Israeli for translating Luljeta Lleshanaku from Albanian.

Five Hundred Years After: What Was Left Unsaid about Sepharad

A journey through Ammiel Alcalay's collection of essays, *Memories of Our Future*, affords the reader accustomed to a plural reading of the syntax, strata, complexities and occlusions within Mediterranean cultures at the end of the millennium, a welcome display of clear-thinking honesty. The beautiful biographical introduction mingling evocations of horrors from past and present introduces us to the diverse, changing space of the Balkans, the Middle East, and North America through authors whose identity has been denied, or is ambiguous or problematic, such as Edmond Jabès, Jacques, Derrida, Edward Said, Mahmoud Darwish, Edouard Roditi, Anton Shammas, Abdelrahman Munif, and Etel Adnan: witnesses to or victims of a history imposed from the outside, its destructive effects spreading, as if via connecting vessels to a weft made of various materials, a site of diasporas, dislocations, and exterminations provoked by religious fanaticism and retrograde nationalism. In this book Alcalay examines frankly and unsentimentally the consequences of the expansionist policies of the state of Israel both on Palestinian and centuries-old Sephardic culture, weaving into his reflections timely references to the absence of self-criticism within Arab culture, to Spanish medieval history, and the devastation of the new Toledo that was Sarajevo by Milošević and Karadžićs' bloody myth-making.

As Jews attained the status of citizenship during the nineteenth century, the living complex Sephardic traditions of Cairo, Fez, Marrakesh, Aleppo, Istanbul, Sana, Sarajevo, and Salonika were marginalized by the new Judaism integrated into the political, economic, and cultural modernity of Europe. Centuries of people rich in experience, contacts, transfusions of languages—Hebrew, Arabic and Ladino, but also Portuguese, Berber, Turkish, Greek, Serbian, Persian, and Uzbeki— were locked into a dead end by the Eurocentric vision of Zionism's founding fathers. Faced with the well-documented reality that, throughout the Middle Ages and well into the nineteenth century, Jewish culture was mestizo and Mediterranean, the perspective adopted by the official Israeli world reminds the author of the views held by those responsible for other historical whitewashes and self-interested amnesia, in Spain and in the Balkans.

The reign of Ferdinand and Isabel is not only characterized by the expulsion of the Jews and the acculturation of the *mudejares:* it also marks the moment when eight centuries of Euro-Semitic culture was lopped from the trunk of European culture despite a key role in its creation. At a stroke, Averroes, Avicenna, and Maimonides lost their professorial status in the Sorbonne and Italy and were consigned to the obscure, remote, exotic fold of the oriental. In a word, Islam in the West and the Spanish-Judaic world ceased to exist with the new frontiers of Europe drawn from the Renaissance. The establishment of the Holy Office to investigate the suspect Catholicism of *Converso* Jews, frequent public spectacles of autos de fe, and the final solution of the Spanish Muslim problem were only the visible side of a more profound, far-reaching phenomenon: the brutal excising of the Jewish and Arab presence that originated in Spain from the neo-Latin culture of the Middle Ages. The subsequent blindness of the Spanish in relation to their own past—first denounced by Anglo-Saxon travelers to the peninsula and later by more lucid Spaniards, from Blanco White to Américo Castro— was rooted, as Ammiel Alcalay perceptively observes, when referring to the ideological aspects of memory, "in the form of fixed, unchanging images: indelible and iconic, their clarity is blinding."

If crypto-Jews and *conversos* are the first exponents of the schizophrenia of modern existential anguish, the Hebrew diaspora from the peninsula was also reinvigorated and nourished by other cultures and languages: their decenteredness—the view from the margins to the periphery—endows it with a unique character, comparable to what we now understand by modernity. The studies of Américo Castro, Albert Sicroff, and Marquez Villaneuva of the specific but diverse spirituality of the new Christians cast a harsh light on the life of conflict that they experienced for almost two centuries. Caught in the dilemma imposed by ecclesiastical authorities who marked out the frontiers of their difference beyond the "regenerating" gift of baptism, while denying them the public expression of that difference, they suffered the inner torment of twentieth-century intellectuals grappling with the hydra of totalitarianism. The radical pessimism of Fernando de Rojas and Mateo Alemán, the irony of Cervantes, and the bitter sermons of Fray Luis de León are distant manifestations of personal strategies of disenchantment, resistance, or evasion. Though the harrassment and destruction of the social class of *conversos* delayed for centuries Spain's entry into the intellectual, political, and economic modernity developing in seventeenth- and eighteenth century England and France, the literary forms created in response by some of its victims anticipated those fashioned by twentieth-century writers and artists, enabling us to read them as if they were our contemporaries. A subtle pattern unites, as if in a complex tapestry, Sephardic diaspora, Spanish and Portuguese crypto-Jews, and new Christians opposed to the oppressive straitjacket of Hispanic national Catholicism and the dogmatism of a counter-Reformation which, as Américo Castro rightly notes, should rather be called a counter-Judaism.

Notwithstanding the "cordon sanitaire" (Bataillon *dixit*) established by Philip II around his kingdoms, subjects and property, books and ideas continued to circulate beyond the boundaries of the peninsula: "in Tlemcen, Sarajevo, Casablanca, and even the Bronx"—writes Alcalay— "poetic forms brought to Cordoba from Baghdad in the 10th century continued to be written and renovated in Livorno, Jerusalem, Bombay, and Brooklyn. Fully alive to the possibilities of each idiom they encountered, these writers made their cities books and lived in words, but never as a means of excluding themselves from the world they inhabited—refusing to use tradition as a barricade, they avidly pursued and confronted the new." From thirteenth-century authors like Benjamin de Palencia, who traveled from Castille to the Yemen, attracted by the culture of their correligionaries, to Francisco Delicado, Antonio Enriquez Gomez, and Leon Hebreo, there formed an unbroken chain of Sephardic and Hebrew-Arab narrators and poets reaching down to the present, across different contexts and languages, embodied in such significant contemporary figures as Edmond Jabès, Anton Shammas, and Edmond Amran El Maleh.

As Ammiel Alcalay notes, Zionist discourse reiterated within the fin-de-siècle intellectual framework, the Europeanizing option of the Renaissance and its rejection of Judeo-Arabic culture. The study of "oriental" Hebrew literature and the work of Jewish writers in a variety of languages was abandoned, despite the fact that the Sephardic population is an essential component of the state of Israel. A mixture of chauvinism, political myopia, and ahistorical paternalism led to the sidelining and concealing of a fertile legacy to which access is only possible through an interdisiplinary perspective, able to encompass different epochs, cultures, and languages. To paraphrase Yoram Bronowski, "offical" Israeli literature works within strictly European parameters, and the work of its best known writers constitutes a mere annex to Western—mainly American—novelists. Others have even claimed that *all* Israeli writers (whether of Moroccan, Iraqi, Egyptian or other origins), have alienated themselves from the Middle East. Thus, as Alcalay notes, "The 'oriental' exists only as folklore and bygone traditions, not as culture or living forms." It is of little importance that the work of numerous Sephardic writers, be they Israeli or not, belies such an assertion. The European-Askenazi literary canon imposes a critical reductionism that negates and excludes. As Alcalay concludes: "To be 'abbreviated' in the multiplicity of our possible range of identities is a form of oppression."

Against such impoverishment, the author of *Memories of Our Future* recalls how the standard framing of Jews from all countries and epochs in a universal, inevitable "Jewish destiny" was in reality the product of the combined impact of Zionist ideology and the terrifying Holocaust. The wealth and variety of Sephardic history located in various cultures and continents fell into a nonbeing similar to that shaped centuries before, on the altar of purifying homogeneity, by Ferdinand and Isabel and the invention of a Europe stripped of its Semitic roots by the oracles and inspirers of the Renaissance. Against the present-day perception of Israeli literature as a simple appendix of European and American literatures, Alcalay proposes another, at once more traditional and modern, characterized by the mutiplicity of roots and its recovery from a long, cultivated amnesia: "It seems to me that the only chance for Hebrew culture is to grow backwards: to bring to bear all the power and richness it can muster from the past by losing the fear of reaching the point of freedom it takes to be "traditional." The modernists hinted at what the postmodern world takes for granted: the collusion and correspondence between African masks and Picasso, Persian tiles and Mondrian. Maybe Hebrew culture's strongest possible subculture, its furthest "underground" and most advanced avant-garde, its true link to a world outside itself, is deeply hidden precisely where most least expect to find it: within tradition. To grow backwards also means to look ahead: by recuperating everything these texts carry within them—the music of shepherds, nomads, muezzins, mathematicians, alchemists, miniaturists, court orchestras, and David's lyre, the light and smell of every city in the Near East purposefully obscured only to remember Jerusalem, then maybe the Gates of Mercy will remain open long enough to remember the touch of all the objects beyond them, long enough to regain the familiar impression of their images and finally recover from this long and painful amnesia."

When tracking the thorny issue of Israeli policy on the settlement of the occupied territories, Ammiel Alcalay forthrightly underlines the devastating effect of its intention to deprive the Palestinians of their right to memory on behalf of a holocaust for which they were not at all responsible, to convert them into undesirable aliens in their own land and to condemn them to be impotent witnesses to the ruin and transformation of their environment. Against the religious reasoning and "militant archaeology" of the proponents of a greater Israel and their concept of a state impervious to its geographic ambit and historical realities, Alcalay maintains that "Any relationship to Israel must include a relationship to the Middle East, to Arabs, to Islam, to unemployment in Algeria, censorship and torture in Egypt, the abandonment of Muslims in Bosnia, to efforts at rebuilding Beirut, to the effect of sanctions against Iraqi children. We cannot continue traveling back and forth from Jerusalem and pretend that Damascus, Tripoli, Sidon, Fez, and Baghdad do not exist."

The essays devoted to the genocide of Bosnian Muslims and democrats finally allow Alcalay to trace a suggestive parallel with events that happened five centuries ago. Isn't the operation in Memoricide enforced by Croatian and Serbian extremists in relation to the Ottoman past a repetition of what Spanish national Catholicism did in respect of the Judeo-Arabic legacy? Doesn't the present refusal of Spanish academic circles to accept the existence of a *mudéjar* literature and the role played by *conversos* and New Christians in various branches of narrative, poetry, and the essay in the Golden Age show that, as the Bosnian-Croatian Ivan Lovrenović writes, referring to the former Yugoslav

Federation, Spanish culture—and the official culture of Israel!—also have "a grave problem related to the recognition of its very content and value; in other words, that it suffers from a grave problem of self-recognition (due to the fact that) it cannot integrate its own differences?"

Could iconic identity—whether Spanish, Serbian, Israeli, Turkish, or Greek—be an attempt to mask the vacilliations and questions lurking beneath? In the light of so many sleights of hand and false genealogies, intellectuals free of mythical, exclusivist, nationalist or religious blinkers must conclude, in the spirit of Alcalay's rigor and honesty, that their land, as Cervantes discovered in his day, is the fertile territory of doubt.

Juan Goytisolo
Translated from the Spanish by Peter Bush

Preludes: An Opening

"weighing the losses, like stones in your hand"

Often I Am Permitted to Return to a Meadow

as if it were a scene made-up by the mind,
that is not mine, but is a made place,

that is mine, it is so near to the heart, . . .

ROBERT DUNCAN, *The Opening of the Field*

1.

In seersucker overalls, I'm trying to balance myself on the huge old Hudson, the sunlight glaring off the hood. 1960. I'm four years old, still blond from my grandmother, the darker genes haven't kicked in yet. The family's only been in the New World nine years. In the next set of pictures, it's 1963. My hair is dark and, in every picture in the series, I'm holding Jip, my stuffed terrier. What happened?

2.

Does the memory of kin you never even knew leave its own implacable trail upon the very texture and fabric of your body, growing as you grow to imprint itself upon your every move? How many times did their muffled voices impinge upon a desire as simple as moving my hand, shifting my weight, or saying what was on my mind? And having overcome or ignored their nameless restlessness, wasn't I simply left with a longing even more unfathomable and indefinite than anything I could actually remember?

3.

There is a difference between things coming to stand in place of feelings and the inability to get the things that, say, a child wants: "It's hardest at night," he said. "When I go to bed I always remember the custom of saying good night to my son. And then when I close my eyes I remember his face the last day I took him to the market. He wanted me to buy him a toy, but I had no money. He looked at me so piteously and I felt so sad. I wanted so much to buy my son a toy. It is this face that I see when I close my eyes and think of home."[1]

4.

The fable of our father Abraham just means unfinished business, long after the garden and the flood and the tower. Abraham's brother Haran died before his father, in his native land of Ur-kasdim. But their father, Terah, died in Haran. Abraham was already seventy-five when he set out for Canaan, going through the Negev and on down to Egypt, even before he changed his name.

5.

Aung San Suu Kyi at the age of about six: long black hair tied in a bowed ribbon falls over her left shoulder. Her left hand clings to a plant, her right hangs limply at her side, only a few inches above the hem of her checkered skirt, a lacy white frill around the neck, the short sleeves slightly puffed. She's wearing white socks, folded over, and proper shoes with laces. Her head is slightly cocked and her right cheek almost seems flushed. Her lips are about to move: it's hard to say whether she feels the acuteness of a wound too deep to articulate, a premonition of the future burden she will bear, if she's just woken up, or is simply being mischevious. There's more weight on her left leg than on her right. "My father died when I was too young to remember him," she would write later on: "It was in an attempt to discover the kind of man he had been that I began to read and collect material on his life. . . . Writing about a person to whom one is closely related is a difficult task, and the author is open to possible accusations of insufficient objectivity."[2]

6.

Last summer there was a scene on Croatian TV, on the late news, that showed a family in the midst of a violent separation seemingly of their own making: a boy who must have been eleven or twelve started boarding a bus with his mother who pushed him up the steps. The father came up behind and pulled her down while the boy ran off the bus and darted across the street to hide behind a tree. As the bus got ready to go, the man pushed the woman, now screaming, back on. He ran over to the boy and they climbed onto another bus. The next day, I was talking about the incident to a friend of mine but neither of us could figure out who was who and where they were headed since the newscasters had left out all the details.

7.

"Draw the map the voyage made. Yes & No, looking with care in the beginning, using what I had been taught at school. Sitting down at my age now—to write. I trust my intuition. Who am I writing to? To explain my detours. Yes, to keep them alive. Look the other way—not afraid to make my mistake and show it. I want to show ambition. I want to show what it is to be in America. Positive & Negative, I scratch through the surface. Children grow up. Mary is gone. Love turns to indifference. Always returning to New York—except for Andrea. Andrea dying in the air in Guatemala. LIFE DANCES ON . . . HOME IMPROVEMENTS . . . LAST SUPPER . . . the map makes itself, I follow, no choice, like exorcising the Darkness come too early. Please line up the chapters now one two three—too late to teach about photography. Just accept lost feelings—Shadows in empty rooms—silence on TV. Silence in Canada. Bad dreams—Black & White & Things, enjoy each minute to the fullest . . . KEEP BUSY. The memory of all. So much of it gone. I wish that the feeling of that Memory will make a sound of music."[3]

8.

They were cut off from everything else, my "studies": the view across St. Nicholas Park, the old massive Gothic structures, the Vietnam vets I hung out with in the cafeteria who studied Ancient Greek. (*The cafeteria almost like grade school, like the school lunches I never ate, preferring bread-and-butter sandwiches with a carton of milk at first and cold cuts later on.*) That far uptown didn't have much to do with downtown, and the life I was leading. The Latin class had become a tutorial, since there were only two of us, me and a girl whose name I don't remember but who turned out to be Croatian and spoke a language as familiar and broken as my Serbian the few times we haltingly exchanged a few words as she rushed off to meet her boyfriend before asking me which lines of Virgil were due: we both bore a burden, and it seemed we were on the verge of becoming other people.

9.

And so the story of the vanquished is turned into that of another victory:

> *I'm on a train. I'd considered not mentioning it, but we are passing ship-building yards—and great steel hulls, & cranes rising from the water: ugly & beautiful, dull & fascinating—and houseboats—stark and dreary but for the small parts made of rich warm highly-varnished wood—and now the train yards—smallish red cars—hundreds of them. We've left Calais behind. On my way to Paris, I've finally gotten used to London. Now it's easy to be there. In Paris, perhaps you know, there's a neighborhood called Le Marais—it is where you see this ✡ on every shop, the children are dark skinned with curly black hair, you read "N'oubliez pas!" on the facade of a grammar school and you can get borscht at Joe Goldenburg's Delicatessen. It's getting to be spring in NY and when I left it was getting to be winter. I think of your life there, envy it in fact—balanced, full well-conceived—like you. At first I hated everything new and strange—now I grow tense at the thought of the throbbing arrogant familiarity of every building and pile of dog shit in NY. I'm coming for a week or so around the end of May—for the unveiling. It's one year—time is all different because nothing has happened this year, just watching it pass. And I fear nothing will change. I'd like you to come to the ceremony. Horrible as it will be, would you be there anyway?*

10.

It was as if the unyielding logic of the grammar, united with the absurdity of the sentences, provided me with the only mental excercises I'd ever encountered analagous to the kind of menial work I'd done so much of, like bundling papers, shingling, wrapping fruit, sanding fiberglass or unloading trucks:

The man said that he himself would praise the girl.

Marcus said that he (Claudius) had not praised the woman.

The girl said that the woman had been praised by the man.

The woman thought that the leader should not be praised by the men.

The girl will deny that she (herself) has praised the man.

The man said that the women were praising their own sons.

The boys believed they were being praised by the leader.

The man praising the woman praised by the girls about to praise the boys about to be praised will come to the city.

You came back to the city, but just as you did I was about to leave and I'd be gone for years. Maybe you did envy me when you thought of me from that distance—You wrote about your choices, and I was happy for you, I would only want you to have the best—but what choices could I speak of?

11.

Not much of a transcript, really. A "C" average in high school, and even that was luck and a certain sympathy some of the teachers had for "a great deal of ability that his record does not really show." Then college: a "C" in Shakespeare my first semester, troubles with the registrar, financial aid, disbarred at some point for an unsettled debt. A lot like my students now who, as Kimiko described them, seem extremely pissed off and must have been considered screw-ups at some point. True survivors. "My life in New York," "your envy." The way up the hill from Broadway, after switching from the express to the local at 96th St. I don't even remember what I carried my books in, it was before knapsacks. A shoulder bag, I guess. Or maybe even my old canvas delivery boy bag with the wide fluorescent orange strap that I used for brushes and spackle knives and the hawk I was so proud of having bought after learning the finer points of plastering from Jokeem.

12.

STORM   CALM

Sails   ——————————   <u>a mission</u>
                                         i.e. to do something
                                         seeking something

<u>shipwrecks</u>}

                                     <u>outside</u>

<u>drowns</u>}

                                     -<u>DREAM</u>-
— — — — — — — — — — — — — — — — — —
appears to Halycone naked &
          dripping — (she sees him as he is)
— — — — — — — — — — — — — — — — — —

          <u>goes to shore</u>

(<u>his last prayer</u>)

                              {<u>body washes ashore at</u>
                              {<u>her feet</u>

she leaps into sea

   reverse?   her death = life (sea)

       jumping to him
       as he is

     unable to be sated?

EGGS IN NESTS ON THE SEA

hatched seven days before &
seven after winter solstice

(Ceyx, King of Trachis, disregarding the entreaties of his wife Halycone [who, as a daughter of Aeolus, knew the power of the sea winds], sailed to Ionia to consult the oracle of Apollo, and was shipwrecked and drowned. All naked and dripping, he appeared to her in a dream and told her of his death. She hastened to the seashore and his body [in accordance with his last prayer] was washed ashore at her feet. She leaped into the sea to kill herself, but the gods, taking pity, changed her and Ceyx into kingfishers and Zeus forbade the winds to blow for seven days prior to and seven days after the winter solstice when they are hatching their eggs in nests on the sea.)

13.

The rich purple woven into robes by Dido, from the same sea: "Will no color content your eye, but such as is stained by the fish *Murex*?"[5] Such common English usage dates back to 1589, 400 years after the Third Crusade:

> We have already spoken of the great concentration of Frankish troops at Tyre. The cause of this was that Saladin allowed them to depart freely from every city and fort that he took and sent them to Tyre with their possessions, women, and children. This created

an enormous concourse of Franks and an inexhaustible supply of money, in spite of the very heavy expenses of the siege. Here monks and priests and a crowd of Frankish knights and nobles dressed themselves in black and expressed great grief at the loss of Jerusalem. The Patriarch of Jerusalem took them with him on a journey through the Frankish domains calling on the people to help, invoking their aid and inciting them to avenge the loss of Jerusalem. Among other things, they made a picture showing the Messiah, and an Arab striking Him, showing blood on the face of Christ—blessings on Him!—and they said to the crowds: "This is the Messiah, struck by Mahomet the prophet of the Muslims, who has wounded and killed Him." This made a deep impression on the Franks and they flocked to the Patriarch, even the women. There were in fact in the army at Acre a certain number of women, who challenged their enemy's warriors to single combat, as we shall describe later; a man who could not himself fight put a substitute into the field or gave money to the limit of his capacity. In this way they collected immense quantities of troops and money.

A Muslim living at Hisn al-Akrad told me the following story— he was one of the garrison that had handed the fort over to the Franks a long time ago, and who then repented of having given the Franks help in attacking Muslim territory and having fought and battled at their side—this man told me that he had gone with a group of Franks from Hisn al-Akrad in four galleys to the Frankish and Greek lands beyond the sea to seek help (for the Crusade). "Our trip," he said, "took us at length to Rome, that great city, which we left with our galleys full of silver." And a Frankish prisoner told me that he was his mother's only son, and their house was their sole possession, but she had sold it and used the money obtained from it to equip him to go and free Jerusalem. There he had been taken prisoner. Such were the religious and personal motives that drove the Franks on. They flocked to battle by any means they could, by land and sea, from all directions. If God had not shown his grace to Islam in the death of the German King on his way to attack Syria, as will appear later, it would have been said one day that Syria and Egypt *had once been* Muslim lands.[6]

14.

Sarranus murex, known throughout the Roman Empire. Purple from Tyre. Dido, the refugee in Carthage: "upon her shoulders / she wears a robe of Sidon with embroidered / borders. Her quiver is of gold, her hair / has knots and ties of gold, a golden clasp / holds fast her purple cloak."[7] My old beat-up copy of Virgil, the spine already broken off when I got it, only some greyish cardboard showed between the nondescript, muddy-colored boards. I kept my notes in it with a mechanical pencil, to get between the lines of the tiny print as I struggled with the text. Dido: a Phoenician woman given in marriage by her father as a virgin to a man who was then murdered by her brother. Dido: a Lebanese refugee, a suicide. The finger-nails of her sister Anna scratching her face and wounding her flesh in lamentation as Aeneas sails off with his son toward Italy, leaving behind the glowing flames of Tunis: "Because the Marquis of Sidon, who was waiting for a dispensation from the pope to put his sister under a Muslim, or if not his sister then his niece, was not suitable as a genuine ally against the English, who were holding Acre under siege. . . . Because the aim of parti-tioning the land into coast and mountain between Arab and Frank was not, under prevailing conditions, to guarantee for the Arabs whatever forts and terrain had remained in their hands but to grant the enemy a respite that enabled him to establish a pattern that sanctioned his transition from exception to rule. . . . And they read the history of forts and citadels con-querors used as signatures to keep their names alive in lands not theirs and to forge the identity of rocks and oranges. . . . Forts and citadels that are no more than attempts to protect a name that does not trust time to preserve it from oblivion. . . . It has had a long history, this double operation of searching for a place or a time on which to put a signature and untie the knot of the name facing the long caravan of oblivion."[8]

15.

every few years there would be a different name to let you out of a differently named hell and you would have to accept it like the last name except the more names you were given the less you knew your own and the longer you had each one the longer it took to realize you weren't really there and the more names you had the less you knew of each one while it was yours as you waited for the door through which you were supposed to be led toward palms and white balconies to another shore where signs marked a division in time and names belonged only to whom they named: you ran and were taken to no door but led back to windows and shown for once and for all that no name reflected back at you and so time passed like that as you walked by tracks that curved down a hill with no palms but only a box outlined on a door with a name written in it: by now you had no way of knowing to whom it belonged or if it had once been yours and now was not or if it still might be so you repeated the sharp motion over and over with a small chipped rock until you fell against the door and alone on the ground by the fence looked at the pattern in the cracked cement searching for the lost outlines of letters that might make a name until you felt the air become a breeze and you watched the sky return to darkness.

16.

"When I came back to Beirut ten years ago, the first thing I did was stop a taxi and say to the driver: "Take me to Damur." I had come from Cairo and was searching for the small footsteps of a boy who had taken steps larger than himself, not in keeping with his age and greater than his stride. What was I searching for? The footsteps, or the boy? Or for the folks who had crossed a rocky wilderness, only to reach that which they didn't find . . . ? The sea was in place, pushing against Damur to make it bigger. And I had grown up. I had become a poet searching for the boy that used to be in him, whom he had left behind some place and forgotten. The poet had grown older and didn't permit the forgotten boy to grow up . . .

. . . I picked mulberries in Tyre. Then our journey came to an end in Jizzine. I had never seen snow before. . . . In winter we couldn't bear the biting cold of the wind, so we moved to Damur. The sunset stole time from time itself. The sea writhed like the bodies of women in love until it raised its cry in the night and for the night. . . .

I cannot carve my name on a rock in Damur, even if it has been used as cover by snipers with designs on my life. I cannot. No, I cannot. Therefore, get this photographer away from the face of the rock. Keep this kind of talk away from a sea still in place. . . . I have no interest whatever in carving my name on a rock in Damur because I'm searching for a boy there, not for a homeland."[9]

17.

How can I even begin to describe Jaffa, as a repository of memories that could never have been mine but which still remain familiar or as material proof of a forbidden and concealed history that is still being lived despite the extent of the defeat? What was I looking for, in Rome, Jerusalem, Egypt, Palestine? The cities, towns, and villages my family once hid out or lived in? The physical presence and texture of places that had once been a part of what I would become? The gaze of Ascanius I had read about in a book, looking back at the kind and beautiful queen who had hoped to kidnap the heart of the father by embracing the son? Could this possibly be what the "distinguished" professor meant when he said that students have to read the Western classics since that is part of "our" "heritage"?

18.

"The term *Tophet* is known in the Bible as the site of human sacrifice. Tophet originally referred to the place near Jerusalem in the valley of Hinnom where those who worshiped Baal sacrificed their children . . .

Recent excavations conducted by Professor Lawrence Stager have shown that the accounts of the horrors of the Carthage Tophet were scarcely exaggerated. . . .

Stager excavated more than 400 urns containing human and animal bones buried between 700 and 146 B.C. He believes that some 20,000 urns, most containing at least one human baby, were interred between 400 and 200 B.C. alone . . .

Only 30 percent of the bones analyzed from the earliest periods were of sheep or goats; the rest were of extremely young infants. By the fourth century B.C., only 10 percent were animal, and older children were sacrificed at a greater rate. Of the single-child urns, 68 percent contained a child between the ages of one and three years; premature and newborn babies made up 30 percent. But 32 percent of the urns contained two or three children. A surprising number of urns contained the remains of three children; two were premature or newborn, and the third was a two- to four-year-old.

The conclusion may be that a stillborn or premature child was deemed unacceptable to the god, and—since the "dedicant" had vowed the offering and could not back out—an older living child had to be sacrificed as well.

On the stele, the genealogy of the dedicating family frequently appears and the vow (NDR) is cited. Paul Mosca, a leading American authority on the Tophet and the Punic language, has concluded that MULK 'IMMOR means the sacrifice of a lamb or a kid, MULK BA'AL is the sacrifice of a child from a wealthy family, and MULK 'ADAM is the sacrifice of a commoner (although this term is not found at Carthage). Such "labels" may indicate a sort of caste system in which sacrifices are rated or classified in value."[10]

19.

In Kerkouane, the Punic archaeological site is covered with a layer of broken murex shells: "In one of the tombs of Arg el Ghazouani—Kerkouane's cemetary—was found the painting of a fortified city thought to be the City of Souls *(Rephaïm),* the subject of a tablet of Ugarit."[5] In Jerusalem, a street called *'Emeq Refaïm* ("Vale of Souls") begins at the gas station forking to the right past Talbieh; now mainly inhabited by rich American and European immigrants, it's only about a ten-minute walk from the Valley of Hinnom, also known as Gehenna, or Hell.

20.

Alexander of Macedon laid siege to Tyre in 332 B.C. The siege lasted from January through August. A variety of accounts estimate that 8,000 people died or were killed during this period; another 2,000 men of military age were crucified after the city was taken and the remaining 30,000 inhabitants were sold into slavery. From there, he went on to Gaza where he also met fierce resistance. After a two-month siege, the entire Gazan garrison was slaughtered and all surviving women and children were sold into slavery. And so Alexander moved on into Egypt.[12] It is said that he still held a grudge against Tyre and, in 323 B.C., the year of his death, he planned to construct an armada of 1,000 ships in order to lead an assault on Carthage.

Carthage remained a thorn in the side of empires: "The years 264 to 133 B.C. witnessed the rise of Rome to the position of greatest world power.

This progress was accompanied by a transformation of the economic bases of Rome. Money economy and speculation supplanted the peasant economy which had hitherto been prevalent. In the year 269 silver coinage was introduced; five years later the first Punic War broke out: the war against Carthage, at that time the greatest commercial power in the Mediterranean."[13] These wars lasted, off and on, until "Carthage was overthrown and completely destroyed in the third Punic War (149 to 146) with all the brutal and hypocritical cruelty of which the Romans were capable."[14]

After destroying the city, the Romans initiated a process of colonization that, by the time of the Jewish historian Josephus in the 1st century A.D., had turned Africa into the breadbasket of Rome: "They continued the development of agriculture but gave it a new orientation. The vineyards and olive groves that had been destroyed at the end of the Punic period were left abandoned to avoid competition with Italy, which then dominated the wine and oil markets. . . . Rome's economy and political requirements made Tunisia a one-crop province, and that crop was wheat. Rome had 200,000 citizens on the dole. They were getting free distributions of wheat, and Italy and the whole empire were suffering from a shortage. Tunisia had to provide 1,260,000 quintals (over 200 pounds per quintal) of wheat annually. This covered two-thirds of Rome's needs and nourished the Roman plebiscite for eight months out of twelve. (The final one-third was taken care of by Egypt.) This contribution permitted Rome to avoid riots and famine—dangerous to the stability of the regime."[15]

21.

"As they have made Jericho a bridge between Israel and Egypt, I ask myself whether they are planning to make Lebanon a bridge between Israel and Syria? For example, they are speaking about building a [coastal] railway line. Is there a railway anywhere in the world having a length of only 200 kilometers? In fact, the railway is [designed] to run between Tel Aviv and Ankara. In the government's ten-year reconstruction plan more than $13 billion is going to be spent on roads and railways and only $250 million on agriculture. Yet 45 percent of the Lebanese live on agriculture."[16]

22.

There aren't any known historical depictions of Dido, also known as Princess Elissa. Punic coins made of electrum, a mixture of silver and gold, depict a woman's face in profile that has variously been claimed as Dido, Demeter, Persephone, or the Phoenician deity Tanit, believed to be of Libyan origin. Her nose is long and angular; her eyes are also long, set deeply into her high cheeks. Her lips are resolute, but bend ever so slightly to the sloping curve of her chin. Her hair is extremely curly, set in a diadem that also seems to have a thick braid pulled through it. She is wearing a long earring, with three hanging pendants. Her neck is thin and elongated; at the bottom of the coin, a simple embroidered lace adorns her clothing. As the granddaughter of King Mattan of Tyre, she would have been the great-niece of King Ahab's wife Jezebel, the daughter of Ethbaal, king of Sidon and a former high priest of the goddess Astarte. It was Jezebel's daughter, Athalia, who was instrumental in bringing forbidden Phoenician practices back to the southern kingdom of Judah.

23.

Phoenician and Hebrew are regional dialects of the Canaanite language. In my son's encyclopedia, it says: "A tiny group of cities perched along the coast of the Mediterranean produced the most famous sailors and traders of the ancient world. These seafaring people were called the Phoenicians. The cities of Phoenicia were linked by the sea, and they traded in many goods, including purple dyes, glass, and ivory. From 1200 to 350 B.C. the Phoenicians controlled trade throughout the Mediterranean." In another entry, under alphabet, it says: "The Phoenicians, who lived about 3,000 years ago in the Middle Eastern country now called Syria, developed the first modern alphabet. The ancient Greeks adapted the Phoenician alphabet, and later the Romans improved it. The Roman alphabet is now widely used throughout the world."[17] Phoenician inscriptions have been found in Cyprus, Greece, Egypt, Africa, Italy, France, Spain, and the islands of Melitus, Gaulos, Sicily, Cossura, Sardinia and Corsica. The following text is from Carthage:

Tariff of payments set up by [the
          men in charge of the payments . . .].

[For an ox, as whole offerings or *substitute offerings*], the priests
[shall have] the skins, and the person offering the sacrifice the *fat parts*
[. . .].
          For a stag [as whole offerings or *substitute offerings*], the priests
[shall have] the skins, and the person offering the sacrifice the *fat parts*
[. . .].
          For a ram or a goat, as whole offerings or as *substitute offerings,*
the priests shall have the skins of the goats, and the person offering the
sacrifice shall have the *ribs* [. . .].
          For a lamb or for a kid or for a *young* stag, as whole offerings or
substitute offerings, the priests shall have the skins [. . .].
          For any sacrifice which shall be offered by persons poor in
cattle, the priest shall have nothing whatever.
          For an 'gnn bird or for a ss (bird), 2 zr of silver for each.
          [For any *substitute offering* wh]ich he shall have to carry to the
God, the priest shall have *necks* and *shoulder joints* [. . .].
          [Upon any] holy [*oblation*] and upon a hunt offering and upon
an oil offering [. . .].
          Upon a *cake* (*fodder*) and upon milk (fat) and upon a sacrifice
as a meal-offering and upon [. . .].
          Any payment which is not specified in this tablet shall be made
[according to the written document . . .].
          Any priest who shall take [. . .].
          Any person offering a sacrifice who [. . .].
          Any person who shall trade [. . . , and who] shall shatter this
tablet [. . .].[18]

24.

A talent of gold, a talent of silver, the sound of crushed shells under our
feet. Shells at the bottom, shells from the top, shrapnel and shards. Any
person who shall trade, any person who shall shatter. This name, this
likeness. That I carry myself. And of you within me. And your curly hair
as we untangle the spreading roots that take us farther and farther away
only that we "may learn what is the winged oak and the decorated cloth

upon it."[19] The fabric a veil we never placed between us to consecrate our union. Now the shells, in a bottle on the shelf of a room you're not in. "Shelf." "Ledge." "Room." "Chamber." "Window." "Portico." "Fabric": "cloak," "shirt," "tunic," "gown," "dress." Clay, brick, lime, slate, mortar, ash, sand, gravel, wood, glass, copper, brass, lead, plaster, burnt umber: the materials of the building you sift through my hands as we survey the wreckage. Walking up the hill from the beach past the lighthouse, the lack of fish and tainted water, the breakers choppy. This sea. This body we drift and skirt, the water rushing past your toes as I run after you in the wind of a winter sun in Jaffa. The chiming bells dangle past garages and welding shops and junkyards, the pavement soaked in oil and the flash of acetylene lost in the din of spinning rims, grinders, generators, jacks, pumps, and compressors. Most of the world is like this road—a place in between other places—the hood open, someone busy peering down into a carburetor as a bus careens around a hairpin turn, picking up speed for the next hill. Today the sun burst through the clouds over the elevated at 4th Avenue and in the distance the girders looked just like the awning of a ruined Roman amphitheater, where the cornice has been chipped away, the inner and outer shells blending with vaults and columns, arches and windows, brackets and arcades.

25.

Lying in the singed grass of the empty meadow near the old rusty tractor all I could hear were the tall cornstalks swaying in a field I couldn't see. Far from the water wheel and the brook rushing over the rocks and hitting the spiles of the footbridge, I abandoned myself to the breeze and the enormous day whose boundary didn't stop at my body but stretched forever in a blend of light that didn't divide the shimmering whirlpool dying to be green from the already parched and dead. In the fall I died. Every fall I died, thrown into the dark pit, the lid suddenly closed tight over the sky, trapped in the black among raw sacks of grain, having killed the bird and knowing it was a sin, not having swam enough: neither a fish unable to emerge dry nor lost in the fathomless blue trying. On the empty road, passing the dilapidated houses I thought of what I would tell them and fixed the designs in my mind: opal wheels revolving in the night, unknown doors at the end of paths skirting the sea, the descent whose access and issue only I knew. On damp gray mornings when they marched us out for our daily air against crumbling walls soaked with piss and scribbled arrows tenderly piercing broken hearts, I described my underwater caves, the sun that warmed me through the glittering aquamarine prism that enveloped and hid me, fearing nothing more than a sudden blow on the back of my head that hounded me like a lost brother, perpetually waiting to slam me into the pit, trap me in corners, and suffocate me until I fell with a dull thud and felt the mix of blood and dirt settle on my tongue.

26.

As I look at pictures of us in different places I wonder what made Virgil tell the version of Dido's story that he told. More than seventy years before the poet was born, right on Byrsa Hill (where the Queen Dido Hotel now overlooks the excavations of Punic houses), as the Romans set fire to building after building, the wife of Hasdrubal—the last commander of Punic Carthage who begged at the knees of Scipio—cursed her husband and, dressed in her finest robes, jumped into the flames of a funeral pyre she had prepared for herself. Legend has it that the widow Dido or Elissa, having escaped the blood feud of her brother Pygmalion and made her way to Carthage (after getting a group of maidens about to offer their virginity at a Temple of Astarte in Cyprus to join her expedition), also leaped into the flames of a funeral pyre rather than submit to a local Libyan king. Even Virgil cannot deny her pride as he put these words in Dido's mouth: "We Tyrians / do not have minds so dull and we are not / beyond the circuit of the sun's yoked horses."[20]

To see the very shadows cast by precisely that sun; to feel the heat of the rocks before evening and their coolness before daybreak, to rub pepper leaves and rosemary between my fingers, to dream of ancestral homes we never knew, gardens fallen into ruin, memorials never erected or left unvisited. I keep looking through the pictures, putting some aside and concentrating on others. An older one, in black and white: you are leaning against a stone pillar in the ruins of the old olive press in Sheikh Badr, just across the road from where we lived; you wear a long black coat—it's winter. Then a more recent one: our son running with a friend along the plaza of smooth paving stones leading up to the stairs below the archway that frames the magnificent golden dome of the Haram as-Sharif in full sunlight. Their shadows are distinct and slant at perfect forty-five-degree angles below the slender cedars where you once nursed him before we left. Another one: this time Mahmoud swings our boy through the air as he grips his baseball hat, screaming with glee— they're right in front of the fountain that never works marking the twenty-fifth anniversary of Sultan Abdul Hamid's rule, near the Muristan and the Aftimos Market. Which chapters of *his* life will these images attach themselves to, like so many barnacles seeking an anchor in the sea of this world?

Now I see us against the background of the city, in exactly the same place, some fifteen years apart. In the more recent picture, the sky is overcast and a new railing adorns the wall of the promenade. We're both smiling, our coats pulled tight against the January wind. The city below is visible as clusters of buildings held in relief by the long lines of the ancient walls that our bodies obstruct. In the other, older picture, the sun is directly in back of our hair and the sky is completely white, flooded by the strength of the light. It was taken by a friend who later killed his wife and then himself with a kitchen knife; she's buried in Tel Aviv and his remains were scattered over the Jersey shore. The silver dome of al-Aqsa is to my left: the edge of the walls at the corner near the Pillar of Absalom blends right into the sharp rocks of the valley whose winding road leads to Silwan. To the right of your shoulder is the wall leading to the Lion's Gate, and below that the landscape is dotted with stones and graves leading up past Gethsemane to the Mount of Olives. As I look into your eyes from this distance, I know who the queen is: she is the thread pulling us back and binding us together, the old flame, my mate, the temptress of fate—*she* is the woman in my life.

1996

Atonement

For David Alkalay, 1897–1982

The only time I ever saw Vienna was through the window of a boxcar. He whacked the onion wrapped in a towel against the table. I tell you, if the government doesn't fall soon, it'll come to the bombing of cities. Casualties will be heavy. He took the onion out and put it between two pieces of bread. I'll give you a hat exactly like this, he said, pointing to the gray visored cap on his head, the best wool.

I nodded: if it fits. I had always, from the first time we met, addressed him in the familiar. Even my father, his brother's son, used the polite form.

A few weeks after we arrived he had arranged for us to meet Cohen, to show us a place Cohen wanted to rent, left empty since his wife had died and Cohen had gone out of the city to live in the country with his daughter. There are a number of things I could say about the place Cohen rented us: the mosaic-tiled floors, the overgrown backyard filled with goats, the steel doors with thick grilles on the windows, the huge chests filled with Cohen's things, the neighbors who sang, threw bottles, and fought every other night, the window near the bed looking onto the street—jammed with buses carrying workers, women with baskets on their heads, and children with their hair cut close, almost to the scalp, to keep clean. But unfamilar habits, the dissonance of an alien language, belong to another tale, one in which I've never had a part. I seem to have assumed a place already mine, or rather, the place resumed its absent space within me, unperturbed, expectant, one might even say anxious to arrive. I was given to see myself through another and those eyes became my river of remembrance, nights my steps, groping blindly, tapping at gates and walls but always denied entrance, left empty-handed, powerless to ask for keys to what I never knew as locks. The city itself had many gates, not only those marking passage along its walls, but others: the Gate of the Dead Brother, the Gate of the Merciful Binding, the Gate of the Many-Colored Coat, the Gate of the Drunken Son, the Gate of the Birthright, the Gate of the Night Journey, and the Gate of the Two Mothers, to mention only some. But the unwounded body has no memory: sea obliterates the sun's heat, sweat retains nothing of the wind or a winter night. Even a body continually wounded, scarred from having things ripped from its soul—wife or child—resists, builds again, clings to life.

They told me I shouldn't fast, especially if it stays like this. He looked out the window at the apartment buildings between the road to Bethlehem and the railroad tracks. That's where we lived when we came, in tents—now I can't even get someone to fix my stove. Laughing, he handed me my weekly kilo of halvah, wrapped in a bag with the magazines he saved for me, but I was already lost in the anticipation of last year's warmth, wrapped softly in white, swaying to the melodies, under the still blades of the fan looming above me, packed in tight with the others, my voice finally my own, drowned out.

In silent devotion the duties of the heart owe allegiance to the printed word, but in the unison of song the spirit is tempered. Before Thee we stand, our wounds light—how is it that to us free passage was given? The Lord is King, the Lord has reigned, the Lord will reign until the end of time.

Sound the horn, the sun is down, announce to me how death released him, without his hat or with it: guide my song to the earth that covers him so I can see whether even there part of what once composed his body still remains so stubborn, continually longing for others, those above, and those consumed by fire.

1982

Of Books and Cities / The Journey

My Mediterranean

My Mediterranean began on the Atlantic coast, first frontier of the New World, in a fishing city called Gloucester settled by Portuguese immigrants. Whenever I was sad, I would ask my mother to take me up to the church of the fishermen, high on the hill, majestic in blue and stucco, with its two open bells ringing in the tide. Gloucester also meant the Greeks: cool drinks at the Anastas luncheonette, seedless grapes hanging abundantly off the white arches across from the movie theater at the Ketchopoulos Market. Boston and my father's sweet tooth led us to the Syrian and Armenian quarter. Later, Atlantic Avenue in New York meant the cassettes of Fairuz and Farid al-Atrache. By then my vocation had already found me: I was in love with words. Although I expressed my identity in a way that was polemically American, embracing the poetics of William Carlos Williams and his contempt for T. S. Eliot and anything continental, I still longed for the meaning that a color could have in Lorca, for the "red earth" of Pavese. My access to those texts came partly from my parents' "secret" language, the Italian they had acquired as immigrants in their flight from Yugoslavia, and the fifteenth-century Spanish that filtered down to me from an older generation. Although my family seemed "European," something was different: my name told me as much. After all, the first name was Hebrew and the last name Arabic and both languages and cultures were very far from any standard curriculum.

Somewhere between words and the world, between the genetic and the sensual, I began to more systematically pave my way along a path already sketched in the blood. This journey wound its way between books and cities. Books took me everywhere: to Tripoli, Istanbul, and Fez—my body made its way through Pesaro, Split, Athens, Cairo, Jaffa, and Jerusalem. Unlike many who had come this way, Jerusalem and Jaffa drew me precisely for the traces of a world no longer with us. Having come to the land where olive trees are uprooted and the bulldozer rules, I remembered a favorite sentence I had read years back by Ford Madox Ford in his *Journey to Provence:* "Where the olive tree grows, *there* is civilization." This contradiction, seen everywhere on the very face of the land and itself rooted in the deep conflicts that confront us daily, planted its insidious seed deep within me. All around me I sensed the utter contempt for traditional economies, ecologies, and the ancient beauty of ancient ways. My ancestral myths had always spun glorious tales of Sepharad, of al-Andalus, of Jews and Arabs, philosophers, poets, and alchemists; my eyes, so used to the abstract forms of American painting, felt close to the invigorating infinity of Islamic geometry, color, and design. But, in the promised land, it was precisely *this* part of the Levant that seemed farthest away. The living manifestations of that Old Levantine World (the native Muslims and Christians, the Arab Jews) either found themselves completely transformed or walked on as ghosts, extras placed in landscapes fit for the consumer market of an exotic but safe tourism. Again, my name provided a clue: in it, Hebrew and Arabic not only existed side by side but were incorporated into one. My heart and my head, my name: all spoke to me of the possible while everything around me dictated the impossible. Yet, everywhere, through the cracks, the Mediterranean light seeped in: I thought of a passage in the novel *Alexandrian Summer* by the Israeli writer Yitzhak Gormezano Goren: "Yes, Mediterranean. Really. Maybe it's by right of that same Mediterranean that I sit here unravelling this tale. Here, in the Land of Israel, bordering the shores of the Baltic Sea. Sometimes you find yourself utterly perplexed—is Vilna the Jerusalem of Lithuania or is Jerusalem actually the Vilna of Eretz Israel? It's because of this I wanted so much to tell the story of the Hamdi-Ali family, and the story of the city of Alexandria."[1] I soon discovered a whole world of writing, one that would appear baffling and strange to the very audience that most

Israeli literature seemed aimed at. This writing had to tell the story not only of Alexandria but of Baghdad, Aleppo, and Smyrna, the Galilee and Gaza, Katamon and the HaTikva quarter, and it seemed to make much more sense when placed within the context of modern Arabic poetry and prose, the North African novel in French, contemporary Spanish, Greek, or Turkish literature: in other words, the writing of the Levant.

But to tell the story of one family and one city in the Mediterranean is not an easy business because no matter what, the fact remains that people and objects, books and ideas, all traveled steadily from one side of the Levant to the other. The career of the tenth-century Hebrew poet Dunash Ben Labrat is not as remarkable as it is typical: a native of Fez with a Berber name, he went east to Baghdad to study before going to Cordoba where he revolutionized Hebrew writing by introducing secular Arabic themes. This triggered an explosion of writing that circulated back and forth from the Eastern to the Western Levant, from city to city, until the twentieth century. This massive body of writing forms only part of the Levantine heritage, but to create living work in the present also means saving the past from the uses it has been put to.

Now the Levantine space is one in which Jerusalem, what George Seferis called "the ungovernable city,"[2] is physically only less than two hundred miles from Beirut and two hundred fifty miles from Cairo, but—at least in any official sense or common pool of reference—still light-years away from the Mediterranean and Arab world it forms a natural and indivisible part of. Besides its stereotypical sun and clarity, the Old Levantine World is now a space of crowded cities, polluted seas, dwindling resources, increasing debt, and other, more ancient and insidious forms of oppression such as the subjection of women. Here the dialogue between men and women has just begun beyond which, perhaps even more significantly, as the Algerian writer Assia Djebar puts it, "the restoration of a real conversation among women"[3] can also begin. Here, among the many voices emerging, we can sense the extent to which the full emergence of women's voices in the Levant will alter our sense of its past, give witness to a present constantly pushed aside and form the kernel for new relations in the future. The Levant, above all, remains a space of immense human richness, a space that can propose new models for a world rapidly losing sight of the dependence of each part upon every other part. The books of the Mediterranean, what we can now in all frankness and without shame call Levantine writing, its ancient fragments and contemporary texts, are still its most vital resource but they must be reoriented within the terms of an altered, more plural political and cultural economy. The journey from my Mediterranean to this one has reached from the very familiar to the very strange: despite everything, as my head and heart tell me, the possible always also remains: to use the phrase of Mahmoud Darwish, we cannot succumb to letting "the surplus value of the slaughter" go unredeemed and we must continue to guard "the plot of the Book against the Prophets."[4]

1988

The Quill's Embroidery: Untangling a Tradition

In a gathering whose emissaries mirror both the more recent movement as well as the more venerable stasis of the Sephardic diaspora—among those formerly of Egypt, Baghdad, Tunis, Aleppo, and Algiers, and more recently of Paris, Montreal, Los Angeles, and Israel, as well as those remaining in the Balkans, the *shearith Israel* from Sofia and Belgrade—I find myself, if not the least exotic, certainly the least attached to a place that can stake claims to a tradition, a place that, at least in appearance, seems so vested that its natives naturally assume residence within the richly textured arabesque this tradition has always been presumed to emerge from. So it is, ironically, as an American, from a position of indigence that I would draw the margins these soundings intend to trace—margins that verge on nativity and estrangement, memory and forgetfulness: the writing and rewriting, the reading and rereading of the past.

Writing and reading, no matter where, have much to do with the unearthing, the grasp, and often the mastery of both presences and absences. Reading as both recovery and relapse; the ink of writing as life-blood, animator, nourishment—the book as fertile ground nurtured by ink.

In Shem Tov Ardutiel's *Battle of the Pen and the Scissors,* written in Spain in the fourteenth century, "on a day of frightening snow, a day of terrible ice," the writer's inkwell has frozen and his pen, in despair at not being able to perform, "to remember what is absent from memory, and stand guard that nothing be lost," recounts past service to his master:

> Have I not written for you excellent things. . . . When my udders were filled with ink I emptied them all on the scroll. Riches I swallowed, and I spewed them forth, and not a drop did I retain for myself. Naked I came forth from my inkwell and naked I shall return. . . . When the ice has been melted and dispersed. . . . Then with joy shall you draw the waterspout of the wall of salvation, and the scroll and its writing will be like an irrigated field.[1]

In the Crimean port of Theodosia, not far, in mind, "from Smyrna and Baghdad," the Russian poet Osip Mandelstam wrote of a "bookish earth,"[2] and dreamed of a place that, within the inherited wisdom of its people, embodied an allegiance to words—sentenced to internal exile, Mandelstem placed the form of his vision and the memory of his biblical ancestry in a Mediterranean world in which Spain was central— sowing dormant seeds, he unearthed his own genealogy.

The Spanish experience, packaged most garishly since the Jewish Enlightenment as "the Golden Age" and exploited by many, often at cross-purposes, remains, like Sinai or the Exodus from Egypt, part of the Jews' collective memory. But like any common, central experience that looms large in a people's past, it too runs the risk of diffusion, dispersion, and finally inertia: this field can become muddy and these furrows turn to drainage ditches that empty out into a still-born swamp, final resting place for what is allowed to go unquestioned and uninterpreted. Paradoxically, the movement of memory too often reappears in the form of fixed, unchanging images: resilient, indelible, and iconic, their clarity is blinding. In his *Commentary on the Mishnah,* also known as *The Eight Chapters,* Mamonides wrote:

> One action may resemble another action, so that the two actions are thought to be identical even though they are not. For example, consider three dark places: the sun shines upon one of them, and it is illumined; the moon rises over the second place and it is illu-

mined; a lamp is lit in the third place, and it is illumined. Light is found in each one of them, but the reason for the first light and its cause is the sun, the cause of the second is the moon, and the cause of the third is fire. . . . There is no notion common to all of them except through equivocation. Grasp this notion, for it is extraordinarily marvelous.[3]

Untangling the strands of the past is not simply an act of recognition, of fitting events into fixed patterns, of just seeing the light; it begins, rather, by apprehending the source of light and follows with an active, incessant engagement in the process of naming and renaming: distilling the light into sun, moon, and fire.

Of all the Jewish pasts, since it is almost impossible to speak of a recent single Jewish past, that of Sephardic Jewry has been recorded, transmitted, and interpreted in a way most alien not only to itself but to the very nature and basis of the more ancient Jewish structures out of which it emerged and grew. Disenfranchised, the head and heart safely removed from the body politic, Sephardic Jewry remains an anomalous and enigmatic entity to the vision of Judaism predominant since the French Revolution, a vision largely shaped by opposition and dichotomy: body and spirit, internal and external, secular and religious. Within this scheme, the history of Sephardic Jewry, the life space of its creative power and the almost singular diversity of its experience have been reduced to a frantic shuttle between light and darkness (the light of the Golden Age, the darkness of the Expulsion from Spain and its aftermath), without ever identifying the source of light or the subtle and sundry tones of its recalcitrant shades. Abridged into isolation (its nucleus distorted—the before and after assigned to obscurity), the longer tale of Sephardic Jewry remains to be told.

This before and after ranges from southern Arabia, Egypt, the Fertile Crescent, Persia, Central Asia, and India to North Africa, Western Europe, and the New World; its cities of residence and accomplishment, among them Kairouan, Fez, Aleppo, Tiberias, Cairo, San'a, Istanbul, Safed, Livorno, Salonika, Amsterdam, and London remained intertwined and bound by a generous surplus of tongues—mainly Hebrew, Arabic, and Ladino but also Aramaic, Latin, Portuguese, Italian, Provencal, Catalan, Greek, Serbian, Berber, Bulgarian, Persian, Marathi, French,

English, Dutch, and more than a few others with much remaining in parchment and newsprint, divan and prayerbook, question and commentary, document and fable.

Of 350 writers in a proposed anthology, only 2 were born, lived, and died in the same city: Sarah Coppia Sullam, a poet from Venice, and Haim Palaggi, a rabbi from Smyrna. The others moved, often frequently, sometimes by choice, sometimes of necessity, in a world much like that envisioned by Mandelstam: a world that embodied an allegiance to words, centered around the Mediterranean. Yet, we have become so accustomed, as the historian Elie Kedourie writes, to "statements cast in the universal mode purporting to apply to all Jews at all times and everywhere . . . to a universal and inescapable Jewish fate,"[4] that it has become an almost arduous task to envisage and accept a world in which passage was not exotic, a world in which autonomy—religious, linguistic, and cultural—was expressed and realized in contexts and under assumption radically different than ours can accommodate.

More than some of the labor in seeing and accepting this world has been undertaken by S. D. Goitein in his great work, *A Mediterranean Society.* In this reconstruction of the Mediterranean world from the tenth to the thirteenth centuries, based on thousands of personal letters and business documents written by Jews and preserved in the geniza of a synagogue in Cairo, he writes:

> I have counted so far about 360 occupations of Jews. . . . There was constant cooperation between the various religious groups to the point of partnerships in business and even in workshops. In order to assess correctly the admissibility of the Geniza records for general sociological research, we have to free ourselves entirely from familiar notions about European Jews. . . . During the "middle" Middle Ages, around 1050, the unity of the Mediterranean world was still a fact. This is all the more remarkable since the European shores of the Mediterranean, including Spain, as well as the African and Asian sides, were split up into many separate units, often at war with one another. However, despite the many frontiers and frequent wars, people and goods, books and ideas traveled freely from one side of the Mediterranean to the other.[5]

Even more remarkable may be the fact that, to a great extent and against great odds, this unity persevered among Sephardic Jews through the end of the nineteenth and into the twentieth century. "People and goods, books and ideas" continued to travel freely: songs originating in Andalucia, Castille, and Aragon continued to be sung in Tlemcen, Sarajevo, Casablanca and even the Bronx; poetic forms brought to Cordoba from Baghdad in the tenth century continued to be written and renovated in Livorno, Jerusalem, Bombay, and Brooklyn. Fully alive to the possibilities of each idiom they encountered, these writers made their cities books and lived in words, but never as a means of excluding themselves from the world they inhabited—refusing to use tradition as a barricade, they avidly pursued and confronted the new: from the eleventh to the thirteenth century writers like Yosef Ibn Zabara and Yehuda al-Harizi, among others, worked within the structure of framed tales that mingled philosophy with fancy, invective with praise, and the hermetic with the evident, much in the style of their successors, Chaucer and Bocaccio. The first poet to write sonnets in a language other than Italian was Immanuel of Rome, using the form in Hebrew over a hundred years earlier than the French or the English; forged in the cauldron of the Inquisition, little attention has been paid to the writing of *marranos, conversos,* and crypto-Jews as reactions to catastrophe, works created by those who were, as Shmuel Trigano writes in *The New Jewish Question,* "both the prototype and the anguished laboratory of modernity; the 'political animal' divided into a private, fantasizing persona, and the universal citizen, abstract and theoretical."[6] Like their more glorified and well-known predecessors in Islamic Spain, Sephardic Jews writing during and after the Inquisition faced this new state of being polymorphously, in many guises and under many rubrics: as crypto-Jews or the offspring of conversos bearing secret messages, writers like Moses Almosnino, Francisco Delicado, and Fernando de Rojas gave birth to and sustained the picaresque; discarding their veils, others like Antonio Enriquez Gomez and Moses Zacuto made Amsterdam center stage for the production of Hebrew and Spanish drama when European theater was at its height; seeking the reasons for persecution in time rather than text, Solomon Ibn Verga and Yosof HaKohen revived and reinvented the art of the Jewish historian; others like Esperanza Malki and Esther Kyra appeared as foreign missionaries and diplomats in the Ottoman court or Renaissance figures, like the poets, musicians, and patrons of the arts in Venice, Deborah Ascarelli and Sarah Sullam;

medical scholars like Amatus Lusitano and David de Pomis, haunted ruthlessly by the very superstition and ignorance they fought against, answered their inquisitors with examples from the unheeded valor of classical antiquity and the New Testament; by undermining and tempering the gentlemanly or spiritual exile of the world of courtly love or the pastoral with the fact of their own suffering and the cutting edge of their art, the humanists Solomon and Abraham Usque overcame the semantic and psychological shackles affixed to the paradox of expressing both shame and rage in the language of their oppressors. Often reduced to the status of a nonperson, skirting and straddling generic, linguistic, and geographic borders, the work of these and other Sephardic writers remain apt and cogent but neglected rejoinders to the dilemma faced by Jewish writers of the generation prior to Kafka's—these writers lived between three impossibilities: the impossibility of writing in German and the impossibility of writing any other way, to which one could even add another impossibility, that of writing per se.[7]

Although an awareness of this tradition as a way of negotiating the obstacles presented by nativity and the hierarchy of dominant and subject languages still lingers, to a remarkable degree, among Sephardic writers (Elias Canetti, for instance, when asked why he chose to write in German, stressed his full identification with the Jewish and crypto-Jewish writers engendered by the machinery of the Inquisition), the inherent impossibilities of the dilemma have only been exacerbated by contemporary catastrophe, entangled allegiance, and rebirth. Quite far from Prague, on a journey beginning in Baghdad and ending in what he describes as "the lovely town of Ma'alot," in northern Israel, the Baghdad-born Israeli novelist Sami Michael has outlined precisely three impossible possibilities (only substituting Arabic for German) in his struggle to write along the margins, between countries and languages. Writing and possibility, however, and the subversion of impossibility, seem to me to comprise a longer, more circuitous tale, one that goes well beyond the borders of particular languages, books, and countries to question the more radical temper of language and the book itself.

In an argument that takes place in Albert Memmi's novel *The Scorpion,* Alexandre Mordechai Benillouche desperately tries to convince his old uncle of the need to color code the commentaries surrounding his sacred texts; adamantly refusing, his uncle insists that:

"All the commentaries are true at the same time, so there is no reason to use colors to differentiate them . . ."

"But," Alexandre argues, "authors contradict each other."

"The contradiction is within yourself," Uncle Makhlouf answers, "it comes from your not having a view of the whole."

"Even so, a commentary hasn't the same value as the original text! A commentary on a commentary hasn't the same value as the commentary itself!"

This time Makhlouf answers categorically:

> . . . only if you don't know how to reconcile the whole. . . . You ask, which is essential, which embroidery? A bad way of looking at things. . . . You end up wondering which is the text and which are the commentaries. You end up doubting the text. Bad. Pernicious. Remember: everything is the development of a single text. And shall I tell you something? Even that text is a commentary. . . . When you need to hear God's voice itself, you have the Text. After all, what is it, if not the permanent presence of the word of God? It's up to you to understand it, as best you can, as you need to. That's why the commentaries may seem different.[8]

Poor and almost blind, a tireless weaver of silk, Uncle Makhlouf, although his text is specific and his presence may be our absence, effortlessly eclipses us: having skipped modernity altogether, he is already well on his way into the "postmodern." His sense of palimpsest, that beneath one text there is always another, strikes the bedrock of Jewish thought but without implying the presence of an Ur-language, as many considered Hebrew "man's," or more precisely, Adam and Eve's first tongue. Commenting on Adam's naming of the beasts in Chapter 2 of Genesis, Maimonides writes: "Among the things you ought to know and have your attention aroused to is the dictum: *And the man gave names and so on.* It informs us that languages are conventional and not natural, as has sometimes been thought."[9] Assuming language to be immanent rather than transcendent, "an aspect of the continuous divine creative force itself," as Susan Handelman writes in *The Slayers of Moses,* "the *Torah* is not an artifact of nature, a product of the universe; the universe, on the contrary, is a product of the *Torah.* One does not pass beyond the name as an arbitrary sign towards a non-verbal vision of the thing, but rather from *the thing to the word* which creates, characterizes and sustains it . . . Jews adhere to signs because reality innately is constituted as linguistic for them. . . ."[10]

To put it another way, the world is comprehensible only through the context the text provides, through language. To go further: the dean of Sephardic commentators, Abraham Ibn Ezra, in a note on Chapter 4, verse 35 of Deuteronomy, wrote that: "The human element of speech is divine or partakes of divinity." Since one of the most important divine attributes is infinity, both text and talk, the letter and the voice retain fluidity and remain limitless. The same logic that not only safeguards but vehemently protests against the word becoming either flesh or spirit also upholds the equality of the exegete: adhering to signs, beginning and ending with the words it expounds, commentary emerges not as reduction or limitation but a way of reinscribing and expanding the parameters of memory and knowledge, perpetual source of possibility and recuperation. In a commentary on Jacob's death, Benjamin Artom, chief rabbi of the Spanish-Portuguese congregation of London in the 1870s, subtly shifts some of the metaphysical assumptions about immortality simply by examining the memorial act in another context, a specifically philological context:

> After his prophetic blessing was over, Jacob said, "I am to be gathered unto my people; bury me with my ancestors in the cave of Machpelah." Can there be any connection between those two expressions—to be gathered unto his people and to be buried with his ancestors? Are they dependent on one another or are they equivalent? Abraham, in accordance with the promise of the Lord, was gathered unto his people, yet his tomb was far from that of his father or his ancestors. To be gathered unto his people means to ascend to the region of immortality; it means to return to our ancestors—to our father, mother, wife, husband, children brothers—to all those to whom the link of life had bound us *upon the earth*; it means to return to the country wherefrom we were sent in the moment of our birth, it means not to die but to live.[11]

Yet, to return also means asking where to and, more often than not, in what language. In *Return to the Book,* Edmond Jabès writes:

In the cometary of Bagneaux, dèpartement de la Seine, rests my mother. In Old Cairo, in the cemetary of sand, my father. In Milano, in the dead marble city, my sister is buried. In Rome where the dark dug out the ground to receive him, my brother lies. Four graves. Three countries. Does death know borders? One family. Two continents. Four cities. Three flags. One language: of nothingness. One pain. Four glances in one. Four lives. One scream.[11]

Locution and location: the Tower of Babel combines two fables, that of utterance, articulate or not, and that of place, which have become almost synonymous with a modernity that finds itself caught, eager to catch up with an inherited wisdom that embodies an allegiance to words but unsure of the markers mapping the path. In the argument between Makhlouf and his cousin Alexandre, the young man clings to a hierarchy that sees commentary and further commentary as regressive, a reduction or diminution of the original text. Makhlouf, however, accepts any writing, whether centrally placed or scribbled along the margins, as inaugural for "writing," as Jacques Derrida notes, "is the anguish of the Hebraic *ruah,* experienced in solitude by human responsibility; experienced by Jeremiah subjected to God's dictation, or by Baruch transcribing Jeremiah's dictation. . . . It is the moment at which we must decide whether we will engrave what we hear. And whether engraving preserves or betrays speech."[13]

This sense of writing as "inaugural" opens both the doors and the floodgates—extending the itinerary and increasing the way stations along the route, it also allows the sojourner to become a possible inhabitant. When Moses admonishes the people of Israel to remember Egypt, both the sojourning and the slavery, perhaps he meant, as the much neglected scholar Abraham Shalom Yahuda implied in his great study on the Egyptian influence on the Pentateuch, inscribe your experience within the very fabric of the language, take the land and the cities and the people with you and make them live in your book—reinscribe Egypt in such a way that you remain responsible for what Shmuel Trigano has called "the Egypt within, the interior exile." Freed by the desert and the breaking of the tablets and graciously exempted by God from the disappointment of seeing the promised land become a monarchy modeled on the banished one, only a child of Egypt like Moses could so thoroughly accept the exterior Egypt, since it posed no threat to him, and eradicate it by permanently inscribing it within the palimpsest. Just as Hobbes called Moses the perfect law-giver, he is, in this sense, also the perfect writer for he never reaches his destination.

This way of acceptance, this manner in which the exterior is internalized without being disowned or renounced is a stance of utmost respect and recognition toward the other, as well as an acceptance of the otherness of one's self: a fertile path furrowed in the very humus of the "bookish earth" by the biblical and rabbinic tradition, Sephardic writers kept well within its course. Sojourning in Alexandria on his way from Spain to Palestine, in a poem dated from the twelfth century, Yehuda Halevi wrote:

> See the cities:
> Behold the unwalled
> villages held once
> by Israel and pay
> homage to Egypt.[14]

This constant referral back to something always anterior but newly circumscribed within the text can be seen as the flip side of apocalypse, or what apocalypse has been taken to be, the tone of defiance and urgency announcing the coming of the end. This flip side seems to say, rather, that the beginning is always at hand and may refer to what Jacques Derrida has characterized as a nonquestion:

> The non-question of which we are speaking is not yet a dogma; and the act of faith in the book can precede, as we know, belief in the Bible. And can also survive it. The nonquestion of which we are speaking is the unpenetrated certainty that Being is a Grammar, and that the world is in all its parts a cryptogram to be constituted or reconstituted through poetic inscription or deciphering.[15]

Much of the certainty of writing in the Sephardic tradition owes itself to the acceptance of this nonquestion, a nonquestion that is also an unquestion—something prior to the act of questioning, Dante's "truth beyond whose boundary no truth lies." There is nothing surprising, then, in seeing how the creative genius of this tradition manifested itself in grammar and codification, two of the great projects of Sephardic rabbis. All the great commentators, in addition to being physicians, poets, diplomats, judges, or astronomers, were first and foremost grammarians. If the world is seen as an act of divine speech, then the study of grammar includes all the disciplines that have become disparate and even conflicting in the Western tradition since all categories of thought must struggle for and find their place of expression in language. Instead of the sterile discipline usually associated with the study of grammar, the Sephardic grammarians practiced their art as if the world depended on it, for it actually does. Humans are both God's speakers and readers, grammar is not the "after-effect" of language but the genesis of meaning—to hear is to understand.

Although cultivated by the learned, the route of this nonquestion was never restricted to them, constantly reappearing in songs, proverbs, fables, and even novels. Disguised in the form of a popular Spanish love song and composed anonymously somewhere in the Mediterranean world, the following Ladino lyric is typical of what hearkens back to something half-remembered but never forgotten:

> If the sea were made of milk
> I'd make myself a fisherman
> and fish for all my sorrows
> with little words of love.
> (Si la mar era de leche
> Yo me haria un peshkador
> Peshkaria las mis dolores
> Con palavricas d'amor).

Here the sea is the mother tongue, speaking love's idiom, and milk the invisible ink, perhaps of Rabbi Eliezer who said:

> If the seas were of ink and all ponds planted with reeds, if the sky and the earth were all parchments and if all human beings practiced the art of writing—they would not exhaust the learning I have mastered, just as the Law itself would not be diminished any more than is the sea by the water removed by a paint brush dipped in it.[16]

Surrounding the nonquestion, like commentaries strung along the margins of sacred texts, are the endless questions announcing what may be most unique about this tradition of writing: its complete and conscious renunciation of originality in the conventional sense. Here the writer can be distinguished not as engenderer of icons but eternal iconoclast, an iconoclast who does not simply destroy but, as Shmuel Trigano writes, "is a creator whose lips form the word that arises again instantaneously." Unwilling to simply settle for either spirit or letter, light or darkness, this tradition has found its medium through questioning the nonquestion. As Edmond Jabès has noted:

> Answers embody a certain form of power, whereas the question is a form of non-power. But a subversive kind, one . . . that will be upsetting. . . . Power does not like discussions. Power affirms, and has only friends or enemies. Whereas the question is in between.[17]

In many times and places, in many idioms, the Sephardic writer has found tradition along the interstices, between the milk of the mother tongue and the invisible ink of a beginning always at hand. This tale of the "in-between" is even more varied than the fragments I have so far tried to recount, and though it must wait for another time, it remains poised for the telling.

1986

The Quill's Embroidery: Poetry, Tradition, and the "Postmodern"

In 1982, in an article on Hebrew poetry, I wrote that: "As the lover's exile from the beloved became a symbol for the Jew in exile, Hebrew poetry itself became a garden enclosing the early unity of the Mediterranean world, long past the almost complete dissolution of that unity."[1] The deeper truth of this didn't really come home to me until I began making the connections from the present backward, rather than from the great tenth-century poet Dunash Ben Labrat and Andalusia on.

After reading "Zohra Alfasiya's Song" by the Algerian-born Israeli poet Erez Bitton, I went out looking for some recordings by this forgotten singer, which I finally found in a small shop in Mahane Yehuda, the Jewish market in West Jerusalem. The owner, Aziz Yifrah from Marrakesh, turned out to be a relative of R. Yossef Yifrah, editor of a collection of *piyyutim* (liturgical poetry) in which some of the great musician Rabbi David Buzaglio's (1901–1975) poems appear. Later, I found my way to Rabbi Hayyim Raphael Shoshanna, a liturgical poet from Morocco living in Beersheba who had just completed a definitive, critical edition of the "Companionship Songs" entitled *I Shall Arise at Dawn*, with an extensive commentary. I had come full circle: my work was cut out out for me—two poles—the marketplace and the academy, and in between a traditional Beit Midrash or House of Study that no longer existed.

Yet, even if the traditional Sephardic way of study, a mode that did not isolate itself from the world but included it, no longer really exists, one can at least say that, despite everything, Jews around the Mediterranean and east of it never stopped writing poetry. As Rabbi Shoshanna writes:

> The People of the Poem—if the ancestors of our kin Ishmael called us People of the Book in reference to the Book of Books, then it must be in reference to the Song of Songs stored within this people, and still comprising an inextricable part of our very selves, that they also call us the People of the Poem.[2]

Within the Sephardic communities, poetry is primary; in the preface to the first volume of Rabbi Shoshanna's collection, Shalom Mashash, the chief rabbi of Jerusalem writes:

> For behold, clearly we have before us the example of such magnificent figures as Moses, Joshua, David and Solomon as being our first poets; and Hezqiyahu was punished for not reciting poetry. And this isn't all, keep in mind that the whole Torah is referred to as poetry, as it is said: "and you shall inscribe to them this poem." And in my mind, anyone whose portion of poetry is lacking, has not fulfilled their duties of worship.[3]

Clearly, poetry here is something quite different from the reduced conception of it we are so familiar with, read by only a select few, uncared for, arcane. Here, poetry retains what it once was to many ancient peoples: the encyclopedia of the tribe. And as such, poets are also, of necessity, grammarians. Herein lies the crucial difference between Hebrew poetry based on Western models and this kind of Hebrew poetry; the "modern" Hebrew poet has relied more on *midrash*, seeking expansion from elipses between events in the text. The traditional poets remain preoccupied with language itself and transform humanly motivated biblical action into a delineation of optative and propositional states of being in relation to the unknowable: toward, away from, before, up to, if.

Poets are kept alive, kept "in print" by serving as intimate interlocutors between the community, the individual, and what lies beyond. This is nowhere more evident than during the holidays, when each community (with local variants) gives voice to the beauty and genius of the whole history of Hebrew poetry. If one considers what the equivalent, in England for example, would be if a good part of the population spent a week reciting selections from Chaucer, Shakespeare, Milton, and another few dozen poets, then one can begin to sense the full significance of just how remarkably cohesive a cultural achievement this is.

Once Hebrew poetry was published all over the world (in Sa'ana, Marrakesh, Baghdad, Calcutta, Livorno, Adrianople, and Split, to mention only a few); now, by word of mouth, we search to find books coming out of places like Qiriyat Yam, Mahane Yehuda, Beersheba, and Rosh Ha'Ayin. There are many hidden worlds within this poetry as well as many clues to solving God's most treasured pun: *'ever ve'arav* (Hebrew and Arab), both unvoweled peoples built around consonants, both each other's vowels, each other's shape and story, each other's tale. In talking of the musical modes upon which the "Companionship Songs" are based, Rabbi Hayyim Raphael Shoshanna writes:

> The ancient poets of Arabia came to the conclusion that every melody that had ever been or might possibly exist could not but correspond to one of the eleven melodic modes. These ancient musicians, with sound, subtle and acute sense, also stressed that each melodic mode corresponded to a particular time of day. And naturally, anyone of judgement and taste can effortlessly feel that the *'ashaq* mode, for instance, is clearly meant for the morning, with the throat's protestations and the voice's resonance after sleep. The subjects of the poems, I refer here to Arabic poetry, of course—also revolve around sunrise, the glitter of the sun, the dew's caress, the smell of the field, wind at daybreak and the battle with nightfall, as it is driven off to give way to the light of day. Thus, you find a melodic mode like the *maya* corresponds to evening and poems set in this mode concentrate on descriptions of twilight and the setting sun, subjects invoking melancholy among those who must put an end to their gaiety and dissolve the bonds of friendship with the coming of night, but joy to those whose designs can only be fulfilled under cover of darkness. There are

melodic modes characterized by delight and pleasure, such as the *hijaz*, while others—such as the dramatically structured *ghariba*—evoke an undercurrent of grief and sorrow.[4]

It seems to me that the only chance for Hebrew culture is to grow backward: to bring to bear all the power and richness it can muster from the past by losing the fear of reaching the point of freedom it takes to be "traditional." The modernists hinted at what the postmodern world takes for granted: the collusion and correspondence between African masks and Picasso, Persian tiles and Mondrian. Maybe Hebrew culture's strongest possible subculture, its furthest "underground" and most advanced avant-garde, its true link to a world outside itself, is deeply hidden precisely where most least expect to find it: within tradition. To grow backward also means to look ahead; by recuperating everything these texts carry within them—the music of shepherds, nomads, muezzins, mathematicians, alchemists, miniaturists, courtly orchestras, and David's lyre, the light and smell of every city in the Near East purposefully obscured only to remember Jerusalem, then maybe the Gates of Mercy will remain open long enough to gaze through them with affection and leisure, long enough to remember the touch of all the objects beyond them, long enough to regain the familiar impression of their images and finally recover from this long and painful amnesia.

1986

Paris / New York / Jerusalem: The Unscheduled Flight of Edmond Jabès and Jacques Derrida

Two T-shirts being sold these days in the Old City of Jerusalem read as follows: "Don't Worry America, Israel Is Behind You," and "If You Don't Visit Israel, Israel Will Visit You." Besides everything also implied by this mobile graffiti, it may also help explain why the work of Edmond Jabès and Jacques Derrida has not received the attention it deserves in Israel. The facts of the case, Israel and her "special" relationship to America, confound both time and space: the Jerusalem/New York route, although no travel agent will confirm it, is much shorter and more accessible than the Jerusalem/Paris line. Culturally, and even more resistant to the laws of physics, is the fact that, except for imported cassettes labeled "Chansons Marocaines" by singers like Sabah Husni, the reverse route (Paris / Jerusalem), is even longer and more difficult to traverse. This new trade route is no longer lined with silk but with the exigencies of power that inevitably seem to translate into one color alone: green. Not that the ancient or medieval silk route was all that innocent either but, at least as far as Jews were concerned, one of its by-products was true mobility.

Faced with the incredibly rich and varied evidence remaining from that world, with no other choice but to simply express one form or another

of amazement when confronted by the sterility of conventional classifi-
cations that attempt to impoverish and reduce the status of such trea-
sures, we might do better by confronting these peculiarly modern
dogmas as they affect not the transmission of the past but of the present
itself. One of the ironies of instant communication, like modern warfare,
is its built-in and ever-present ability to outdo itself—the lines can be
jammed, and interference is not only carried out along the shortwaves
of the superpowers. We are still both in and not in the age of phrenol-
ogy, that nineteenth-century pseudo-science that determined intelligence according to skull measurement. We live in a world where many
of the ways of measuring have simply become markers indicating the
extent and degree of *mismeasurement* involved. Events, even those left us
in the form of traces from the past, have outpaced conventional ways of
classifying, understanding, placing, and coming to terms with them. In
a study tracing the history of scientific attempts to measure human
intelligence, Stephen Jay Gould writes that these scientists "did, indeed,
study 'man' (that is, white European males), regarding this group as
standard and everybody else as something to be measured unfavorably
against it."[1] Anomalous in so many ways, Israel is no exception here;
still drawing much energy from the nineteenth century, from both its
determinism and romanticism, Israel continues to maintain, with only
some variants, fossilized European models.

Between measuring skulls and manufacturing heat-seeking missiles, the
countless hosts that hold dust and heaven in balance exert a questioning
pressure. The pressure of the question, the constructive thrust of skepti-
cism is clear in the deconstructive work of Derrida and Jabès, Each in
his own manner has sought new ways of measuring between the arch and
the ruler. Formerly privileged colonial subjects (Derrida in Algeria and
Jabès in Egypt), they have themselves subjected the strictures of other
kinds of domestication to a thorough interrogation. Jabès's central concern has been with the form of literature, with the shape and structure of
the book: how much meaning does a book dictate simply by virtue of
itself, by being a book? What is a book, where does it begin, where does
it end; how and why does one enter it or exit from it, as a reader, as a
writer? What is the time of the book and the time of the story, the time
of the writing, the time of the reading, the time of the writer reading and
the reader writing other books within the space provided by the book
itself? And writing between other books, against them, in knowing igno-

rance of them—those characteristic traits of Jewish writing—the acts of subversion and usurpation, of linguistic autonomy, are carried on intensively in Jabès. Yet for all its restlessness and questioning, there is a certainty to this writing which finds its basis within the nature of the question itself, at the in-between where the question rests.

It is this state of being in-between that characterizes the space inhabited by the books of Jabès. Between prose and poetry, fable and testament; between the friends of the song and the enemies of the song that constituted both the real and the imaginary audience of the troubadours. The delicate and richly allusive language of Jabès follows a line marking both the beginning and the end point in the unending crisis of the Western lyric since at least Petrarch. Yet, it is precisely Jabès's inheritance of part of a Semitic tradition, that is, the transference of the burden, the task or the fun of simply solving riddles, that distinguishes his divergence from that well-beaten path. In Jabès, the play of sound and word, the puzzle of names and naming, yields another crisis—that of choice. Here, the riddles are closer to those we know from Samson and Delilah, not the series given throughout the story, but the dense irony of their names themselves, of the enigma of naming, of linking the significance of name and act.

The work of Jacques Derrida has been most heavily criticized precisely on the grounds of its playfulness, on the grounds of his concept of play, of the enormous space he has opened between name and act, between the enigma of naming and the puzzle of the sentence in all its parameters. Yet, despite the controversy centered around his thought, despite one critic going so far as to say that his thought "dislikes residence and offers itself as a philosophy for nomads," there is, at this point, no doubt that many whose work will reshape the ways we think about philosophy, literary theory, and a variety of other disciplines, have already found a home within the spacious confines of Derrida and taken up residence there.

The scope of Derrida's work is global, its space is non-Euclidean and its time one in which artificial intelligence, hieroglyphs, video, and cavedrawings remain suspended within the black holes of the new physics; its critical intent is to de-center privileged and hierarchical modes of discourse that have, at various times, occupied such spaces as the terms metaphysics, history, humanism, anthropology, and linguistics can serve as labels and reinvest the texts that comprise the life span of these terms within an altered order. This altered economy reinstates the fact of writing, of what Derrida calls the "trace," or the "text," as much more than what it has been reduced to, a notational system that simply serves as a pale substitute for the living word, the presence, life, nature, or the transcendent spirit. Both literality and mystification confound Derrida; for him, writing is the system of any order, not just that of the phonetic alphabet, and his tale of writing (most clearly articulated in his major work, *Of Grammatology*), would include everything writing can note inclusively, prior to searching outside the trace. This sense of precedence, this idea of the world as book is much more than a lavish conceit or metaphor and reaches the bedrock of Jewish thought:

> It is customary that when a human being builds a palace, he does not build it according to his own wisdom, but according to the wisdom of a craftsman. And the craftsman does not build according to his wisdom, rather he has plans and records in order to know how to make rooms and corridors. The Holy One, blessed be He, did the same. He looked into the Torah and created the world. (*Bereshit Rabbah* 1:1)[2]

At the same time, writing is also the violence at the heart of any system simply because of everything designation *excludes*. In this sense, like Jabès, Derrida also finds himself in between but his question is closer to what he calls the "no-question; the unpenetrated certainty that Being is a Grammar, and that the world is in all its parts a cryptogram to be constituted or reconstituted through poetic inscription or deciphering."[3] Derrida, ironically, reads a denser past, one that serves a future already with us, simply because he is fully here now. Reading Derrida and Jabès is also a writing lesson and initiates an anthology that, in Derrida's words, "is also a lithography." A sense of event rather than a redoubling of metaphor, for the figure that ends Derrida's "White Mythology" ("Heliotrope also names a stone: a precious stone, greenish and streaked with red veins, a kind of oriental jasper"), refers to the "third row" on "the breastplate of judgement; the work of an artist . . ." (*Exodus/Shemot,* 15–19).[4]

1988

Perplexity Index

Golden Doves with Silver Dots: Semiotics and Textuality in
Rabbinic Tradition by José Faur. Bloomington: University
of Indiana Press, 1986.

Having tracked the fate of this book closely, serving in the joint effort to
find a publisher after first encountering it in manuscript several years
ago, it is most gratifying finally to see the end result in the light of day,
outside the circle of a few once dedicated admirers. In a curious way, as
in many such cases, the book may have meant more to us then than it
does now, as it begins (so one hopes) to gain meaning for others.
Certainly readings, of any book, differ radically through circumstance.
Maurice Blanchot has written of "exchanging a few emotional words"
with Georges Bataille after "being convinced (over-whelmed to the point
of silence) at what was unique" about one of Bataille's works: "I spoke
not in the way you talk to an author about a book of his you admire, but
in order to make him understand that such an encounter was enough
for my entire life, just as the fact of having written the book should have
been enough for his." But Blanchot goes on to say: "Admiration, reflec-

tion, comparison with other works—the things that perpetuate a book are the very things that flatten or equalize it." Herein, it seems to me, lies the raw, even aching problematic occupying the margins of Faur's remarkable work.

To begin: *Golden Doves with Silver Dots* is an unquestionable *tour de force.* I can think of no one whose erudition in rabbinics is matched by an equal erudition in science, philosophy, linguistics, structuralism, and poststructuralist theory. And make no mistake about it, neither is this rabbinical erudition of the standardized academic kind we have not only come to expect but even come to think of as unsurpassable or thorough in its approach.

Faur, as an heir to a Hispano-Arabic tradition that didn't expire in either Babylonia or Spain (encased in some cordoned-off museumlike space labeled the Golden Age) but flourished throughout the Near East, the Balkans, and Western Europe until the twentieth century, brings back to mainstream Jewish thought that which overwhelmingly always has been the mainstream of Jewish thought and rabbinic writing: an essentially textual, linguistic, encyclopedic, and poetic approach that is more akin to non-Euclidean math, the New Physics, postmodern art, and deconstruction than any of the correspondent "systems" Judaism has either been reduced to or boxed and packaged in since the time of Spinoza.

In *Spinoza and Interpretation,* David Shasha writes: "From a world of books comes a series of readings which seek to replace the Book with a set of mechanical operations translating into reason and ontology; the absence of linguistic theory exposes the non-Hebraic character of Spinoza's philosophy and contemplation replaces interpretation. Philosophy has rarely had to take the brunt of criticism for our 'real' problems, it is much too speculative for that, but I would positively assert that Spinoza was at the forefront of a (then) burgeoning tradition that created a world (even though creation is, for them, impossible) far more confused and embittered than the one it so swiftly and readily rejected. They even renamed the medieval period the 'dark' ages. For a tradition with such contempt for words, it is indeed odd they manipulated them so often."[1]

As Faur points out in "Freedom, Language and Negativity," a chapter concentrating on Maimonides: "The philosopher approaches the truth as if it lies beyond the perimeter of the text and a context: truth is absolute, transcendental and all-embracing. For Maimonides there is no truth outside a text and context. A text—any text—demands an *a priori* commitment to its significance as the *sine qua non* for the possibility of an interpretation; the text is a book, a particular book, 'the Book'."[2]

Long past being engulfed in the wake of Finnegan ("Nomad may roam with Nabuch but let naaman laugh at Jordan! For we, we have taken our sheet upon her stones where we have hanged our hearts in her trees; and we list, as she bids us, by the waters of babalong"),[3] and totally inundated by forms of "new-speak" so insidious we may no longer have the wherewithal to contain or even recognize a fraction of the complex occasions standing behind them, our more accurate avatars (Borges, Canetti, Derrida, and Umberto Eco among them), may be writing new Guide(s) to the Perplexed, heralding a revival of that particularly medieval mix of tale and teller, sign and meaning, semiotics and semantics, in a way much closer to Faur's brilliant exegesis of the original sense of Maimonides' title, *Dalalat al Ha'irin,* which might translate better as Perplexity Index, a realm identified with the Desert, where "it is not possible to get one's bearings."

Faur's project has been to reorient, regain one's bearings, and articulate what, until modernity, have been basic concepts of traditional Jewish thought, understood by a majority of Jews at varying levels: a few subheadings of the five chapters comprising the book should give some sense of the range covered here: Visual and Auditory Thinking; Spatial and Successive Organization; Thought and Experience; Calling Upon the Name of God; Freedom and Creation; *Halakha* and *Haggada;* The Formulation of the Oral Law; "Written" and "Oral" Texts; Cosmology and the Tora; Authentication of Tradition; Transmission and Change.

These concepts are often conveyed with unparalleled clarity, as in the following: "By excluding the vowels from the text of Scripture, Hebrew tradition was in fact excluding semiotic reading. It was also excluding parasitic exegesis, the type of static reading peculiar to the 'readerly' text discussed so brilliantly by Barthes. It is hardly possible to conceive a more 'unreadable' text than one made exclusively of consonants! The same distinction applies to the 'commentaries' on the Book. A commentary may be anaesthetic; its object is to make the text 'readable'; therefore, it presupposes literary innocence on the part of the reader. The 'explanations' are designed to act as a soporific whereby the reader surrenders his own criteria to that of the author and becomes totally passive. The 'unreadable' type of commentary presupposes total alertness. Its object is to point out hitherto unforeseen posibilities in the text, to formulate new alternatives by further perforating the original, and thus to raise the level of perplexity. This type of commentary bears no resemblance whatsoever to the original. It requires superior erudition and scholarly sophistication merely to note in what way it is actually expounding the original. Consider, for example, the Mishna and the Talmud, the most authoritative compilations of the oral law. Traditionally, they were considered the official *perush,* 'commentary,' of the Tora. It is a remarkable fact that they bear absolutely no resemblance at all to the Tora, in either structure, language, or style."[4]

There can be little doubt that *Golden Doves with Silver Dots* will become a classic among students of literature, literary theory, and the history of ideas, providing fresh, untainted access to the dense and luminous world of rabbinic thought; it is also, as Susan Handelman points out, a work that "both 'Orthodox' and 'non-Orthodox' Jewish scholars can read, admire, and learn from." Nevertheless, that aching sense alluded to earlier seems to point to the absent and ideal addressee of the book—the retreating and even disappearing exponents of traditional Jewish and particularly Sephardic thought Faur so eloquently interprets: the sages themselves, their students, and congregations. Faur's primary concern is with meaning, yet where this meaning is both directed and received may serve as a more accurate indicator of just how critical an impasse the Jewish concept of community from which such thought emerged has come to. Blanchot writes: "Perhaps life continues," while Adorno wrote: "Our perspective of life has passed into an ideology which conceals the fact that there is life no longer."[6] We remain stuck here, somewhere between the marketplace, the street, and the academy, waiting for the now defunct House of Study, the traditional Beit Midrash that always stood between those two poles, serving as seed and filter, shield and garment, to reassert itself, put theory back into practice, reprocess the oral tradition and read the vowels back into unintelligible consonantal texts.

1986

Desert Solitaire: On Edmond Jabès

.

I once had the distinct fortune of meeting Edmond Jabès and his wife Arlette in Jerusalem. Ostensibly I was there to ask some very specific questions about Edmond's education, but I also just wanted to converse with a poet who, by then, had become such an ethereal presence for me. My copies of the *The Book of Questions,* a mock-up of the Gallimard edition (red and black letters bordered by a simple red and black frame), were well-worn. But the *Book's* innovative mix of fragmented narrative, crystalline prose, distilled aphorism, rabbinical colloquy, and searing poetry had not quite prepared me for how much this gentle and urbane couple reminded me of my grandparents. I had the sense that were I to have visited their apartment, I would have known precisely where to find the sweets. A certain etiquette, decorum, warmth, and pride marked a character not exactly European nor completely Middle Eastern but something in between, like the terrain Jabès himself came to claim as the nonplace of questioning.

A Sephardic Jew born in Cairo in 1912, Jabès did not leave Egypt until he had no choice, in 1957, at the age of forty-five. He lived the remaining thirty-four years of his life, from 1957 until his death in 1991, in Paris. The nature of the balance between these two places only struck me *after* our meeting. Coming down from their room at Hebrew University's Mount Scopus guest house—with its magnificent but highly contested view of the old city dominated by the Mosque of Omar on one side and the Judean desert fading off to Jericho on the other—this elegant couple gravitated, almost imperceptibly, toward the television set in the lobby. It was a Friday afternoon, which meant that an Egyptian movie was on and a group of Palestinian workers from the hotel sat on the couch, watching and commenting. Neither Edmond nor Arlette could hide their delight at the black-and-white images of their former Cairene life on the screen. Soon they were among the workers, gossiping away in Arabic about the famous stars. This incident spoke volumes about what had always seemed left unsaid regarding the particular historical, social, cultural, and political context informing the trajectory of Jabès's work.

Grasping this context presents particular challenges for Americans. To begin with, the relationship of Jabès to his own Judaism, and of that personal relationship to public Jewish intellectual life in France, is inconceivable within the parameters of Jewish discourse in this country. That an Arab Jewish writer such as Jabès—extremely active in antifascist movements in Egypt from 1929 until 1948, and a contemporary of Paul Celan, Maurice Blanchot, Jacques Derrida, Michel Leiris, Emmanuel Lévinas, and Pier Paolo Pasolini—could be granted a prize by the Foundation for French Judaism, is a phenomenon that has no parallel here. Simply put, no ready-made slot exists in which to place an Arab Jew, someone who was both a Levantine heir to Rimbaud and French poetry read through the filter of Egypt, and a European re-reader—through the filter of exile in France—of the Kabbalah, Arabic poetics, and Auschwitz. All of these points not only mark Jabès's map of the tellable, but determine how it can be told, for, as he writes: "You cannot tell Auschwitz. Every word tells it to us."[1]

This insistence on discovering the wound in *every* word carries with it the effort to democratize language. Often Jabès levels the semantic field to such an extent that words of import and consequence rest on an equal plane with the seemingly insignificant. Both *A Foreigner Carrying in the Crook of His Arm a Tiny Book* and *The Book of Margins* perpetuate this project in different and vital ways. A collection of varied pieces, many of them commentaries or colloquies with other writers, *The Book of Margins* is a metacommentary, a kind of *Mishna* that codifies the method of Jabès's other work both explicitly and by analogy. Explicitly, in "Extract from a Speech," Jabès succinctly defines his position:

. . . For all my being bound to the French language, I know the place I occupy in the literature of our country is not strictly speaking a place. It is not so much the place of a writer as of a book that does not fit any category. . . .

This absence of place, as it were, I claim as my own. It confirms that the book is my only habitat, the first and also the final. Place of a vaster non-place where I live.

A word emerges from the silence of all the others, and this silence is also the desert.

If I had to define the words in my books, I would say they are words of the sands—of sand—made audible, visible for a brief instant, words of intense harkening and very ancient memory.[2]

As he has insisted so many times, terms like "sand," "desert," or "silence" are not vague abstractions but the very texture of his memory in recollecting the times when, as a young man in Cairo, he would venture into the desert to both find and lose himself. These words become part of a personal vocabulary—not a mythology but a foundation. Like the moveable Ark of the Law traveling through Sinai with the Hebrews, his key words make up a nomadic set of references that pitch their tent within the space of the book. Once these laws have been established, we can proceed by analogy:

So: a reading before the book, by the author, and a reading after the book, by the reader.

On the bottom of the sea, an undeciphered text fascinates the writer. So daring his dives! And if the words brought to the surface are black it must be because, as with the frightened octopus bloated with venom, once caught, ink is their dazzling weapon.[3]

This "dazzling weapon" is, as Jabès reminds us, what the rabbis defined as the Book: "what the black of fire carves into the white of fire."[4]

A Foreigner Carrying in the Crook of His Arm a Tiny Book is a pure distillation of the poetics and narrative that characterizes Jabès's major work, *The Book of Questions*. Here, however, Jabès has managed, as he wrote, to get "rid of the burdensome "I" in favor of the almost anonymous "We." This "we" is the foreigner, the stranger in each of us made palpable by the longing and sensuality of Jabès's own exile:

> He has just turned seventy-five.
> Paris slips under his feet.
> Precocious season of death.
> Cold hardens the cold.
> By day, he follows his shadow,
> by night, his life shading away.[5]

And again:

> "This man coming toward us is a foreigner."
> "How do you know?"
> "By his eyes, his smile, his walk."
> "I see nothing different from the rest of us."
> "Watch him. You'll understand."
> "I won't take my eyes off him."
> "He owes his nearsighted eyes to the infinite, his hurt smile—
> smile of a very old wound—to the past buried in his memory, his
> slow walk no doubt to fear, to distrust. He knows flight is illusory.
> Look. He stops, considers, hesitates."[6]

Closer to autobiography than any of his other work, *A Foreigner* also soars
further and further from Jabès as narrator, Jabès as Jew, to fully embody
both, as ciphers and containers of our age's profound sense of displacement:

> I left a land not mine
> for another, not mine either.
> I took refuge in a word of ink with the book for space,
> word from nowhere, obscure word of the desert.
> I did not cover myself at night.
> I did not shelter from the sun.
> I walked naked.
> Where I came from no longer had meaning.
> Where I was going worried no one.
> Wind, I tell you, wind.
> A bit of sand in the wind.[7]

Despite a certain proficiency in the technocratics of entry-level
deconstruction among certain of his followers, broader readings of Jabès
that take all the implications and resonances of his work fully into

account have barely gotten off the ground. Jabès begs to be read within the deeper and more embedded historical texture of Levantine Jewish writing instead of within the decontextualized and merely exemplary use of "rabbinic" or "midrashic" textuality. His work also begs to be read in the context of contemporary rereaders like Adonis, who—leaning on the theory of the great medieval Arab theoreticians and philosophers like al-Jurjani and Ibn Arabi—claims that language and poetry are not stages "in the history of human consciousness," but constituents of this consciousness. As Jabès writes:

> He said: "To the philosopher I prefer the thinker, and to the thinker, the poet."
> When I asked him for his criteria, he replied:
> "The philosopher is born with philosophy, the thinker with thought, and the poet with the world."
> And he added: "This is not all. The shallow valley of language dreams of full-grown forests; the rock, of teeth, needles, crests; the grain of sand, of reliable dunes; sea salt, of resined horizons.
> "Nearer the sky, the poets' words."[8]

For us, Jabès must be read within the context of Rosemarie Waldrop's remarkable, decade-long travail of translating his work into American English. An exile from her own native and adopted languages, German and French, Waldrop has achieved more than a great translation. She has expanded the possibilities of American poetic and narrative discourse itself by accomodating the opaque and extremely abstract counters of Jabès into an idiom that has always, and vociferously, resisted accommodation to such qualities. Her committment to the creation of such space must, as well, be seen in the light of Jabès's own intentions and testament. Part of this testament, bleak as it may sound, can be summed up as a motto for the next millennium as we remember past holocausts, witness those of the present, and brace ourselves for those to come. As Jabès writes in "The Unconditional": "What resists is what happens to die a more dignified, more ample death." And he insistingly reminds us that "Every book is a log"[10] which, we must remember, can burn, be burned, or used to keep a record in, a testimony of time.

1994

For Edouard Roditi

Sometime in the early 1980s after coming back to New York from several years in Jerusalem, we were surprised to find a letter from Edouard Roditi. I had been familiar with his work—poetry, translations, interviews with artists, the biographies of Wilde and Magellan, and various articles on a variety of subjects—for quite some time. I had no idea how or why such a venerable figure would have any reason to get in touch with me. The letter itself concerned a translation that my wife Klara and I had done of a common friend of ours, David Albahari, then of Belgrade. As we would later learn, this letter captured much of what characterized Edouard's curiosity, knowledge, and truly remarkable generosity: he commented on the origins of some words that appeared in our text and their sources in some particular aspect of Vienna during the Austro-Hungarian Empire; from there, he immediately went on to inquire as to our family origins. This classically Sephardic trait had two complementing and conflicting intents: first, to display his own illustrious family tree with the very pride that Elias Canetti so eloquently ascribes to his mother in the unforgettable opening chapters of *The Tongue Set Free*. And, then, in almost direct contrast to this pride, in hoping against hope that there might actually *be* some family connection since there are, after all, so few of us left, and family is, after all, still family.

But for Edouard the concept of family had no bounds. He created a vast network of people spread over various continents and remained a faithful correspondent and connector between and among all of them. He immediately also inquired as to our activities, our interests and projects, with the promise that, the next time in New York, he would be sure to visit. Still only knowing him by letter, we took this with a grain of salt. But, lo and behold, soon after that we got a call from a phone booth saying—in his inimitably elegant way—that he had arrived and would like to drop over. Hemming and hawing, we expressed concern that he might have trouble getting to us as we were then living in a six-flight walk-up. "No problem," he replied. Within less than a quarter of an hour he appeared, got through the buzzer and presented his imposing figure at our door, not showing the least strain. This would be the first of many enjoyable meetings until the sad announcement of his death. Even until the last few times we saw each other, he maintained the same resiliency, the same presence of mind and body, only complaining about how so many of his close friends seemed, as he put it, "to be getting old."

Whether or not this trait remains a legacy of the Inquisition or hearkens back to some even more atavistic biblical code from the years of wandering in the desert, everyone knows that all true Sephardi Jews possess unique and private archives where they gather evidence to be brought forth into the light of day at some trial of a nature and date even less pronounceable or specific than Kafka's. Both Edouard and I fit this bill; having just spent a few years in Jerusalem, my archive was brimming with texts and tales whose letters were intent on burning a path into the sand, while Edouard's archive bore all the traces of someone who had meandered for decades through the lore of a dozen countries, languages, and cultures, with the familiarity of someone preparing a meal in their own kitchen. Together we planned and wrote up an enormously ambitious project simply titled *SEPHARAD*.

Our aim was to present a kind of *Norton Anthology* of writings by Sephardi and mizrahi Jews, in two volumes of between 600–800 pages each. All in all, some 400 writers were to be included. Many of the texts would be translations from the major languages these writers worked in—Hebrew, Arabic, Judeo-Spanish, and French—as well as over a dozen others such as Aramaic, Latin, Judeo-Persian, Portuguese, Greek, Italian, Dutch, Turkish, Serbo-Croatian, Bulgarian, Georgian, German, and Provencal. The need for such a collection seemed beyond question; in addition to the hundreds of lesser known writers we planned to include, we were well aware that there was no single source available giving access to the diverse range of well known Sephardi/mizrahi creators. Our aim was to treat writing as writing, accepting the premodern concept of the learned person as a polymath, equally comfortable writing verse, a mathematical treatise, a legal response, or a letter. At the same token, we would treat "folklore" as the accumulated wisdom and honed mastery of generations of artists. There was to be no generic hierarchy, our intention being simply to present paradigms that could at least provide a hint as to the depths of this massive ocean of writing and the breadth of the Sephardi/mizrahi geographic, historical, cultural, political, social, and emotional experience. The publisher we were in contact with, a major university press, greeted our proposal with initial enthusiasm. As the proposal moved to the press's academic advisory board, it also met with great enthusiasm. Much to our chagrin, what seemed self-evident and crucial to us both as intention and need, met stern opposition in the form of a dissenting voice who ultimately prevailed in convincing the rest of the board not to accept the project.

There was an implicit and explicit political message to our work that many were neither eager nor even willing to hear. Our work simply assumed and illustrated that the highly ideological period of Zionism was an aberration and not the norm, that one could not look back at Jewish history—and particularly Sephardi/mizrahi history in the Levant—through a lens solely focused by the sites of a primarily European ideology. Our attempt was to present, if you will, a "Sephardo-centric" look at Jewish culture without, however, displacing one version of history for another; the idea was not to vie for a bigger slice of the pie but redefine the nature of the pie itself. The threat that acceptance of such a point of view might pose is self-evident: the academy would, literally, need to revise its whole sequence of study; languages and regions that have become the exclusive domain of experts, for example, would have to be brought back into the general curriculum, to become accessible to a wider public.

Moreover, we simply assumed that people—any people—can only anticipate and envision a future according to how the past is represented and transmitted. Thus, our selection of contemporary Sephardi/mizrahi writing amply portrayed the symbiotic nature of the Arab Jewish identity and its expression of pain and suffering over the internal and external divisions between the terms "Arab" and "Jew," and the wounded humanity inhabiting those terms. If our suppositions were to be accepted, then contemporary Israeli culture and literature, for example, would have to be studied in its wider Middle Eastern context. Many of the fictions we have come to accept as fact, in face of overwhelming textual and historical evidence testifying to contrary or contradictory experiences, would simply have to be dispensed with. All of these were issues that were close to Eduard's truly pluri-cultural experience and way of looking at the world.

Unfortunately, Edouard died before we could make further headway on our grand project. With him, also, went a storehouse of irreplaceable knowledge, languages, texts, and cultural nuances that no institution or book can fully embody. Rather than discourage me, my experience with our proposal only proved to me just how wide a net would have to be thrown in order to begin changing the terms of the discourse and get to a point where a project like ours would be fully embraced and welcomed as a sorely needed and valuable contribution. It was during this period that I began mapping out the very wide parameters of what would become *After Jews and Arabs: Remaking Levantine Culture*. My goal was to create a context in which the writings we had intended to include in *SEPHARAD* could be made intelligible.

Yet it is only now, having been asked to contribute some memory of Edouard to this collection, that I realize to just what extent he influenced my approach to intellectual endeavors and cultural work. In Edouard's approach, the simple fact of possessing certain knowledge—of languages and their cultures, for example—engendered a particular responsibility. Translation meant not only the thrill of transforming poems close to one's heart, but the willingness to serve as a technician, the way Edouard had at the Nuremburg trials. Book reviewing, for example, was not simply a matter of opinion but a way of carving out space that could have some influence in providing access to alternative ways of knowing the world. The work one did covered an enormous range of possibilities and permutations, none of which should necessarily take precedence, no matter how tempting or natural that might seem. Ultimately, the relationships that one maintained (one's "good name," as it were), mattered much more than anything that could be "achieved." These are lessons that Edouard lived unassumingly and they are ones I hope I have managed to take to heart and put into practice.

1995

Behind the Scenes: *Before* After Jews and Arabs

The movement toward studies that went into what eventually became *After Jews and Arabs: Remaking Levantine Culture*, published in 1993, began—faintly—in the late 1970s, and picked up speed and intensity in the mid 1980s. One form of the manuscript was finished, as my doctoral dissertation, in 1988. The circumstances of that writing, I would like to think, were somewhat different than much of the academic writing I generally encounter, either as a reader or within formal academic contexts. In retrospect, I find that *After Jews and Arabs* is a book that has seriously been read by a lot of poets, and used as the tool I had meant it to become, because it has a poetic and musical structure. Its most sensitive and intelligent assessment (written by Peter Lamborn Wilson) was, in fact, published in *Sulfur,* the journal edited by the poet and translator Clayton Eshleman, arguably the most important American literary editor of the past 30 odd years. While my textual models included works like *Call Me Ishmael* by Charles Olson, *Can These Bones Live* by Edward Dahlberg, *The Shape of Time* by George Kubler, *The Souls of Black Folk* by W.E.B. Du Bois, *Blues People* by Amiri Baraka, *Genoa* by Paul Metcalf, and *My Emily Dickinson* by Susan Howe, there was a deeper echo that had to do with the modes in which "traditions" and "innovations" can be juxtaposed to stand out in relief. It was a musician, the guitar player Marc Ribot, who queried me about this and understood that I had in mind the kind of formal issues brought up by composers like Albert Ayler or Cecil Taylor.

At any rate, I was a writer (shades of the elated, belated, and painful declaration by William Carlos Williams, "I *am* a poet! I / am. I am. I am a poet, I reaffirmed, ashamed."[1] That is, the quality and design of the writing were as important to me as what it was I was trying to say. I was lucky enough to have the support and wisdom of teachers who were also writers and translators of the first order, particularly Allen Mandelbaum (most well known for his translations of Dante, Ovid, and Homer, but also a poet whose linguistic and cultural sensibility is unique on the American scene), Frederick Goldin (a powerful inter-preter of the Troubadours and Minnesangers), and Burton Pike (recog-nized, most recently, for his pioneering work on and translation of Robert Musil). During this period, I had spent close to seven years in Jerusalem where, ironically, I had forgotten just how narrowly circum-scribed American cultural space was regarding any kind of alternative views on the intellectual, social, and political history of the Middle East in general and the relationship of Jews, Arabs, Palestinians, and Israelis in particular. This is where even starker shades of another declaration cast their distinct outline, in the form of Mahmoud Darwish's unequiv-ocal lines: "Put it on record. / I am an Arab."[2] Framed within my own personal context such a declaration might have seemed far-fetched, but within the collective endeavor I had undertaken—that is, an examina-tion of, as I wrote in the preface to *After Jews and Arabs,* "the relation-ships between Jews and Arabs on the literary, cultural, social, and political planes . . . and the relationship of the Jew to the Arab within him or herself,"[3] it came as a threat. In short, my manuscript began to circulate in an environment that was not only indisposed toward it for-mally but actually downright hostile toward it on ideological grounds.

Needless to say, attempts to get the manuscript published were met with enormous resistance. These attempts lasted close to five years before the book was finally taken by the University of Minnesota Press. While this proved to be a very frustrating experience, I took umbrage in the fact that the vehement, viscious, and intellectually dishonest nature of the reactions to my work meant that it really was threatening and could actually effect change once it began to circulate. The bottom line boiled down to a very simple equation of power and authority: if my premises, assumptions, and conclusions gained in popularity, many of these people would simply no longer hold any legitimate authority in what they were teaching or writing without taking cognizance of my work or attempting to engage in a dialogue or a debate over it. If anything, it is this cowardly behavior that has most frustrated me. I feel that the field in which I am engaged—however one defines it, whether as Cultural, Middle Eastern, or Jewish Studies—has been very much impoverished by the absence of an open debate on *After Jews and Arabs*. I have tried, in a variety of ways, to ferret these anonymous critics out of their ivory bunkers and by-lines, but to no avail. After the Oslo Accords, an enormous victory for mainstream Zionism and a politically disastrous decision for the Palestinians, a new approach was taken. I was suddenly being asked to participate. It was quite comical to begin getting invitations for speaking engagements or article submissions from people who, only the week before, wouldn't have dreamed of asking me to do anything. I am not sure whether what follows (extracts from two of the original anonymous reader's reports, and my rebuttal to the second, more substantial report) will finally bring out the critics to engage openly with my work but at least, in Mahmoud Darwish's words, it will be there for "the record."

> This book does not represent new research but a very personal view of the situation of what the author calls "Mediterranean and Arab Jews." It is a rather strange combination of history, literary analysis and quotes from a variety of literature worked into a pastiche containing the author's own dislike of Israel, Zionism and Ashkenazic Jews. There is, therefore, no group of "specialists in the author's field" who could welcome its publication.
>
> There is a great deal of culling of quotations, but I would not call it scholarship. It is a highly romanticized work of the "picture of a vanished world" genre. The author does not mention by name the most important work on the major part of his many subjects, *The Jews of Islam* by Bernard Lewis. Since I didn't receive a copy of his notes, I don't know whether he quoted from it. Much of what Lewis, the outstanding scholar in the field, writes contradicts flatly statements by Alcalay about the socioeconomic status of the Jewish communities of which he writes.
>
> If one is interested in the personal views of the writer—I don't know who he is but I assume that he may be of Iraqi Jewish ori-

gin—it is a valid perspective on a little known subject. Not an important work in my view.

The style is florid and at times unintelligible. The spelling is horrendous in places: the author hasn't learned the basic "i before e" rule, etc. The "organization" is such that I found it difficult to follow some of the author's arguments. What gives it some power, however, is the strong emotional component. The author feels the subject strongly.

I cannot see this fitting into the publishing agenda of the Press. It is not a scholarly work nor is it a more personal work by a noted figure that would make it interesting to a broad public. It will be of interest primarily to people who want further ammunition to use against Israel although the author sees his message as a broader critique of what modernity has done to the Middle East in general.

While I will let much of this go unremarked, I find the racist assumptions here to be most telling: that is, there seems to be some correlation in this reader's mind between his or her assumption that I am of Iraqi origin (which I am not, unless of course one goes back to the tenth century, in which case I might be, and which would only further prove many of the points I was trying to make in the book), and the "strong emotional component." I bring this up because it comes up, again and again. This first report, because of its brevity, must have relied on its author's reputation and authority in the field since there doesn't appear to be any need to even attempt proving its suppositions or claims. The writer of the next report, however, decided that my work posed such a threat that it needed to be misrepresented, in detail:

The main goal of the ms. is to provide a new view of the historical relationship between Jews and Arabs on the literary, cultural, historical, social and political planes; to shed light on "the relationship of the Jew to the Arab within himself or herself"; to examine the relationship of the Near Eastern or Oriental Jew "to a native space, namely, the Levant." Although a great melange of evidence is marshalled for support, much of it is highly selective, some of it quite tendentious, and often it is grossly misinterpreted. (See my attached report).

Although polemical works are always stimulating, I do not think this is a significant contribution to the field. The author tries to disarm potential criticism by claiming to be an amateur. But that does not relieve him from responsibility for knowing what has been done in the field. He certainly has read a great deal, but he has also missed a great deal. Many of the false or exaggerated claims would not have been made if he had gone further. (See my attached report).

The dense style and the bombast preclude any general readership. Although this may appeal to some comparative literature people who have no acquaintance with the field, it can by no means be termed "useful" because it is so tendentious. (See my attached report).

READER'S REPORT

Ammiel Alcalay's manuscript is highly problematic. There is certainly room for a new and fresh examination of the social, cultural and literary interaction between Jews and Arabs over historical time and geographical space. And indeed the literary aspects of this interaction (which seem to be this author's strong suit) are perhaps the least studied till now (except within certain discreet topical limits). Unfortunately, this manuscript fails to deliver. This is very much a piece of what might be called "popular French intellectual writing"; it never lets the facts get in the way of a good theory and it is enamored, even self-absorbed in its own rhetorical flourishes. The text is frequently couched in a dense, almost unreadable style, heavily salted with a few favorite catchwords which appear over and over again. "Space," "duration," and "memory" are prime examples of this. And of course, there is "palimpsest," which is often used metaphorically, although never literally. The pseudo-intellectual jargon is from time to time punctuated—rather jarringly —with popular and journalistic expressions (e.g., "x-ray vision") which is totally out of character with the purported tone. The manuscript is simply a total mishmash throughout. The first chapter tries to break out of the confines of the "rigid paradigms" of the historical disciplinary approach and moves back and forth from Maimonides to Osip Mandelstam, to Brenner, to the Description d'Egypte of Napoleon's scholars, to the *Guide Bleu* of the 1930s, to Edmond Jabès, and Tahar Benjelloun [sic]. Throughout these ramblings, the author makes all sorts of historical and political points that are never really developed, much less proven, but which really ought to be. Sometimes these points are taken up in the lengthy asides of the footnotes. Unfortunately, it is here that one sees the author's woefully inadequate knowledge of what has already been done in the field. He is frequently dependent upon highly unreliable secondary works, some of which are scarcely more than political tracts. Marion Woolfson's *Prophets in Babylon,* is a case in point. Many of the gross generalizations regarding the lack of comprehensive studies on the multifaceted social relations "both within the Jewish communities and in relation to their societies" show appalling ignorance of the works of anthropologists such as Rosen, Geertz, Loeb, Deshen, Shokeid, Goldberg, and Bahloul, as well as historians, such as Zafrani in France, Ashtor and Hirschberg in Israel, Brown in England, Cohen, Schroeter, Stillman, Udovitch, and Valensi in the U.S.

The one major historian with whom the author is apparently familiar, and for whom he rightfully shows a great deal of admiration is S.D. Goitein. Chapter two, in fact, contains a very lengthy excursus on the Cairo Geniza and cites a potpourri of details from Goitein's magisterial work *A Mediterranean Society.* This section of the manuscript, however, does not gel very successfully with the rest of the text and should be excised. The author is clearly out of his depth here. If there is the embryo of a publishable book here, it is in the first and final chapters.

The author's strength is in describing how the Levant has been seen through 20th century literary works, how Arabs and Jews viewed each other during the period of the rise of their respective nationalisms and in the period following the emergence of the State of Israel. Even here, however, there are some glaring weaknesses, for example, although the author is familiar with Israeli society during the 1950s and '60s, when Middle Easterners were at best ignored, and at worst suppressed, he is totally out of touch with Israeli society of the 1970s and '80s, when the situation changed dramatically and the Middle Eastern element began to be reclaimed and to assert itself both culturally and politically. (The author cannot retort that these decades are outside his highly idiosyncratic time limits—i.e., from the appearance of Dunash's wine song in ca. 965 to the Yemenite laments in 1951—since he is never bothered by such temporal restrictions when it comes to airing his pet peeves).

What is most disturbing even in these stronger parts of the manuscript, is the thoroughly polemical tone and nature of the discourse. The author chooses only what fits his vision and conveniently ignores everything that does not. His one-sided depiction of the Arab in Israeli literature is a case in point. It fails to indicate that there was a range of attitudes from the romantic paternalism of Smilansky to the varied depictions in Yizhar, Shahar, Horgin, and others. Had he availed himself of other studies, such as G. Ramras-Rauch's *The Arab in Israeli Literature,* rather than mainly Fouzi El-Asmar's [sic] more partisan work, he might have presented an account of greater academic integrity. He might also have tried to give some sense of perspective by dealing with the image of Jews generally and Israeli [sic] particular in Arabic literature.

Sometimes in reading this manuscript, I was not sure whether it was out of ignorance or the narrowness of polemical vision that the author makes some of the statements that he does. He laments the fact that the texts of Hebrew writers of Arabic milieu are ignored, mentioning three examples: Burla, Shami, and Kahanoff. Of the three only Burla is a truly first rate littérateur, and it is simply false to say that he has been ignored. His novels are read in Israeli high schools and studied in universities in Israel, Europe and the United States. As for the other, they are really more mémoiristes, and even their work cannot be described as totally ignored. (There is in fact an interesting survey of these and other writers' recollections of their Islamicate backgrounds by Jacob Landau which the author has obviously not seen.) More contemporary writers of this milieu, such as Sami Michael and Amnon Shamosh are not only widely read, but have had their works dramatized on Israeli television.

The author's hang ups so completely overwhelm the text at times as to make it ludicrous. Referring to the laureate of medieval Andalusian Jewry, Judah ha-Levi, he writes: "Yet like so many other works of the Levantine period these poems have been read less than used like the perennial elephant of the Jewish joke—to handily answer one of the many forms of the "Jewish question," as another piece of evidence fit into the mold of an already predetermined set of assumptions. At its most vulgar, Halevi is made into some kind of proto-Zionist; this metamorphosis, naturally, precludes emphasizing the fact that he was also known as Abu al-Hassan."

Speaking of vulgarity, the entire passage is crude, no less than it is false. The Arabic cultural formation of Judah ha-Levi is emphasized almost everywhere, whether in popular or scholarly writings. Passages such as this abound. They may score points with some people who have a political and cultural axe to grind (for example the readers of *Khamsin*, a polemical journal of dubious scholarship the author seems to read), but certainly not with any serious scholars. I fear that this book will do no better with the general educated reading public than with serious scholars. It is full of pseudo-intellectual jargon and bombast. For example, he states at the very outset that he is creating a model that "is ecological through the reclamation and recycling of antithetical episodes that can perforate circumscribed versions of history and serve to inform a forward looking future." That is sure to attract a general reader!

Polemical works can make very entertaining reading. They can be intellectually challenging. This ms., alas, is not in that category. It should not be published by a self-respecting academic press. It will, I am sure, eventually find a publisher among one of the small, politically-oriented presses in Paris or London.

There is, obviously, much that can be said about such a report and I proceeded to say it, as evident from the text that follows. Perhaps the only detail that I did not cover in my meticulous response was this writer's last point, that my manuscript would "eventually find a publisher among one of the small, politically-oriented presses in Paris or London." This was, in fact, a possibility I considered but it was very clear to me that such an option would even further neutralize the kinds of pressures I hoped the book could generate. The very terms in which this equation is stated point this out clearly: that is, the author of this report sees no contradiction or irony in encoding the word "political" to mean "not our politics," even as he or she is in the very process of excluding me from any access into that very political realm. At the risk of tedium, it seems to me that reproducing my response here in full serves diverse purposes that go beyond a merely documentary value; the title then used was not *After Jews and Arabs* but *Re:Orienting/Writing the Mediterranean*; in addition, the page numbers refer to the manuscript:

Re:Orienting/Writing the Mediterranean has primarily been an effort to shift the focus of a remarkably diverse literary and intellectual history (that of Jews and Arabs in the Near East) from the exclusive tutelage of an extremely narrow field of academic scholarship to the general community of literary scholars and students, from the traditional philological or "orientalist" approach to that of cultural studies and literary theory. In fact, this shift in literary focus has already occurred in other fields such as Asian studies, African and Afro-American studies, and Latin American studies, yet, as one of the reader's reports points out, "Middle Eastern studies has been, for the most part, remarkably absent from these debates." Unquestionably, any revisionist work is bound to meet some resistance along the way; my own awareness of this, along with the often heated emotional responses that the subject I have chosen to research sometimes elicits, made me all the more cautious regarding the scholarly and methodological foundations of my work. Given this, I sensed a definite bias towards my project in the second reader's report, a bias that, upon a close examination of the reader's objections, seems to rest more on an authority that would rather not be questioned or scrutinized than on intellectual rigor or scholarly evidence.

Before surveying some of the particular inaccuracies contained in the report, a few general comments seem in order. Throughout, the reader utilizes what might be termed a "hit and run" method, making a point without fully substantiating it. This, combined with an ad hominem critique only supported by tautological arguments that never get beyond judgemental and evaluative language to actually specify the reader's *own* contentions or position, all go into leaving the impression that this report is highly defensive but not very analytical. At the risk of being overly tedious, I would like to indulge in a point by point examination.

After summarizing the main goal of the work (in answer to question 1), the reader characterizes the evidence for my contentions as "highly selective, quite tendentious and often grossly misinterpreted." Yet, these claims are never fully substantiated in the body of the report. As far as selectivity goes, the reader states that I showed "appalling ignorance" of a number of anthropologists and historians; however, as I will document in detail further on, many of these figures are not only mentioned or cited but heavily relied on in my work. As far as being "tendentious" is concerned, the reader *never* states specifically what arguments are referred to nor why my work is generally characterized as "polemical." By then stating that I have "grossly misinterpreted" things, one can only come to the conclusion that this reader believes there is a correct and an incorrect interpretation to the very complex events, historical processes and texts that I present. This, in itself, is a highly suspect position in *any* academic context, and even more so in a field ("the social, cultural and literary interaction between Jews and Arabs over historical time and geographical space") in which the reader him/herself states that "there is certainly room for a new and fresh examination." "Indeed," the reader goes on to say, "the literary aspects of this interaction (which seem to be this author's strong suit) are perhaps the least studied till now." What is, perhaps, most puzzling about this report (a point that I will also go into further detail on when answering the objections to my second chapter), is that while the reader states that the "literary aspects" are my strength, these very literary aspects—as well as their conceptual and theoretical underpinnings—are all but ignored in the report. This, along with what appears to be an aversion to critical or literary theory, would lead me to believe that the reader's primary field of expertise is *not* literature; even were it a subsidiary field, the reader's language and terms of reference would seem to indicate that he/she is quite unfamiliar with and wholly outside the parameters of current debate, a debate that, I might add, has strongly influenced the practice of historical, anthropological and sociological writing, all fields that the reader emphasizes.

In answer to question 2, the reader states that "The author tries to disarm potential criticism by claiming to be an amateur." This is a reference to the second paragraph of my introduction: "*Re:Orienting / Writing the Mediterranean* is an amateur's attempt to shed some light on a realm that has been left in the hands of experts and ideologues too long." Given my range over literary, historical, theological, philosophical, sociological and anthropological works in over half a dozen languages, only a reader hard pressed to find fault would not see the irony involved in this introductory statement and not internally anticipate quotation marks over both "expert" and "amateur." Beyond even this more subtle point, I was surprised that the reader could not detect a reference to an article of mine from 1983 ("The Quill's Embroidery," *Parnassus: Poetry in Review;* Volume 11, Number 1; Spring/Summer 1983; pp. 85–115), an article that has come to be considered one of the most insightful introductions to Hebrew poetry written in English, where I discuss the late Professor Haim Schirmann's suggested mandatory equipment for the exegete of Hebrew poetry, a set of equipment that he almost comes to claim, tongue in cheek, impossible to acquire within one lifetime. Oddly enough, like the general lack of literary reference mentioned above, the reader barely mentions this primary concern and subject of the book, namely, Hebrew poetry.

Further on in this same paragraph (in answer to question 2), the reader states that "He certainly has read a great deal, but he has also missed a great deal. Many of the false and exaggerated claims could not have been made if he had gone further." To begin with, and this is another point that will entail many specifics, the reader has read the manuscript quite selectively since many of the sources he claims I am ignorant of are, in fact, prominently cited. Moreover, these purportedly "false and exaggerated claims" are never specified. The certainty displayed here regarding truth and falsehood is, I daresay, a boundary I never overstep as examples I intend to quote on subjects I *think* the reader seems to be referring to will clearly indicate. Nor, for that matter, does the reader ever specify what makes this a "polemical" work rather than, as the first reader characterized it, a "radical critique, at once substantive and methodological, of a dominant version of the present sustained by a particular, and equally dominant, grasp on the materials of the past." Scholarly rigor notwithstanding, one had hoped that enough revisionist work has been done to make such claims to exclusivity a thing of the past. Yet, the reader continually characterizes the work judgementally ("very much a piece of 'popular French intellectual writing'—it never lets the facts get in the way of a good theory"), without specifying the particulars: we are led to believe that there is, actually, only one set of facts (but can only assume which set since the reader never tells us), and, moreover, we are given to believe that my work rests on some grand "theory," rather than a continual questioning of assumptions along with a rigorous examination of both more traditional and neglected materials.

Given some of the objections brought up in the body of the report, I would assume that the "false and exaggerated" claims the reader alludes to have to do with the relationship of Jews and Arabs as well as the transmission of the history and culture of Sephardi and Oriental Jews. This is substantiated by paragraph 2 on the second page of the report where the reader discusses my "one-sided depiction of the Arab in Israeli literature" as "a case in point." To begin with, the reader misrepresents my sources by saying that I relied mainly on the work of the Palestinian writer and critic Fawzi al-Asmar; in fact, all of the quotes I actually *used* in the section under scrutiny came from an Israeli critic, Ehud Ben-Ezer. In addition, I also cite the work of Risa Domb as well as Lev Hakak. Even given such a clear inaccuracy, this would not seem to me to be the point here. What appears to be at stake, in the reader's terms, is some sense of balance given to differing points of view and interpretations of the historical relationship between Jews and Arabs. Yet, even the most cursory (but unbiased) reading of my work shows that my statements are continually qualified and problematized; in fact, almost anywhere one turns, qualifications are made to particularize the general experience that I depict. Although the following examples are completely out of context, they should give some sense of what I mean.

Beginning with my introduction, I anticipate precisely the kind of objections that the reader seems to allude to without ever really specifying them: "Any attempt to "right" such volatile terrain, however, exposes one to accusations of righteousness, the replacement of one exclusivity for another. Setting something straight, of course, also presupposes that something's gone wrong, that once things were one way and now they're another. This, too, leaves the work open to a broadside, categorical critique in which the very structure of the work can be seen as a set up: once there was unity and harmony, now there is fragmentation and dissonance. Yet, the central categories that concern me—the qualities of mobility, diversity, autonomy and translatability possessed by the Jews of the Levant for a very long time—*have* eroded drastically. The marker for this, of course, is literal and unequivocal: most of the Jewish communities of the Mediterranean and Arab world simply no longer exist. Those that do are but a mere shadow of their former selves. . . . While I would obviously hold the qualities noted above as positive, they relate solely to themselves and do not necessarily imply further harmonies or idealized relations between either Arabs and Jews or Jews and themselves. The paradigms chosen to illustrate these qualities simply provide a catalog of possibilities that, given the constrictions of the present context, seem almost inconceivable . . . *Re:Orienting* is not about victors and victims: to pit a powerless and gnawed at "East" against a voracious "West," with its consuming imagery, energy and capital, is to propose an argument as blind in its reliance on essences as the one it purportedly was trying to topple." (pages iv–vi). As an aside, the reader objects to my "highly idiosyncratic time limits," again, completely out of context and conveniently ignoring my own very specific qualifications: "I have suggested a time span within whose limits (with befores and afters), a certain fluidity exists. This fluidity does not signal an ahistorical aversion to the specificities of time and place, but is an attempt (within a very broad framework), to mirror the conditions of space, at least as I have presented them, in the Levant. My sole justification for this is decidedly historical: Jews lived and traveled, settled down and created from one end of this realm to the other throughout the 1000 year period in question." (page vii).

But back to the main point of contention; by citing things out of context and choosing to emphasize certain aspects of my work while ignoring others, the reader leaves one with the impression that *Re:Orienting* is a grossly oversimplified, "one-sided" book. Again, quoting myself out of context, I would hope that a few examples can serve to give the general flavor of the kinds of qualifications I have been particularly careful to make in anticipation of just these kinds of objections. On page 21, in a discussion of some of the factors leading to the mass emigration/expulsion of Jews from Arab countries: ". . . often, as in other periods throughout the history of the region, wealthier Jews could find themselves in a much better position than poor Muslims while the fate of poor Jews was often more closely linked to that of the Arab masses. Amongst Jews themselves, there were distinct divisions between the more culturally Arab working class (who lived in the traditional old Jewish Quarters, the *hara* or the *mellah*), and the more Europeanized middle and upper classes who tended to live in the newer quarters." Continuing on this topic (page 22), I go on to state that: "Here, the warring parties managed to find common ground. The increasingly reactionary Arab regimes also had their proverbial two birds and they, too, could be killed with one stone: by expelling the Jews, they could confiscate a substantial amount of wealth and property; at the same time, the Jewish question could be manipulated as a scapegoat to mask their own inert rhetoric, indifference and lack of resolve regarding the question of Palestine which, in turn, could help deflect attention from the more pressing, volatile and brutal power struggles and social conflicts transpiring in their own countries."

Again, out of context, the reader dwells on two issues, one of which has already been cited above: my "one-sided" depiction of "the image of the Arab in Israeli literature," as well as what I claim to be the neglect of "Hebrew writers of Arabic milieu." Just for the record, my discussion is not of "the image of the Arab in Israeli literature" but how a specific Hebrew novel that could not possibly be "Israeli" since it was written in the 1920's, sets one parameter of a fairly fixed set of characteristics. At any rate, on page 30, immediately after introducing these topics (pages 25–29), I take great care to specifically address the fact that ignorance of the "other" is not a one-sided phenomenon: "It is not only in Jerusalem that the number of people born into a new reality has multiplied: all over the Arab world (except in Morocco), there are fewer and fewer people who can still recall either the diverse Jewish cultural presence or the full range of *human* encounters with people who just happened to have been Jews; at the same time, there are more and more people for whom Jews can only be seen through the dull film of "Zionism," "Israel" and war." The discussion of the writers whose work I contend has been neglected is also taken completely out of the context in which I discuss it, that of being made into representatives of a particular kind within a subordinate culture by a dominant culture. In addition, there is a further inaccuracy regarding the work of the three writers in question which, though seemingly minor, just adds to the very generalized nature of the report. The reader "corrects" my categorization of them by stating that "Of the three only Burla is a truly first-rate littérateur. . . . As for the others, they are really mémoiristes." Disregarding the constant need to put things in a hierarchy, the fact is that Jaqueline Kahanoff wrote a novel and essays (in English, not Hebrew, as one might conclude from the report) as well as memoirs, while Shami only wrote novellas and short stories.

Another example relating to my purported lack of balance can be found in the section on Beirut in chapter 1, where prominent attention is given to the detrimental effects certain ideological trends had on Arab culture; on page 67, "But unlike certain tenets of Arab nationalism which, like Zionism, attempted to reduce and homogenize a plethora of social, historical, economic, cultural, ethnic and religious differences under the all embracing rubric of either "Arab" or "Jew," these writers expressed their vision of a borderless and uncensored Arabic as a way of speaking for people without a voice." By choosing to ignore my own often very critical discussions of events and texts emerging from the Arab world, the reader misrepresents my own sense of context and balanced argument entirely. Further examples of this abound, for instance: "Despite the short shrift given Muslims by the *Blue Guide,* during the 1,310 year period dating from the Arab conquest in 638 until 1948, there were only 129 years in which Jerusalem was *not* under one form or another of Islamic sovereignty. While this is not to suggest that such sovereignty was in any way uniform, ideal, or free from the practice of various kinds of occupation or exploitation . . ."(page 94). Again, in discussing the 1950's in Israel: "The implacable fate of the Jew writing Arabic in Israel was to remain unread: on one hand, the increasingly high and feverish pitch of official nationalist Arab culture cut off outside avenues of expression to anyone even remotely connected with "the Zionist entity;" on the other hand, fewer and fewer Jews found the means to maintain the level of Arabic needed to contend with works of literature." Here, as I believe everywhere else, I try to point in *at least* two directions at the same time in order to do justice to the representation of incredibly complex phenomena.

In the second paragraph of page 1, the reader states that "The manuscript is simply a total mishmash throughout." There follows a list of a number of authors, again taken completely out of context and without supporting evidence, that is supposed to serve as final proof for an argument the reader has not yet fully or even partially clarified. The seeming disparity of the authors is made an end in itself ("from Maimonides to Osip Mandelstam, to Brenner"), as if such a range already presupposed some kind of incoherence. Almost at random, I chose a book to see what range of authors or sources might be quoted or referred to within the space, not even of a chapter, but a few pages. The book, *On the Art of Medieval Arabic Literature* by Prof. Andras Hamori of Princeton University, is considered one of, if not *the* finest exposition on Arabic literature currently available. In the words of the great scholar Franz Rosenthal: "Professor Hamori's book is distinguished by the fact that it attempts to take Arabic literature, mainly poetry, seriously and to apply the canons of modern literary criticism to it. There are hardly any books in English comparable to it, and few in other European languages." In a discussion of a certain genre of Arabic poetry, Hamori mentions Spenser, Ariosto, Homer, the Serbo-Croatian epic and Heidegger in the space of two pages (74–75). Again, in a discussion of pre-Islamic Arabic poetry, Hamori mentions R. P. Blackmur, *The Death of Arthur,* Chaucer's *Troilus,* Plato, Socrates, Homer and Chinese poetry of the "Double Ninth Festival," all in the space of three pages (20–22). Does the mention of these things together immediately connote incoherence? Possibly, but certainly not in the specific context that Hamori has chosen to use them.

The reader then goes on to write that "Throughout these ramblings the author makes all sorts of historical and political points. . . . Sometimes these points are taken up in the lengthy asides of the footnotes. Unfortunately, it is here that one sees the author's woefully inadequate knowledge of what has already been done in the field." Despite my painstaking and, as I stated earlier, possibly tedious examination of the report, it is only at this point that the reader's bias, through the obvious contradictions engendered by selective reading, becomes clear. After having given the impression that he has read the text *and* the footnotes thoroughly, the reader states that "He is frequently dependent upon highly unreliable secondary works, some of which are scarcely more than political tracts. Marion Woolfson's *Prophets in Babylon* is a case in point." Entirely skipping the very valid question of just what constitutes either a "highly unreliable" source or a "political tract," the reader has chosen to mention a work that I referred to only once in a footnote (Chapter 1, footnote 11, p. 107). The report then goes on to state that I show "appalling ignorance" of a number of anthropologists and historians. Oddly enough, I mention many of these figures more prominently than I do Woolfson. The work of one of the anthropologists that I am purportedly appallingly ignorant of, in fact, is used to form a significant part of my argument in two chapters (the anthropologist in question is Harvey Goldberg; see chapter 2, pages 132–135; also see chapter 3, pages 262–264, particularly footnotes 14 and 16, pages 288–289). While the passages mentioned in the text heavily rely on Goldberg, in footnote 14, I state that Goldberg's "whole introduction is well worth referring to as an example of a highly sensitive reading of completely forgotten material." Another example is the case of the great historian Elihayu Ashtor, someone who also appears on the reader's list. Yet, in the footnotes to chapter 2, he is mentioned twice (footnote 3, page 240) and footnote 5, page 240, where I call his *The Jews of Moslem Spain* (in 3 volumes), "the standard work on the "golden age" of the Jews during this period." Not to know this, of course, would truly be an appalling indictment of one's lack of knowledge in the field. There are other examples, as well: Shlomo Deshen, an anthropologist, is mentioned on page 109, in footnote 18 to chapter 1. Clifford Geertz, Joelle Bahloul, Haim Zafrani, Norman Stillman and H. Z. Hirschberg all figure prominently in my bibliography. On page 3 of his report, the reader mentions an article by Jacob Landau "which the author has obviously not seen." The tone of assurance is even more striking here given the fact that on page 242, in footnote 29 to chapter 2, I specifically refer to the article in question: "For a survey of some examples of this genre of memoir, see Jacob M. Landau's "Bittersweet Nostalgia: Memoirs of Jewish Immigrants from the Arab Countries." Right after this, the reader mentions two contemporary Israeli authors whom I am also apparently unaware of, Sami Michael and Amnon Shamosh. Michael is discussed on pages 303–304, where I note that he has become a significant writer on the contemporary Israeli scene. The works of Shamosh are also mentioned in the bibliography; what any of this has to do with dramatization on Israeli television is well beyond my grasp.

Yet, even more disturbing than these blatant innacuracies are the assumptions and inferences drawn from such a selective reading. The fact that the reader is careful enough to point out that a publication date is missing in a footnote or that a quotation goes over from one page to another (noted with an exclamation point), while assuming I am ignorant of scholars, writers and articles that I mention prominently, can only lead one to conclude that some form of bias is at work here. An example of this can be seen on page 3 where the reader has taken a quote completely out of context in order to make another point that is, again, left unsubstantiated: "The Arabic cultural formation of Judah ha-Levi is emphasized almost everywhere, whether in popular or scholarly writings. Passages such as this abound. They may score points with some people who have a political and cultural axe to grind (for example the readers of *Khamsin,* a polemical journal of dubious scholarship the author seems to read), but not with any serious scholars." What kind of an axe? Which serious scholars? Which popular or scholarly writings? None of this is specified, nor is the innocent receiver of this report at any time given a fair representation of the range of sources that I did consult and that I am familiar with. In fact, this kind of argument is a gross misrepresentation of the range of my own scholarship for the huge areas it simply neglects to mention. For, as a reader of the journal *Khamsin,* I am also the reader of *The Hebrew Union College Annual, Jewish Quarterly Review, Revue des études juives, Encyclopedia of Islam, Encyclopedia Judaica, The Jewish Encyclopedia,* and numerous other standard sources. Why is *Khamsin* singled out (although only two issues are cited throughout), when other standard sources that are referred to more often are never mentioned? And why is the context of the quote, which has to do with the way cultures are transmitted by dominant groups and ideologies for particular purposes, never mentioned?

There are many other questionable aspects: in the second paragraph on page 2, the reader states that "although the author is familiar with Israeli society during the 1950s and '60s, when Middle Easterners were at best ignored, and at worst suppressed, he is totally out of touch with Israeli society of the 1970s and '80s, when the situation changed dramatically and the Middle Eastern element began to be reclaimed and to assert itself both culturally and politically. (The author cannot retort that these decades are outside his highly idiosyncratic time limits . . .)" Here, the reader simply seems to have conveniently skipped the last sections of the last chapter which specifically address the late 1970s and 1980s (see pages 305–329). Moreover, a recent article of mine ("Israel and the Levant: "Wounded Kinship's Last Resort"), provides one of the most thorough surveys of "Oriental" Israeli culture in the 1980s to appear in English, not to mention my socio-political study (published in 1987) on political attitudes of Jews from Arab countries which has become a standard in the field ("La communaute sepharade en Israel et le processus de paix," *Perspectives Judeo-Arabes;* No. 7; August, 1987; pp. 47–85).

An even larger issue that must be addressed here has to do with the question of literature itself. It is certainly odd that while the reader acknowledges the "literary aspects" of the field to be my strength, chapter 2 of the book (which deals extensively with Hebrew poetry and Jewish literature as well as the relationship of Hebrew and Arabic poetics to literature in the romance languages), "does not gel very successfully with the rest of the text and should be excised. The author is clearly out of his depth here." This seems like a major contradiction, yet, again, no evidence is given as to why I am "out of my depth;" it is simply stated as fact and linked to my use of the work of S. D. Goitein, "The one major historian with whom the author is apparently familiar." This kind of disparaging remark is nowhere warranted by the range of sources that are used even within the particular section where Goitein is used as a primary source (only 24 pages of a 130 page chapter). Some of the sources in the historical section of the chapter (comprising 40 pages including the Goitein section), include: Eliyahu Ashtor (mentioned earlier), Walter J. Fischel (a pioneer in studying the economic and political life of Jews in medieval Islam), Oleg Grabar (the foremost historian of Islamic art), Muhsin Mahdi and Ralph Lerner (two of the most respected authorities on medieval political philosophy), Jacob Mann (another pioneer in *geniza* studies, and a standard in the field), Jacob Landau (mentioned earlier), and Harvey Goldberg (mentioned earlier). This is just a partial listing and does not even begin to mention the range of sources consulted (and included on the bibliography), but not cited. These include many standard sources such as Salo Baron's classic *A Political and Religious History of the Jews* (12 volumes); Itshak Baer's *History of the Jews in Christian Spain;* the work of Fernand Braudel on the Mediterranean; Andre Chouraqui's work on North African Jewry; Norman Daniel's indispensable studies on the relationship of Islam and the West; Bayard Dodge's standard work on medieval Muslim education; Renzo DeFelice's work on the Jews of Libya; the extremely important but often neglected works of Levantine Jewish historians like Abraham

Galante, Moise Franco, Joseph Toledano, Michael Molho and Joseph Nehama; the classic orientalist works of Ignaz Goldziher; Marshall Hodgson's monumental *The Venture of Islam;* the work of Philip K. Hitti and Albert Hourani; Reuben Levy's classic *The Social Structure of Islam;* the works of Bernard Lewis and Maxime Rodinson; Andre Raymond and Janet Abu-Lughod's important works on Arab cities; Norman Stillman (mentioned earlier); the works of Georges Vajda, Moise Ventura, Harry Wolfson, Zvi Werblowsky and Gershom Scholem on Jewish philosophy and mysticism; and Yosef Yerushalmi's important work on Sephardi and Marrano Jews, to mention only some.

Not to even mention the range of sources I bring to bear on the major part of chapter 2, that is, the literary part, seems, at best, disingenuous. My own qualifications in the field are not without distinction: I had both the luck and honor to be a student of the late Dan Pagis for a number of years when I was at the Hebrew University in Jerusalem. Pagis brought the study of medieval, renaissance and post-expulsion Hebrew poetry into the modern age through his ground breaking works, *Secular Poetry and Poetic Theory: Moses Ibn Ezra and His Contemporaries* and *Change and Tradition in Secular Poetry: Spain and Italy.* Through studying with Pagis at Hebrew University, I passed the standard apprenticeship of those drawn, or better yet, magnetized to classical Andalusian Hebrew poetry. This meant a thorough knowledge of the standard works by scholars like Haim Brody, David Yellin, Shimon Bernstein, Ezra Fleischer, Yehuda Ratzaby, Haim Schirmann, Nehemia Allony, Shaul Abdullah Yosef, Dov Yarden and Ben Zion Halper, as well as keeping abreast of the latest developments in Israeli, Spanish and Anglo/American scholarship, the three major sites of research. All of these sources are generously referred to in chapter 2 of *Re:Orienting.* Nor is this all: in addition to covering the classical period in Andalusia, there is an extensive discussion of Arabic poetics and its relation to both Hebrew poetry as well as the development of the romance lyric. Having been a student of both Allen Mandelbaum and Frederick Goldin, my sources here, as well (in Italian, Spanish, French and Provencal), meet all the standards. The chapter closes with a completely original piece of research on a Marrano poet who translated Petrarch in 1567; this is followed by an extensive discussion on the extant poetry of Jewish women in the Levant and how some recognition of these works might change many of our assumptions about the whole period. Yet, the reader's report mentions none of this, despite the contention that the "literary aspects" remain my "strong suit."

Finally, throughout the report, the reader criticizes my writing through labels, not analysis; some of these epithets include "dense style and bombast; almost unreadable style, heavily salted with a few favorite catchwords; pseudo-intellectual jargon." There are others, as well, but they never seem to fully explain what the reader's objections actually consist of. Here is a case in point: the reader states that the few favorite catchwords are "space," "duration," and "memory." These are simply brought up as final proof of the reader's argument without any legitimate grounds for discounting the use of these particular words. Again: "The pseudo-intellectual jargon is from time to time punctuated—rather jarringly—with popular and journalistic expressions (e.g. "x-ray vision") which is totally out of character with the purported tone." This is very difficult to grasp since the reader never specifies what my "purported tone" is supposed to be, nor is this made any clearer by the reader's own characterization of my writing. In addition, all of the quotes, phrases and even single words are taken completely out of context. It is quite interesting to note that this reader chose precisely the same sentence (as a primary example of "pseudo intellectual jargon and bombast") that the first reader chose as an "apt description" of my methodology. Not to blow my own trumpet, but that the quality of my writing should be attacked is, indeed, the oddest part of this report as I hope some of the following quotes might illustrate. Outside of the praise that one is always flattered to get, particularly from established figures whose work has been so essential to my own development, the important point about these quotes is the fact that they come from scholars and writers for whom writing itself, and style, are not, by any means, negligible qualities.

"Ammiel Alcalay is that rare thing—a gifted prose writer and poet, an accomplished intellectual and a true, as well as inventive, comparatist."

Edward Said; Old Dominion Foundation Professor in the Humanities: Columbia University

"It is rare that someone has both an articulately perceptive grasp of cultural and political particulars and an art capable of their transmission in all the determining context of their fact. Ammiel Alcalay is far more than the usual cultural historian, or political scientist, or, simply, scholar of complexly "comparative literature."

Robert Creeley; SUNY Distinguished Professor; Samuel P. Capen Professor of Poetry and the Humanities; member American Academy and Institute of Arts and Letters

"As an accomplished poet, social commentator and historical investigator, as well as a tireless researcher, Ammiel Alcalay has pulled together many of the strands gathered during years of prodigious scholarship to present a view of the Middle East that is starkly at odds with that put forth in the establishment press and academic journals. Painstakingly, brick by brick, he has reconstructed a shared literary and historical tradition that has linked Arab and Oriental Jewish thought for the better part of a millenium."

Victor Perera; Lecturer, Journalism and Spanish Literature; University of California, Santa Cruz

"Since the early 1980s I have been following the cultural involvements of Ammiel Alcalay with exceeding interest and admiration. . . . His translations of Hanagid and Halevi (among others), reflected, in the most intricate manner, his loyalties and appetites. However, in retrospect, this seems a mere honing of the tools for the main project that Alcalay took upon himself in recent years. I followed closely the writing of his *Re:Orienting / Writing the Mediterranean,* not only because I was a subject of scrutiny, but, mainly, because of the extreme relevance of this pioneering study to the current cultural scene of the Middle East. His reading of that turbulent region ranks among the most creative and imaginative readings of history that I, being so obsessed with the same subject matter, have ever come across."

Anton Shammas; Visiting Lecturer, University of Michigan at Ann Arbor

"I am impressed by the breadth of his knowledge, his uncompromising lucidity, and his commitment to the Mediterranean—a region too often maligned, idealized, or ignored. Alcalay's scholarly and creative production is, especially for a comparatist of his age, astounding . . . Alcalay's writing is superb. The activity of reading—or remembering a history—becomes in these pages nothing less than a quest for knowledge. The reader is jolted out of the comforts of received polemic, as Alcalay questions our conventional ways of thinking not only about the Middle East, but about Western civilization and European culture."

Joan Dayan; Chair, Department of Comparative Literature; Queens College; 1990 Shelby Collum Davis Center for Historical Study Fellow

Along with this response, I sent the following letter, dated March 1st, 1990:

Enclosed is my rather lengthy rejoinder to the second reader's report on *Re:Orienting*. I really wanted to make sure that nothing got by on this so it took me a little longer than I thought it would.

It may simply be that I've gotten used to this kind of a reaction to my work from certain quarters, but only after thoroughly examining this report against my own work did I truly realize just how vicious and personal an attack this particular one actually is. I've run my reply by a number of people and I don't think that it should in any way be offensive to anyone—I've kept quite strictly to the specifics of the arguments involved. However, you obviously know your editorial board better than I do and I'd appreciate if you went over it and let me know if you think there's anything there that might rub someone the wrong way. I think, though, that this reply utterly demolishes the reader's credibility and exposes the kinds of bias involved.

As an aside (and I wouldn't in any way want this to interfere with the editorial process nor do I know whether this is standard procedure or not), I think it might prove a valuable exercise for the reader to see my reply, if for nothing else at least to know that not everyone is willing to be bullied and cowed into silence by "authority." Nor would I want this to be construed as some kind of vengeance on my part. I just became more and more amazed at the audacity (dare I say *men*dacity) of the reader's claims as I examined them point by point. Disagreement is one thing, academic arguments *with* proof are another, but selective reading and willful misrepresentation simply have no place in this kind of a process.

The appeal failed and the book continued to circulate until it came out, as I mentioned, in 1993; although it was named one of the twenty-five books of the year by the *Village Voice Literary Supplement* and one of the year's choices by the *Independent* in London, the book was generally ignored in academic and mainstream venues where the work of its "anonymous" critics regularly appeared. On the other hand, *After Jews and Arabs* has had an influence disproportionate to its circulation: like the method of poetry, those who read it have paid attention, with the idea of using the information it contains for their own purposes. The book has also forced Israeli literary scholars to reconsider some of their assumptions, while engendering a concerted effort among mizrahi writers, scholars, and activists to publish standardized editions and anthologies of neglected or forgotten writers that can be used as textbooks. At the same time, it has opened a window onto a very neglected aspect of Jewish culture within the Arab world—while there are numerous indications of this, a formal and symbolic marker was an invitation that I received to participate in a conference commemorating the fiftieth anniversary of the Nakba, the disaster of 1948, held in Beirut. Unlike the kinds of invitations that I was getting after the Oslo Accords, this one carried profound meaning for me. Finally, the book has also, thankfully, mattered quite a bit to younger scholars and writers who are in the process of expanding upon its scope and, hopefully, going on to challenge some of its premises and conclusions through the kind of open exchange that has always characterized useful intellectual discovery.

1989 / 1999

Forbidden Territories, Promised Lands

On Arabesques

Arabesques, by Anton Shammas. Translated by Vivian
Eden. New York: Harper and Row, 1988.

Once upon a time one might have hoped that things could have been
the other way around—that Jews would continue as integral and
innovative partners in the creation of Arabic culture—writing plays,
poetry, and novels; making music and art, publishing newspapers:
reading and speaking and thinking and singing in the mother tongue.
Irony of ironies: the possibility of a future, if the tolerated and often
encouraged level of madness doesn't finally overtake us, has graciously been proferred by a true native son, a Palestinian Israeli, in a
form (the arabesque) that is as integrally a part of this place as of the
postmodern world.

Before speaking of the book itself, an extraordinarily dense Chinese
box of a novel that pans from villages in the Galilee to Beirut, Paris and
Iowa City, a word about its reception. Needless to say, it has created a
stir: reactions have run the gamut from glib patronization to outright
adulation. The prominent Israeli critic Dan Miron's piece in *Ha'Olam*

HaZe seems representative of the former: "By using Hebrew, Shammas distances himself from those outstanding attributes of the Arabic tradition, rhetorical and emotional abundance," though, he adds, a bit is gained since modernity has sloughed off "outmoded and static forms." This miserly view from the top simply perpetuates another received idea. Shammas's style, in fact, often achieves that most powerful quality of Semitic languages (Hebrew and Arabic) when written in their own syntax: the ability to embrace contradictory states within the tense enactment of event or relations between people and objects. Dan Miron goes on to say: "A reader of Shammas must ask himself whether his barren quality is the result of personal inhibitions or if a wider problematic is at work here, a social or even national one—is Shammas's aridity the price he has paid for cutting himself off from his social and linguistic roots and adapting a foreign linguistic and cultural system?" While Shammas is given credit for his portrayal of "the behavior of people and animals" (presumably similar in such places), this is attributed to "the intuitive understanding of a villager," since, "from a psychological point of view, Shammas has not yet reconciled himself intellectually and emotionally with his past." Would one accuse the American-born, Hebrew-writing Israeli poet Harold Schimmel, for instance, of cutting himself off from his "social and linguistic roots" by writing in Hebrew and not English? Of course not, after all, he's one of "us" and the essence of a Jewish soul must ultimately express itself in the "Jewish" "language." Without being too hasty in jumping to conclusions, there seems to me to be a code at work here, expressed more vulgarly elsewhere, and which can be delineated in the following terms: He deals so beautifully with village life—who wants to hear about his two days in Paris and visiting Proust's grave and going to the Iowa Writing Program and meeting his lost double, thought dead in Beirut, and his identity and after all doesn't he know who he is, it's right down there on his ID card isn't it? The assumptions behind such thinking, dare one utter it, reflect a kind of positivist logic whose natural culmination finds itself (who, us?), in racial purity laws or the equally ludicrous but no less sinister position in which one cannot be a "Jewish" writer outside of Israel or in a language other than Hebrew. And along comes this Shammas guy who isn't even a Jew or a Muslim but a Christian and he throws a monkey wrench into the whole works . . . scary, isn't it? Apparently, to some.

At the other end of the spectrum, the critic Yael Lotan puts her finger on exactly what some *do* find scary: "In Israel, Hebrew literature has been tribal literature, dealing with tribal matters. Attempts to deal with extra-tribal affairs have, until now, failed due to this provincialism. Only the existence of Jewish readers around the world, along with the natural curiosity of others about life in this little country, was able to push it to the forefront; however, there is also a non-Jewish population which, following the natural course of things, finds itself mixing in to form an integral part of Israeli culture. This would be inevitable even if the country was absolutely isolated, not to mention that it finds itself within the heart of the Arab world, no matter how hard one tries to evade that fact. That Hebrew and Arabic are closely related and half, or more than half of the Jewish population is of Middle Eastern origin only speeds up the process. . . . Maybe a day will come when an Israeli theater troupe will tour Arab countries and present plays alternatively in Hebrew and Arabic. Maybe a day will come when Israeli writers—Jews too—will prefer writing in Arabic, since their readership will be incomparably greater than in Hebrew."[1]

This puts us in the realm of truly frightening prospects: cultural exchange (with our neighbors, not Germany or Finland), pluralism even; perish the thought. But innovative artists change maps, realign branches of affiliation, affect both retro and prospective readings. By making Hebrew a *lingua franca* that just happens to dominate this particular region for the time being—and which can be used due to the exigencies of political and cultural vicissitudes by anyone who happens to be trapped within such circumstances—Shammas has both opened a path for what might come ahead and presented solid reason to reread, a little more thoroughly this time around, the ethnocentric assumptions that have so long and exasperatingly governed most (un)critical readings of Jewish writing. Like all good writers, Shammas anticipates possible readings of his work within the text itself. By not only accepting but even celebrating his own exile within language, he fully realizes the condition and problematic of writing anywhere: in this, he breaks the blockade of contemporary Hebrew prose.

Commenting on Maurice Blanchot, Gilbert Sorrentino has written "His writings investigate the absolute responsibility the writer has to language. Civilization has convinced us that to speak is to control that which is spoken of; Blanchot's entire occupation has been to call this glibness into question. He has shown us that the void writing creates between itself and the world can never be filled adequately, the writer's hope to tell a story is futile, yet this void is, infinitely and mysteriously, the only space in which literature can exist. In Blanchot's words: 'to discover the language of literature is to search for the moment which precedes literature.'"[2] In many ways, *Arabesques* is precisely about finding this constantly recurring and elusive moment, about pulling differently colored threads through a labyrinth of form divided, here, into two parts: the Tale, and the Teller or, in more contemporary terms: the narration and the narrator. By going back in time from the village of Fasuta in a world where Beirut was the urban point of reference, and forward, past Sabra, to Paris and Iowa, Shammas emerges as both teller of tales and narrator of texts. He includes the nineteenth-century novel(s) some would preferred he continue writing (the detective story, love story, story of the double: Hardy, Willa Cather) by interrupting, interrogating, and, finally, through sheer bravado, outdoing them. Instead of relying on the found manuscript, the lost relative himself (Michael/Michel Abyad) offers the teller of tales the book of his own life when they finally meet in Iowa City, so far from everything that has separated them this long.

The form and language of the novel are not mere surrogates in the hands of Shammas, but intimate partners. The first section, and the remaining sections that compose the family chronicle dating from the mid–nineteenth century, embed their fable in words that themselves are part of the past: here, the archaic and the magical coincide. The eyes of the child (observer/narrator), process all the information—colors, sounds, smells, feelings—and release it through the art of a medieval storyteller. But just as the storyteller was often not content to rest on the merits of the tale without at least suggesting the consequences, implications, or moral of its action through a commentary, so Shammas employs various means to reprocess that primal information, to rescue it from its interment in the past, static and eloquent in its beauty but ultimately inapplicable to the only place where it has use, the present.

Ostensibly, the narrator goes forth in quest of a lost relative but the search ends up as an essay in recuperation, an attempt to assemble the shards of that long shattered primal vessel. The narrator isn't driven by false nostalgia, but the need to make some sense out of the delicate and layered experience that comprises the life of those Palestinians who stayed "inside" after the disaster of '48. These layers include the airtight world beyond, represented by Beirut, both as it was and is; the West Bank, with all the attendant ambivalence and confusion involved in that relationship; and Israel itself, with the incessant hope and disappointment it offers. A number of these themes mirror and fold in on themselves: the characters and objects that were part of the primal vessel, the magic lamp of childhood, possess a kind of subterranean vision. They see from underground up and often take to the road, both in flight and search, wandering through the same strata as the narrator. Other characters, those from the "afterworld" (Israelis and others the narrator meets along the journey), can only see in reverse: they have to try and reconstruct Anton the narrator by finding those parts of himself he is still in search of. Paris and Iowa City are two way stations on this journey. As Shimon Ballas has pointed out, they interconnect with another underlying theme twisting and coursing its way through the maze: a love story or, rather, a story of unrequited love, something that has always served to limn the ultimate frustration in reaching final union, whether it be with oneself, the past, or a promised land.

The give and take between the betrayal of telling and the need for things to be told permeates the book (from standing like "a mute dove" before his Uncle Yusef, holder of keys to many mysteries, to the complex net woven in Iowa between Bar-On, an Israeli, Paco, a Palestinian from Nablus, and Anton, the writer/narrator, now the "Jew's Jew" at the International Writing Program). Shammas doesn't neglect the haunting power things have over us: an inlaid Damascene box, flasks of olive oil, horses (white and red), strands of hair (red and black), a blue handkerchief, the pillow of a baby thought dead and, most of all, names themselves. Laila Khouri, an elegant Christian woman from Beirut ends up Suraya Said, a widowed Muslim in the West Bank whose deaf and dumb twins posses a stunning eloquence; Anton (the narrator) sees a picture in the September 27, 1982, *Time* magazine of Michael/Michel (adopted in Beirut in January 1928 a few days after Uncle Jiryis Shammas went off to Argentina, thinking his son Anton dead) riding a motor-scooter through the carnage of Sabra, a partly decapitated horse leaning into a trough in the background. Anton (the narrator) then discovers Suraya Said (Laila Khouri) through Abdullah al-Asbah (once Abdullah Said) forty-four years after al-Asbah had gotten a shave in his father's barbershop in Fasuta, an English rifle between his legs, his gaze fixed on three white horses hitched to a goat shed in the distance.

By acknowledging the power names and naming have, Shammas doesn't succumb to their damning edicts but remains autonomous, always opening another trap door in the labyrinth and letting the feathers (once quills) fly off into the wind to reinscribe themselves wherever they happen to fall. In another context ("Algerian Literature: Horizon 2000"), Jamal Eddine Ben Cheikh wrote: "Our Palestine is within and the language we have to express it guards its secret voice."[4] By guarding the secret voice of his own language, Shammas counters complexity with complexity to reinforce the relentless lesson given about the fragility and caprice of circumstance and the absolutely random swapping of fate once a whole life order has been shattered and fragmented, both politically and naturally, through the pain of growth and loss.

1986

After the Last Sky

After the Last Sky, by Edward W. Said. Photographs by
Jean Mohr. New York: Pantheon Books. 1986.

The habits of violence are indeed various—the point of a knife, the end
of a stick, the velocity of a bullet, the push of a button—but violence
encompasses more insidious means as well: the practice of exclusion,
misrepresentation, dispossession, oblivion. "Terrorists" hijack planes
but "ideologies," in the form of states and other acceptably licensed
power structures, hijack a people's collective memory, or at least make
the attempt. Nevertheless, events pile up and, as Edward Said writes in
his most personal and acute work to date: "Palestine is a small place. It
is also incredibly crowded with the traces and claims of people. And the
more recent the people, the more exclusive their claim, and the more
vigorous the pushing out and suppressing of all others."[1]

Anyone hoping to find slogans to justify an easy dismissal of Said's
claims, singular and collective, will have to search elsewhere. *After the
Last Sky* (a line from the Palestinian national poet Mahmoud Darwish),
is not a book of words accompanying pictures but a labor of love woven

into a pure, unwavering texture; it is a work that triumphs over something photographers, consciously or not, have always faced: the dilemma of what Michel Foucault has called "the indignity of speaking for others." Jean Mohr, the Swiss-born photographer best known for his work with John Berger, seems to possess a sixth sense, a living hand extending beyond the lens to hold back the violence a camera can inflict in the implicitly voyeuristic invasion that "taking" someone's picture involves. The juxtaposition between Said's text and Mohr's photographs, what the words evoke and the images confirm, works almost physically: as you turn to follow a sentence going from one page to the next it meets a picture that bids nothing but the desire to touch—face, hand, shoulder, man, woman, child, maybe even Mohr's extended gaze that more often than not seems to play tricks, to tell you there's nothing special here, just an ordinary scene, just a simple person. And herein is precisely where the power and magic of this collective statement lies—no matter how displaced or dispossessed, a decisive border separates the native and the tourist, something that may not be much to hold onto but, as the Palestinian writer and human rights lawyer Raja Shehadeh writes in *The Third Way:* "We who have lived a silent love for this land are left with the grim satisfaction of seeing that the Israelis will never know our hills as we do. They are already making endless, ignorant mistakes. For all their grand rhetoric, they are strangers."[2]

It is this silence in face of such grand rhetoric that Edward Said's remarkable text manages to maintain. By jettisoning the baggage of erudition and documentation he is so capable of marshaling, Said leaves an even more certain testimony, odd hope in a time that may seem hopeless, but hope that offers no formula, proffers nothing so crass as a "political" position without at the same time taking refuge in a liberality that ignores the politics of power in favor of some amorphous good. This voice, at once speculative, inquisitive, tender, and expansive, no longer *needs* the facts but draws on a much deeper source (like the time of innocence, before the catastrophe, depicted so exquisitely in the exiled Palestinian writer Jabra Ibrahim Jabra's *The Ship,* where two boys are drawn naked into what seems like the earth's womb, the water and rock of Silwan spring). While others desparately dig and document dead artifact, this "fertile memory" continues reaping the timeless union between place and time in which the "proof" of archaeology is superfluous.

The Palestinian experience, and how Jews act in face of it, may be at the heart of a fuller recuperation of the Jews' own tradition, of regaining something other than the purely literal or ritual meaning of "home" and "exile," presently victims of an auto-hijack. After a group of pictures of people working—a street-vendor, student, doctor, and technician—Said writes: "Mohr's photographs here are evidence of a Palestinian ecology that is neither symbolic nor representative in some hokey nationalistic way; rather, we are presented addressing our world as a secular place, without nostalgia for a lost transcendence. . . . Homecoming is out of the question. You learn to transform the mechanics of loss into a constantly postponed metaphysics of return. And all of this alongside and intervening in a closed orbit of Jewish exile and a recuperated, much-celebrated patriotism of which Israel is the emblem. Better our wanderings, I sometimes think, than the horrid clanging shutters of their return. The open secular element, and not the symmetry of redemption."[3] Secular: from *saeculum,* breed, generation; akin to the Latin *serere,* to sow; existing or continuing through ages or centuries—so much closer, one is tempted to say, to the concerns of life in the here and now, the traditional preoccupations of the practice of Judaism, than the land idolatry and hubris so prevalent in the more extravagant claims lately made for God by the faithful, whether through ideology or a grotesque distortion of religion.

After the Last Sky is about the evolution and ecology of human, specifically Palestinian identity, within the context of its changing and diverse experience; it speaks pertinently, as well, to an evolution taking place or that ought to take place within Jewish identity resulting from Israel's treatment of and relationship to Palestinians and the totalizing Zionist ideology of consensus. As Said writes: "For all this vigilante propaganda, there is something desparate, something tuly horrendous in the price it exacts from its adherents. If you need a virtual thought police to champion a cause, something is wrong. I do not want the same thing for us, and in fact I do not know any Palestinian who does. If our lesser status as the victims of a major Victim has any consolation, it is that from our relatively humble vantage point we can see our adversaries going through the enormously complicated procedures to get around us or pretend we are not there."[4]

In bits and pieces, fragments and diaries, poems, novels, lyrics and performances (Fawaz Turki's *The Dispossessed,* Salah Tamari's record of incarceration at Ansar Camp; the work of Walid Khalidi, Emile Habiby, Mahmoud Darwish, Ghassan Kanafani, Samih al-Qasem, and Sahar Khalife, among others; the songs of Mustapha al-Kurd, the theater of El-

Hakawati), a body of testimony attesting to the fact that Palestinians *are* here (and there) is growing.

Having learned the wisdom of Treblinka ('Faced with two altenatives, always choose the third'), Raja Shehadeh writes: "I have the horrible suspicion that I am more aware of the concentration camps, think about them more and dream about them more than the average Israeli of my age does."[5] I also have the suspicion, maybe not so horrible at all, that the memory of catastrophe and the refutation of Adorno's statement that there can be no poetry after Auschwitz, is being served more honorably in an entirely "nonofficial" post-Holocaust literature written, ironically enough, by Palestinians; *After the Last Sky* is an eloquent and timely addition to this body of work.

1987

Who's Afraid of Mahmoud Darwish?

Under normal circumstances, Arabic literature of any kind passes virtually unnoticed in Israel, despite the fact that a few of the most well-known contemporary Arab writers (Emile Habiby and Samih al-Qasem, for example), are Israeli citizens. But the publication of "Those Who Pass Between Fleeting Words," a poem by Mahmoud Darwish, the Palestinian national poet adopted by the Israeli "peace camp" as a "moderate" (and himself a former Israeli citizen), has sparked a furor across the entire political spectrum. That poetry has been turned into a lethal weapon may be the only sigh of comic relief and hope in an atmosphere where daily tragedies have taken on the sickening pall of life as usual: acceptable reactions to Darwish's poem seem to conclude that after the bombs and guns and stones, the natives have now had the audacity to attack "us" with words. The old adage "sticks and stones may break my bones but names will never hurt me" no longer seems to hold true, at least when applied to the delicate sensibilities of Israeli liberals.

Even this poem initially aroused little interest. It first appeared in the Hebrew daily *Yediot Ahronot* in Smadar Peri's translation on February 19, 1988. A month later Israel's second largest daily, *Ma'ariv*, published a new translation by Shefi Gabbai. In an accompanying article, Gabbai maintained that Darwish's poem saw the uprising as a way for the Palestinians to take "all of Palestine, from the sea to the Jordan river." Darwish believes "Israel to be in a state of dissolution," Gabbai went on. "He advises the Israelis to pack their bags and return to the Diaspora along with the coffins of their dead, since the Palestinians reject even any traces of the Jews."[1] This was more than enough to sound the alarm. The fact that none of these statements actually appeared in Darwish's poem and that Gabbai's translation itself was sprinkled with inaccuracies—as the translator, scholar, and peace activist Matti Peled pointed out in a fine article—were minor details. By then the information and history-making machines were in full operation. Four months into the uprising, with the convergence of the world press and the beginnings of a real anti-occupation protest movement developing within Israel, Darwish's poem floated in like a weather balloon to test the atmosphere.

The scale of the reaction only attests to Darwish's acute political/poetic intelligence, not the freedom of his emotions, as even some of those "supporting" the poet apologetically claimed: only the slightest excuse was needed to reunite Israeli public opinion and shore up any breaches in the consensus. Darwish's poem proved precisely the thing to curb both the fear and the euphoria of those first months, to make everyone realize that the passage to any kind of resolution would be a long haul.

The press has had a field day with the poem, and everyone whose good intentions felt wounded had to put in their two cents. The *Jerusalem Post* featured headlines like "When the Moderate Turned Bitter," and "Unrepentant Poet." A columnist in *HaAretz* wrote: "If Darwish wants to expel us from here, we won't be left with any choice but to expel him first." Figures like Amos Kenan, Yoram Kaniuk, and Natan Zach more or less read the eulogy, putting Darwish to rest as a potential partner in any Israeli/Palestinian "dialogue." Haim Guri, a poet who himself was a hero in the Palmach (the military force whose 1947–49 operations contributed to the destruction of over 350 villages and helped put Darwish and over half a million other Palestinians in the limbo they still find themselves in), masterfully and in true liberal fashion turned the issue on its head:

> I fear that this poem by Darwish is liable to give the right the Knesset seats it needs for a possible majority in the elections; the poem returns us to the true demons, it speaks truth, poems do not lie. . . . And it was written by an Israeli Arab, close to Hebrew liter-

ature, who understands what this country has meant to us from the time of the covenant with Abraham. The future looks bleak and dangerous and Darwish's poem only lends substance to this. Israelis will require much understanding, strength and patience to face up to the demons chasing within themselves—and to poems as these.

Beyond the liberal camp, comments on the poem came from all sides. Oddly enough, even those associated with the Israeli Communist Party expressed themselves in a vaguely apologetic fashion: after all, "it was a poem and not a political statement," they said, or again, "given the gravity of the situation in the territories, it could only be expected that someone might lose their restraint." The right, naturally, found the poem cause for celebration: it was discussed in the Knesset, mentioned by Prime Minister Itshak Shamir, spoken of on television. The most ironic aspect of the whole incident is the fact that Mahmoud Darwish, probably the most popular poet in the Arab world but virtually unknown outside of a tiny circle in Israel, had become a household word overnight. The power of poetry certainly works in mysterious ways. . . . What, though, is one to make of all this commotion and who, precisely, are the demons?

A well-known phenomenon seems at work here: the hysterical over-reaction to the poem simply serves as a remarkably accurate litmus test of the Israeli psyche, vividly illustrating the extent to which the concrete, brutal history that led to the fulfillment of the Zionist "dream" remains entirely suppressed on a collective level. Israelis are *still* unable to make even the vaguest gesture in the direction of Palestine, to acknowledge the expulsion of its inhabitants and the transformation of the country into an alien stronghold, truly hostile to the ecology and culture of its environment, not to mention its former population or any other "non-Western" elements. While the right tends to be a bit more honest in acknowledging some aspects of this past, liberal thought goes to great lengths to cover the tracks of the institutionalized brutality that is part and parcel of any power struggle. This is always done by attacking, from the standpoint of wounded justice, any expressions that seem to fall outside the bounds of some idealized sense of "fair play." And here, too, the rhetorical maneuvers of Haim Guri are standard practice: it is the oppressor who needs "patience," and "understanding"; the "demons" are not in *me* (I'm OK), they're out there, objectified in the right, in Darwish and his poem.

This kind of position always collapses conflicts into two equal sides, where people on each side supposedly have the same "objective" space to move in and the same set of possibilities from which "choices" can be made. Without belaboring the obvious, major differences do remain between guerrilla warfare (whatever ugly forms it may take) and systematic violence carried out by a sovereign state (destruction of villages; bombing of civilian areas; seizure of land; limits on movement, expression and political activity; house demolition; crop destruction; arbitrary arrests and torture of prisoners; and the denial of family reunification and the right of return to one's birthplace).

Yet the most intolerable aspect of being on the receiving end in these "battles of equals," the most psychologically brutalizing fact, beyond the litany outlined above, may be the devastating feeling of not even having the right to your own memory, of being made to feel a complete alien in your own home, of seeing things you knew once one way slowly transformed, destroyed, or vulgarized. These are the feelings that Darwish's poem eloquently addresses. Besides glossing over this central theme in the carnival of simplicity attending the poem's interpretation, none of the commentators thought to specifically refer the "fleeting words" of this poem (along with the ensuing ambiguities) to Darwish's bitter lines directed at his own leaders in a work written after the evacuation of Beirut: "We have a country of words. Speak so we may know the end of this travel."[2] The poem, like the Palestinian, remained caught in a one-dimensional limbo.

As any rabbi worth his or her salt will tell you, literal interpretations come at a very low stage of development and if one need to seek "violent" texts, there is nothing closer to home than the Book of Books, which says, among other things: "He dislodges many nations before you—the Hittites, Girgashites, Amorites, Cananites, Perizzites, Hivites and Jebusites—you must doom them to destruction: grant them no term and give them no quarter."[3] Such a text, in the hands of settlers or other ideological archaeologists with the apparatus of a state behind them, becomes much more than a stone: it becomes the blueprint for a colonialism sanctioned by the word of God. In this sense, Darwish's poem touches a more tender nerve by both outlining and provoking the difference between the letter of the law and the principle under which the law can or will be enacted.

This subtle difference, it seems to me, lies at the heart of the rhetoric of Palestinian/Israeli relations: the Palestinian speaks of a homeland as an irrevocable and undeniable possibility without specifying its borders; the Israeli, while never actually defining the real borders of the state, insists on precisely measuring and parceling out the land acre by acre. As Darwish himself said in response to his critics in Israel: "The Israeli is the one who determines for the Palestinian their language and aim; why does the Israeli information apparatus need a poem like mine to test its brilliant ability to falsify and deny the humanity of the other?" This poem, perhaps more clearly than any of Darwish's previous work, is an adamant refusal to accept the language of the occupier and the terms under which the land is defined. Unlike "the language of the Palestine within that guards its secret voice,"[4] once described by the Algerian writer Jamal Eddine Ben Cheikh, the language of Darwish has come out of the interior here, with new confidence, into the full light of day.

To quote an Algerian writer, though, is to simply confuse most of the Israeli intelligentsia even further. Here, as in politics, Israeli writers find themselves most at home with writers whose work emerges from dominant cultural modes: to fully comprehend the work of Darwish, who comes from the tradition of political exile embodied by poets like César Vallejo, Nazim Hikmet, or Yannis Ritsos (and *not* Joseph Brodsky), is truly an effort for those weaned on bourgeois Anglo-American and European literature. For such exiles, there is no such thing as a pure, objectified art; no "engaged" or "disengaged" writing: their work is simply one part of the very condition of those who do not rest on some vague laurels or operate within the apparatus of assumptions that power, in the larger sense, can provide.

One of the few sane voices to be heard in the Darwish fiasco was that of Yossi Shiloah, an actor and member of the *mizrahi* peace and social justice movement, the Oriental Front. Shiloah had recently staged a one-man show called *The Voyage,* based on the texts of Darwish, Ghassan Kanafani, Emile Habiby, and other Palestinian writers—the first production of its kind. As someone who has fought his own cultural battles, Shiloah's authority on this issue was genuine: his disappointment was not with Darwish, but with the Israeli left "which laid bare the little racist hidden within each of them." He went on to say:

If Mahmoud Darwish hadn't written this poem, would tens of Palestinians *not* have been killed? Would the houses of Beita *not* have been destroyed? They treat Darwish just the way they treat Palestinian children. It's all very nice to pat a Palestinian kid on the head and say how unfortunate he is. But if that same kid picks up a stone to fight for his freedom, he suddenly becomes the enemy.

The deeper difference between Shiloah's reaction and most others—even some of those defending Darwish—is that Shiloah identifies himself emotionally and culturally with the "enemy." As he stated regarding his own work:

> I am in search of my roots, my identity, and I cannot find it within Isreali culture; if I do, then it is only negatively. I went to Palestinian Arabic literature in search of my culture and, being *mizrahi*, found that I feel much closer to certain Palestinian poets than Israeli writers. Since the beginning of the conflict, no initiative has been taken in Israel, neither in the theater nor in the educational system, to bring the cultural and spiritual dimension of the Palestinian people to light. I reject the common idea that the two peoples are "condemned" to live together. This is a coercive, negative concept. There is nothing negative or coercive about life in common. On the contrary, one contributes to the equilibrium of the other.

Like any literary text, Darwish's poem puts its cards on the table. Like dream-work, the analysand must read his or her own life back into the signs provided by the dream and struggle to accept responsibility for the acts the dream refers to: is it enough to just read back mechanically the usual fears and traumas, to point to the demons out there without specifying the very real consequences of their existence? Again, one must go back and state the obvious: those Israelis sincerely seeking a political statement from Darwish need only turn to the PLO and its official statements—they certainly do not need to stumble into facile interpretations of his very complex work which, in any case, is derived from a tradition too unfamiliar to them to speak of intelligently. The attack on Darwish is just one aspect of the official contempt for any kind of political/human recognition and acknowledgement of the other, the specifically Palestinian Arab other, expressed more and more in the "lynch now, ask questions later" atmosphere whose logical conclusions are indeed much more terrifying than any poem could ever hope to be.

1988

Israel and the Levant: "Wounded Kinship's Last Resort"

Ironically, the latest junkets featuring liberal Israelis and recently domesticated Palestinians threaten to finally collapse the intricate history of Jews and Arabs in the Middle East into two streamlined, easily recognizable blocs: enlightened, idealistic, and well-intentioned Zionists ("wounded spirits" as the title of a symposium on Israeli culture in New York had it); and articulate, mild-mannered, well-dressed Palestinians ready to interpret the desires of their less articulate, less well-dressed, stone-wielding, and still somehow overly Arab constituents in the occupied territories. This battle of equals can now safely be fought live via satellite or in the anesthetized atmosphere of convention halls and conference rooms, far from the new methods of riot control, crowd dispersion, and political repression. Yet the majority of both populations simply falls through the cracks in such an equation. On the Israeli side, this means *mizrahi* Jews: factory workers and building contractors, neighborhood and development town dwellers, synagogue-goers and crack addicts, taxi drivers and Arabic-speaking interrogators, petty bureaucrats and social activists.

The historical status of Jews in the Middle East remains a point of contention. One thing, however, remains indisputable: after the Islamic commercial revolution of the ninth century, Jews—no matter what ups and downs they may have gone through at different times in different places—continued to live in cities and communities throughout the region, right up until the twentieth century. With the gradual displacement of religious, communal, and cultural affiliations by a national entity as the focus of world Jewish life, these Jews found themselves increasingly cut off from their native domain. Without going into the complexities of this process, it can also be said, as Ilan Halevi put it in his *History of the Jews,* that only the 1967 "occupation broke the geo-cultural isolation of Israel in the Arab world."[1] With this, the Jews native to that world found themselves in quite a different position within the social hierarchy than they had been in the old, "beautiful little Israel," hermetically sealed off from its Arab and Mediterranean environment.

For Israel's educated elite, 1967 marks the beginning of the end of their version of the Zionist dream, that "rampart of Europe against Asia, of civilization against barbarism" Herzl so fervently desired. The coming to power of Menachem Begin and the Likud Party in 1977 only confirmed their worst fears: they were no longer waiting for the barbarians; the barbarians had already come, in the form of *mizrahi* Jews seeking their share of the collective pie.

For Israel's *mizrahi* majority, these two dates have an entirely different significance. Begin's victory signaled the end of Labor hegemony over the *mizrahim* and the beginnings, however tenuous, of a democratization process that at least paid lip service to the possibility of social and cultural equality. Ilan Halevi describes well the new dynamic created by the occupation of 1967: "They who had attempted to forget the language of their parents could now, thanks to their knowledge of Arabic, do good lucrative business in the occupied territories, speculate and trade, and even move up in a military and police hierarchy in which knowledge of Arabic became a professional advantage of extreme importance."[2]

But these hierarchies of power found themselves in direct confrontation with cultural memories and affinities. Schizophrenia became institutionalized: a middle-management security service worker could hum the tunes of Farid al-Atrash, Umm Kulthum, or Muhammad 'Abd al-Wahhab one minute while using a Palestinian subject as the object of misplaced rage the next. As the occupation continues—and with the democratization of repression during the uprising—this relationship has become even more pointed, cynical, and ugly.

Despite such brutal contradictions at the heart of these structures and relations, it seems that almost any scratch on the veneer of Israeli culture and society reveals a distinctly Levantine texture, opening a window onto that suppressed world that once simply constituted a native domain. As Bracha Seri, a poet and activist born in Yemen, put it: "Jerusalem on high / and San'a down below / are one. / One is my city . . . / The same openness / the same majesty . . . I longed to kiss / "these strangers," / our "enemies," / to whisper my thanks / that they exist / as in days gone by / never to return."[3] This sense of identity and gratitude is a far cry from the lyrics of a song like Naomi Shemer's "Jerusalem of Gold," in which the Old City, empty and deserted, comes to life only after the Jews have "returned" to it.

It is music—what the American poet Nathaniel Mackey has called "wounded kinship's last resort"[4]—that has proved the most resilient manifestation of this Levantine character. In the alleys of the open marketplaces, at the central bus stations, out of suitcases, kiosks, flimsy stalls, or tiny shops, virtual walking encyclopedias of popular Middle Eastern culture sell cassettes and videos in every dialect of Arabic, in Turkish, Greek, Farsi, and Kurdish. Down past the genteel tourist traps in the restored seaport of Old Jaffa, dozens of clubs in the seedier part of town feature Moroccan, Iranian, and Turkish stars. The tradition of synagogue music accompanied by large Arab orchestras flourishes; all-night songfests and contests, in which singers try to outdo each other, climbing scales higher and higher or challenging each other to more and more daring feats of improvisation within the framework of whatever Arabic *maqam* they happen to be using, take place all the time.

This music has always existed on the margins, as part of a subculture, but it was only in the late 1970s and early 1980s that the term *mizrahi* music even entered the general Israeli vocabulary. This came about largely through the efforts of Shlomo Bar and his group *ha-Breira ha-Tiv'it* (The Natural Choice), despite the fact that he played something quite different from what has come to be called *mizrahi* music. Bar's overpowering stage presence took Israeli audiences, used to primarily blond and blue-eyed singers and choirs ethereally harping on about making the desert bloom or some forever lost and misty "there," entirely by surprise. His hypnotizing performances, in which he almost seemed possessed by the music, reached beyond the confines of protest music into that fertile and poignant realm of "wounded kinship," with its self-censorship and collective amnesia.

Following the appearance of Bar, the mid-1980s saw the explosion of "cassette music." First sold in the bus stations and open-air markets, this music for a time seriously threatened Israel's major record company. The cassettes (by such singers as Zohar Argov, Haim Moshe, Jacky McKaytan, Maragalit Zanaani, Itzik Kala, and others), produced in makeshift basement and garage studios, outsold by far anything that mainstream singers were doing. Although it could not strictly be classified as protest music, its very tone and raucousness was a shout serving to renew old affiliations and assert the legitimacy of pent-up emotions.

Because of the commercial potential, white singers and groups began using (not to say stealing) *mizrahi* material, inserting Eastern instrumental motifs and Arabic words. Naturally, these songs got more airplay, larger and better quality pressings, more promotion and, last but not least, more money. This led to the next stage in which some of the original "cassette" singers (along with other, newer ones) began producing more marketable music: some of the high notes got lower and weren't carried as long, the beat changed, strings were added, original or religious lyrics were replaced by the material of established songwriters.

On the commercial plane, the perfect mix was achieved by a singer like Ofra Haza: only after having gone through the process of assimilating the codes of acceptable Israeli pop culture was she allowed to produce a record of Yemenite songs. Removed from the context of any kind of social struggle or testimony, the work of such an artist is perceived as a benevolent gesture toward roots which, though exotic, can then be seen as part of the common Israeli heritage. This holds true as well on the less commercial plane: in fact, insofar as artists or performers involved in the practice or recuperation of non-Western forms do not express explicit social or political opinions, their work is sure to be co-opted by the mainstream, a feature of the cultural richness and diversity brought about through the ingathering of the exiles. This curious phenomenon can only be seen as a last-ditch effort to divert attention from the massive structural fissures that threaten the very stability of Israel society itself, for it is only against such drastic realities that the old guard could even imagine considering the entirely outlandish and taboo notion of a vital, plural, and creative Middle Eastern culture.

Even here, much of what is most interesting—whether or not there is an overt or implicit political consciousness at work—still involves the conscious use of non-Western materials in a way that is not gratuitous but earned. On the more popular end of things: the heartfelt wailing of

Yehuda Poliker, either accompanying himself on the Turkish *baglame* or joined by his hard-rocking band; the spirited mix of punk and new wave with songs like "The Night Train to Cairo" by the group Mashina; or the unique mix of instruments and tempos presented by The East/West Ensemble. These are light-years away from what used to pass for with it Israeli pop culture of even five years ago. On the less commercial side, a garage band like The Brotherhood has even gone so far as to use voice-overs of Ben-Gurion within the setting of a Laurie Anderson–like arrangement, and sing a song in Turkish dedicated to filmmaker Yilmaz Güney. This penchant for mixing various contemporary artistic meta-languages with material from a little closer to home extends to other media as well. While Israeli film is nowhere nearly as developed as the contemporary Arab cinema, there are indications that younger filmmakers are starting to use the material of popular native traditions as a structural base for new forms. This can be seen, for example, in the use of Turkish thrillers in *Yononas,* a prize-winning short film by Benny Turati.

These tendencies are evident on the literary scene as well: one of the more interesting things to appear recently is the Israeli-edited French language journal *Levant,* dedicated to presenting writers from the whole Mediterranean basin as well as the Arab world. The first two issues included the work of Tahar Ben Jelloun, Mohammed Dib, and Adonis, among others. Nor has a publication like this arisen out of a vacuum: despite enormous obstacles and against great odds, native Mediterranean and Arab Jews—on different levels and in different ways—have maintained certain connections and allegiances. The Algerian-born poet Erez Bitton revived the practice of reciting poetry accompanied by music as his work eloquently limned the parameters of another Hebrew, a language far from the fashionable phrasing of Tel Aviv's Dizengoff Street and its slavishly imitative modes that set the tone for the country as a whole. The poetry of Shelley Elkayam charted the further recesses of plain language in a Hebrew that finally felt native by simply relying on knowledge localized and encoded in her own experience as a seventh-generation resident of the land. Ronny Someck, one of the youngest Israeli poets born in the old Levantine world, counters the dominating forms of foreign popculture by ironically domesticating and personalizing the indigence of local myths. Sami Shalom Chetrit, another young poet born in the old world, consciously stakes out the material considered quintessentially Israeli and relentlessly subverts it in one of the most powerful Hebrew poem to emerge from the *intifada*. Using the parameters of the Bible and the

Palmah, here the victim is no longer Isaac (long a staple image of modern Hebrew poetry) but a son of Ishmael; and the casual, jeep-riding "heroes" are nothing but thugs in combat boots.

While Arabic as a primary language of Jews proved to be one of the ideology of return's true victims (with only Samir Naqqash, an Iraqi-born novelist still writing serious work in Arabic), writers like Shimon Ballas and Sami Michael made the transition into Hebrew, producing work that seems to have much more to do with contemporary Arabic or North African francophone literature than with the work of their own Israeli contemporaries. This holds true as well for younger writers like Yitzhak Gormezano Goren, not to mention Anton Shammas, the Palestinian novelist who has written in Hebrew. Nor does this even take into account the popularity of other Palestinian writers like Emile Habibi, Samih al-Qasim, Siam Da'ud, and Sahar Khalifah in Hebrew translation. The work of all these writers spans many worlds, worlds once considered forbidden territory, illuminated only on occasion by the foreign gaze of domination, contempt, and ignorance. Here the voice belongs to the subject again, inscribing versions of the past and present that go against the grain of official discourse and the sanctioned guidelines for exportable Israeli cultural products.

Alongside (or, better yet, beneath) these more visible forms, a whole other cultural world exists, outside even the context of contemporary Israeli writers whose concerns have decidedly been shaped by their experience as native Middle Easterners. Against more obstacles and greater odds, nonassimilating (that is, predominantly working-class or "aristocratic") *mizrahim* have managed not only to preserve some part of the culture but even continue producing it in both oddly frozen and new hybrid forms. Far removed from the deadening pallor of metrical polemics in academia (where doing research on eighteenth-century North African poetry, for example, is seen as radical revisionism, since only eleventh-century Judeo-Islamic culture, albeit in a completely decontextualized form, is acceptable), people continue writing original *muwashahat* (a medieval Arabic poetic form). In addition to the countless collections of new liturgical poetry (no longer printed in Livorno, Baghdad, or Smyrna but now in Or Yehuda, Beersheba, and Bat Yam), *mizrahi* Jews continue to produce thousands of books.

These works reflect the same kind of genre displacement typical of the Levant since the advent of colonialism, but often contain a polemical urgency along with a fiercely recuperative tone. Almost none of this material (which includes autobiographical political memoirs in both Hebrew and Arabic; historical and sociological works falling well outside the academic mainstream; community histories; childhood memoirs centered on cities or particular neighborhoods; and local, community-based newspapers and journals) is published by commercial presses or generally available except by word of mouth or through direct contact with the authors or publishers themselves. Once thoroughly documented, a good case can be made for this alternative line constituting the primary culture of a good part of the population, yet it remains largely ignored and rarely cited even in purportedly thorough historical accounts of Israeli culture.

The most significant and potentially liberating alternatives to the existing structures of Israeli society have emerged either directly from the *mizrahi* experience or from some consciousness of its importance as a key but missing element. Running on a shoestring and operating on the margins, these alternatives include projects like David Hamo's Haifa-based magazine of social and political criticism, *The Other Newspaper;* Erez Bitton's cultural journal *Aperion;* Charlie Abutbul's Jerusalem-based Morasha theater and Keshet sound studio; Benny Zadeh's Tel Aviv–based neighborhood paper, *Pa'amon;* Mony Yakim's now defunct but influential public forum, New Direction, once based in the notorious HaTikva Quarter; Moti Abu's Shahar youth movement; HILA (The Israeli Committee on Education in *Mizrahi* Neighborhoods and Development Towns), an extremely important grassroots organization that challenges the present inequalities in education; the People's Alternative College (along with its alternative media center), founded by a collective in Tel Aviv; and Barbara and Shlomo Swirsky's vital Breirot Publishing Company, as well as their broadly-based new project, the Adva Institute for Reorientation. In addition, the umbrella activist/peace groups East for Peace and the Oriental Front include most of the people involved in other more particular projects.

Each sphere of activity briefly surveyed here, despite the enormous differences in purpose, intent, and form, displays an unequivocal concern with questions of nativity. And nativity writ large—that is, the historical presence of *mizrahi* Jews and what they have produced in that part of the world, including Israel—waits poised, like a time bomb, ready to shatter and make obsolete the hegemonic but ultimately more tenuous forms that have served as models until now. The sheer amount of material that lies dormant, ready to be recycled and reinterpreted once the subject begins creating itself within the terms of an altered social, cultural, and geopolitical economy, is truly staggering. Despite signs of frustration, despair, and exhaustion, the scene is indeed diverse and exciting. It is this energy of possibility, of blending and mixing, that finds expression in the activities of the groups and individuals actively remaking and redefining the terms of Israeli culture.

1989

Forbidden Territory, Promised Land

A History of the Jews, by Ilan Halevi, Translated by A. M.
   Berrett. London: Zed Books, 1987.

Israel: The Oriental Majority, by Shlomo Swirski. Translated
   by Barbara Swirski. London: Zed Books, 1989.

Israel Cinema: East / West and the Politics of Representation,
   by Ella Shohat. Austin: University of Texas, 1989.

Each of these books, in very different ways, deftly maps those large
regions that have become the forbidden territory of contemporary
Jewish discourse: the never metaphysical, always concrete geopolitical,
economic, and cultural relations between the "central" and the "marginal," whether under the rubric of the Promised Land and the Diaspora,
West and East, North and South, Ashkenazim and Mizrahim, Israel and
Palestine. Although only Ella Shohat's book specifically defines itself as
dealing with representation, all deal with forms of representation, with
the whittling away of received ideas, and the analysis, recuperation, and

construction of alternative versions of history. These are books that stand neither *inside,* as polemical partisans, nor *outside,* in a vacuum of supposed objectivity, but *alongside* their subjects, always ready to point out avenues of possibility, to delineate the space available for a critique (and a self-critique) that can lead to empowerment. In short, they reassert the value of the book as tool and weapon.

The briefest biography of each writer goes some of the way toward outlining the specifically complex problematic of their subjects, and their relationship to it. Ilan Halevi, an ex-Israeli Jew of Middle Eastern origin now living in Paris, wrote his stunningly original *History of the Jews* in French. Shlomo Swirski, an Argentinean Jew of Ashkenazi origin now living in Tel Aviv, wrote his already classic book (originally published in 1981) on Israel's *mizrahi* majority in Hebrew. Ella Shohat, an Israeli of Iraqi origin who "descended" to New York to pursue an education that would have been virtually impossible in Israel, writes in English.

What can be defined as the political activity of each writer, the modes in which they have deemed their efforts to be most effective, also reflects the very diffuse and interdependent nature of the problems at hand. Shohat has chosen a reading of history within an academic setting on a solid scholarly basis; her exacting analysis of Israeli film—with its unrelenting insistence on the particular political implications of the power relations between film and audience, producers and consumers—will surely force American film critics and scholars to rethink their own politics regarding the accepted imagery of the contemporary Middle East as well as the reception of any "marginal" cinematic tradition. Shlomo Swirski, on the other hand, has left the academy (at least in Israel) well behind him. Formerly a professor of sociology at the University of Haifa, he has (along with the book's translator, Barbara Swirski) concentrated most of his efforts on the establishment of Israel's most important alternative publishing house, Breirot, along with an intense commitment to grassroots work in Israel's *mizrahi* community. Ilan Halevi, in addition to his writing, serves in a rather astounding but certainly refreshing capacity: as the PLO representative to the Socialist International, he is living proof of what the Palestinian writer Raja Shehadeh has called "the third way," a way unimaginable to most, but entirely possible.

Halevi's *History of the Jews* offers an uncompromisingly original perspective in a sweeping but acutely intelligent condensation of an enormous amount of material. Unfortunately, the English title seems to betray his own aims by making the reader expect a comprehensive history; the French title, *La Question Juive: La Tribu, La Loi, L'Espace (The Jewish Question: Tribe, Law and Space)*, better prepares the reader for the kind of conceptual trajectory Halevi has marked out for himself. In this framework, Jews do not possess some primordial essence that melodramatically and solipsistically sustains them on their march through time. Halevi's method, rather, focuses on crucial episodes and fissure points that have shaped the social formation of different kinds of Jews, in relation to each other and to the particular geography, peoples, and forces of the worlds they have inhabited. By keeping the present at hand (and the tangled net of circumstances leading to it), Halevi provides a remarkably liberating reading of Jewish history.

This present is framed by the development of the Zionist movement in its European circumstances; the Zionist encounter with Palestine; the slow but steady erosion of the status of Mediterranean and Arab Jews as true natives in the region; the expulsion of Palestinians from Palestine along with the forced immigration of Jews from the Arab world; and the gradual but unintended emergence of Israel within the Arab world as a consequence of the occupation of 1967. It is within this matrix that Halevi offers some of his most striking insights, as in the chapter titled "Israel":

> The overlapping of social and ethnic cleavages, together with the fact that Israeli capitalism has been built under the label of socialism, has created a situation in which the pacifism of the privileged classes strengthens popular chauvinism. In the present state of the conflict, there is almost no link between the political crisis engulfing the highest echelons of the state, the moral crisis affecting petty-bourgeois youth, and the structural social crisis of the Israeli formation; no articulation between the political and reasoned opposition of some, and the individual and deviant desertion of others. Light years separate the educated young Ashkenazi Israeli who expresses his moral outrage before the excesses of the occupation, and the uneducated young Oriental Israeli who, in his practices and in his behavior, disrupts the national social and ideological consensus.[1]

While some may criticize Halevi's knack for extrapolating the whole from the part, identifying tendencies through very particular paradigms, there is no question that his work is infinitely less reductive of this vast field than most of what scandalously passes for Jewish history these days. It is delightfully ironic that Halevi, whom some Jews regard as a renegade, seems to possess an ample dose of that quality Gershom Scholem deemed essential for the study of things Jewish—*ahavath yisrael*, a love of the Jewish people.

There is not one episode on which Halevi doesn't throw some new light, forcing readers to reconsider their own hierarchy of assumptions and values. At times, reading Halevi's text is simply exhilarating: often poetic and compassionate, the writing itself skirts the margins of catastrophe without ever resigning itself to any of the dead ends that so many traveling this route have encountered. By flipping the Russian joke on its head ("The best historian is the one who can predict the past"), Halevi has managed to write a future-centered history that neither romanticizes the past nor trivializes the seemingly indomitable forces of the present that slowly but certainly pull the shade lower and lower on that very future.

Unlike in France, where the sheer presence of a large community of North African Jews and a deeper connection to the Arab world as a whole have generated a very different level of awareness, there has been precious little untainted material on Israel's Arab Jews available in English. The fact that the United States is the most favored audience for the Israeli liberal elite's often vicious ideological onslaught against the "primitive" nature of *mizrahi* Jews makes the need for alternative sources on this topic more urgent. Make no mistake about it: these stereotypes—at varying levels of vulgarity—permeate precisely those approaches that claim to be most conciliatory toward Palestinians.

It is, as well, indicative of the state of discourse in the United States concerning Israel that we have had to wait so long for an English translation of some of the work of Shlomo Swirski, one of Israel's most accomplished and innovative sociologists. Swirski has conducted his investigations into Israeli society from a class perspective, something that has obviously contributed to this neglect. Perhaps even more than this, one suspects it is Swirski's absolute refusal to mystify, his ability to embed complex theory within seemingly simple formulations and his practice of always allowing his subjects to serve as the screen and arbiter of their own efforts, that truly irritates his former colleagues. This economical combination of theory and practice is nowhere more clearly presented than in *Israel: The Oriental Majority.*

A model of clarity and precision, the structure of Swirski's book provides a key to its method: Part One (The Ethnic Division of Labor) comprises the analytical section while Part Two (Oriental Activists Speak), almost twice as long, comprises interviews with a representative range of people whom Swirski calls a "potential elite." The structure takes on the functions of textbook, classroom, and blueprint for action at the same time—precisely the functions it has served for a generation of Israeli social activists. These are not the usual spokespeople for the usual crowd with their usual funding and open access to the media, but individuals trying to effect change within a brutally divisive and oppressive system of social institutions that categorize from birth those of "European" and those of "Asian" and "African" descent, regardless of whether they are second- or even third-generation Israelis.

Swirski's task has been to refute assumptions that run so deep they have even become, as we witness in the interviews, part of the psychological and cultural makeup of the *mizrahim* themselves. To do this, he has gone to that most favored ammunition dump of the state's faceless ideological machine, the Bureau of Statistics. He does not simply serve up a menu of counterstatistics; rather, each of his seemingly plain but elegant sentences conceals and embeds both fact and theory, as here: "While the fifties saw the proletarianization of the Orientals, the mid-eighties saw the Israeli class structure turn into a combination of the First and Third Worlds, where managers and engineers are paid three to ten thousand dollars per month, while workers and low-grade employees earn one tenth that amount."[2]

Nor is Swirski ever reticent to approach things from an apparently obvious angle: in the chapter titled "The Development Towns of Israel," for example, before going into an analysis of investment patterns, he simply asks, "Are the industries in the development towns developing?"[3] Again, in refuting the slanderous stereotypes regarding the "mentality of the Orientals" and their "latent hatred of the Arabs," Swirski simply points out that "all the wars against the Arabs and the Palestinians have been conducted by an overwhelmingly Ashkenazi establishment."[4] Discussing the recruitment of *mizrahim* to positions in the military government following the occupation, an essential element in understanding how class issues affect Israeli politics, Swirski points out that:

> Orientals did not do these jobs out of "latent hatred of Arabs"; for
> many, the jobs meant an opportunity for advancement in a situa-

tion in which such opportunities were severely limited. However, for Ashkenazi commanders and administrators, viewing the Orientals as they carried out the tasks assigned to them from above, it was convenient to attribute the latter's consciousness to "hatred of Arabs." Such a stance enabled them to present themselves as having a higher order of humanity than their underlings and as having a monopoly on humane feelings and lofty ideals. It also allowed them to ignore the fact that they were the ones in charge of the policy of control and expropriation.[5]

As both a dedicated activist and a detached analyst, Swirski has maintained a level of integrity all too rare on the Israeli scene. His work is essential reading for anyone interested in the forces that shape Israeli society.

The remarkable thing about Ella Shohat's *Israeli Cinema* is that it manages not only to sustain but even pique our interest in films we might not have the desire or opportunity to see. She accomplishes this by using the films as raw material for the subtext (and subtitle) of her own book: *East/West and the Politics of Representation.* Shohat has produced an impressively "representative" work, one whose subject—Israeli film itself—by no means limits its significance. In fact, with its combination of condensed plot analysis deftly exposing the ideological significance of recurring images, and its skillful weave of social, cultural, and political history, the book serves as a model for the intelligible presentation of any national cinema.

Beginning with film itself (the fascination with "exotic" footage of the Orient, an intriguing look at the development of movie theaters in Palestine, and conflicting attitudes toward cinema), the book ends with a detailed survey of the latest group of Israeli movies, "the Palestinian wave." In between, Shohat manages to categorize virtually all extant Israeli films in groupings that provide a context to illuminate both the films themselves and the issues they raise. Here, for instance, is an excerpt from her analysis of *Hill 24 Doesn't Answer,* one of the films from the "heroic-nationalist" genre:

> Seen largely within combat circumstances, the Arabs are almost always presented in long shot. When the battles take place at night, the spectator is completely distanced from their humanity. Their great numbers, in soldiers and tanks, contrast with their minimal impact on the spectator. Although set during the British

Mandate over Palestine, when the British were seen as enemies and violently resisted by Jewish underground movements, the film has British soldiers exert more presence than the Arabs and treats them more sympathetically. This appointing of sympathy and interest reflects a broader attention given to European history and culture, completely marginalizing that of the Arabs, an orientation continuous with policies outside of the cinema.[6]

The issues raised by Shohat, however particular they might be, all come back to the question of power and control, imagery and its intended audience. In recounting the representation and misrepresentation of *mizrahi* Jews on the Israeli screen, Shohat has forged an exemplary approach to the study of popular culture, its stereotypes, and the reception of that culture by the very subjects of its imagery. Reading her description of the *Bourekas* genre, a particular form of Israeli kitsch aimed at the *mizrahi* public, I was reminded again and again of the American artist Robert Colescott's painting of a black family attentively listening to the *Amos 'n' Andy Show*, at the same time spellbound and horrorstruck at the notion of participating in their own degradation. Although the readings Shohat offers of these films are both humorous and moving, they never lose sight of either the intent of the imagery or the humanity of its viewers. In fact, the generosity of all Shohat's interpretations—even for some very objectionable films—makes the utopian allusions concluding her book all the more powerful and credible:

> The filmmakers take for granted the Zionist rejection of the Diaspora without offering any deeper analysis of the Israeli Jew as a multidimensional precipitate of millennia of rich, labyrinthian syncretic history lived in scores of countries. One is struck by a kind of cultural superficiality in Israeli cinema, a lack of reflection concerning issues that have preoccupied Jews over the centuries, issues which often have cinematic resonances. . . . True cinematic polyphony will emerge, most probably, only with the advent of political equality and cultural reciprocity among the three major groups within Israel—European Jews, Oriental Jews, and Palestinian Arabs. But until the advent of such a utopian moment, cultural and political polyphony might be filmically evoked, at least, through the proleptic procedures of "anticipatory" texts, texts at once militantly imaginative and resonantly multivoiced.

Having applied such an unyielding gaze, Shohat has cleared the ground for these very unsettling but highly evocative suggestions. The very thoroughness of the project, and the fact that such few films emerge untainted by the ideological consensus, adds a whole other dimension to her intent—that of artistic possibility. It is only at this point that younger Israeli filmmakers can finally begin to see, and then construct, that whole plethora of images so conspicuously absent from the collective screens of their childhood.

1990

In True Colors

Faithful Witnesses: Palestinian Children Recreate Their World,
by Kamal Boullata. New York: Olive Branch Press, 1990.

While Arabic writing, cinema, and music are slowly becoming available in the United States, many traditions of contemporary visual art from the Middle East still remain largely inaccessible. It is quite fitting that one of the few books of contemporary Arab art now available should feature the work of Palestinian children. After all, it was the "children of the stones" who, as a regular feature of the evening news during the first year of the *Intifada,* rapidly became lodged in public consciousness. But other events overshadowed their bold initiative, and these children have now taken a backseat to reports on the aftermath of a full-scale war, the vicissitudes of shuttle diplomacy, and superpower politics. Their experience has been represented in all its vivid complexity by *Faithful Witnesses* (1990), Kamal Boullata's impressive compilation of paintings by Palestinian children with accompanying text and photographs.

The book, magnificently designed by Lily and Kamal Boullata, demonstrates the entangled character of Palestinian history through its very layout. The text is presented in three columns, with English on the left, French on the right, and Arabic (reading from left to right) in the middle. Photographs of the children at work on their paintings, as well as of village scenes, demonsrations, and Israeli troops are all in black and white. Only the paintings are in color. This design adds a touch of irony to the power of these young artists: what they have created out of simple tools—pigment, watercolors, magic markers, crayons, and paper—seems immediate and forceful, while what has been produced and shot by expensive, technologically sophisticated photographic equipment seems contrived and distant. In fact, the brilliance of this collection lies precisely in its juxtaposition of self-representation to depiction by outsiders, no matter how sympathetic they might be.

Very little that we have seen so far either in the mainstream media or the formidable literature on the Palestinians can prepare us for the astounding aesthetic decisions made by five to thirteen-year-old children as they experience such everyday dangers as being shot at, tear-gassed, beaten, or having parents taken away in the middle of the night, as in eleven-year-old Maher Lahham's eerie *By night they came and took Ali's father away.* The constraints of the crisis situation affect the very colors that the children deploy, as they take part in a deadly battle of wits in which the use of the Palestinian national colors (green, red, and black) constitutes a criminal offense. In trying to pinpoint the remarkable will toward autonomy that the children display, John Berger writes:

> The first language of painting tells everything it tells as if for the first time. The "voice" with which it speaks of tear gas or subma-chine guns is the same as it uses to speak of a cloud or a house. . . . In the Occupied Territories schoolchildren know, before they learn Euclid, that space is what you carry with you past the guns, and that not even death can take this space away with you.[1]

Boullata has faithfully managed, where others could have failed, to convey this internalized cultural space that is carried past the guns. To present the art of children without imposing the rigid conventions and subterfuges of adulthood is, indeed, a difficult task. By sticking to the signs that the children have given us, Boullata's text extrapolates a poetics and aesthetics of that vision that is related both to the children's concrete conditions as well as their references to Arabic cultural traditions. Boullata also avoids presenting the children's work as many adults would have it seen: as documentary evidence of suffering or political commitment removed from any artistic or spiritual intent. The work expresses both suffering and intense political commitment, but never reductively, as a slogan or an image meant to evoke pity might.

In *Tear gas in my eyes,* a girl clutches her eyes in the foreground of a dramatic and colorful painting filled with swatches of orange, red, and purple. Boullata writes:

> Observing a moment in her outer world, one eight-year-old, Sahar Mansour, simultaneously tells us about her inner experience of it in *Tear gas in my eyes.* Unnoticed by three boys leading a demonstration away from us, three tear gas bombs have just exploded around the girl. Just as the boys have no eyes to see the girl (who for the occasion is wearing a skirt made up of the Palestinian flag, the girl, now covering her eyes, can no longer see her three colleagues. Alone, she stands at the center of this red-hot world, facing us as if we were her mirror, the girl is making sure we see how tear gas burns her eyes.[2]

By consciously implicating the viewer, a painting such as this goes beyond the demonstrative to actively engage us in many of the crucial questions regarding cultural production, its purposes, and intended audiences. This sense of detail and measure as well as the underlying presence of such issues is exhibited in all of Boullata's commentaries.

Of particular interest are paintings that refer to traditional Arabic and Islamic motifs. As in the story of Sheherazade, these children know that in order to live they must continue telling their tale for, "from the popular fables of *Kalila wa Dimna* and Aesop the Palestinian child has learned that 'any excuse may serve a tyrant' but that ultimately 'the truth outlasts the sun.'"[3] The book ends with a series of night paintings that are the most haunting images in this collection of moving and powerful works. In thirteen-year-old Bilal Sulaiman's *Return of the purple man;* twelve-year-old Muhammad Najjar's *Running away from Lydda, 1948;* thirteen-year-old Murad Subhi's *Return to Am'ari refugee camp under a starry sky;* and eight-year-old Sahar Mansour's astonishing *Night flight over Jerusalem,* the dignity, integrity, and sheer inventiveness of the young artists is fully evident.

Boullata's subtle and acute presentation of these paintings, not to mention the paintings themselves, provides much food for thought about many of the issues central to current imagemaking. His examination of the use of traditional motifs, for example, relates to questions about the adherence to and deviation from artistic sources. Perhaps more important, his knack for providing a larger context for many of the paintings illuminates our sense of the vexed relationship between an artist and his or her audience, the individuals and their community, and political and artistic activity. In addition, it is a book that is as suitable for young readers as it is for the adults among us willing to learn from this singular combination of wisdom and courage.

1991

Culture without a Country

In 1895, ten days after the first Paris film screening, movies were shown in Alexandria, Egypt; ever since, the cinema has been an integral part of cultural activity in the Middle East. Despite the fact that the native film and video industry has both used and redefined "Western" standards and images, it is remarkable to what extent imagery from that part of the world has been codified, not to mention rigidly controlled, for mass consumption in the United States. Very little has managed to slip through the cracks in the wall of colonial, orientalist, or ethnographic vision, which has served up such images as the drooling, bloodthirsty, hook-nosed, scimitar-wielding Ali Baba of comic fame, the keffiya-wearing "terrorists" of action films, and faceless masses of "Shiites" or stone-throwing Palestinian kids standing by on the evening news. In late twentieth-century America "Arabs" have been defined predominantly by others. Although its title doesn't really do justice to the range of tapes presented, "Uprising: Videotapes on the Palestinian Resistance," organized by Elia Suleiman and Dan Walworth, provides a rare opportunity to directly encounter images produced in the Middle East. The importance of exhibiting and analyzing such work continues to increase, as the barricades restricting the free flow of images are erected more steadfastly:

one need only witness the absurd controversy surrounding PBS's broadcast of the rather innocuous *Days of Rage* (1989, by Jo Franklin-Trout), with its disclaimers and wraparounds calculated to protect people from access to alternative information.

The tapes presented in "Uprising" range, in both approach and technique, from the traditionally framed documentary to the radically personal seizure and molding of material long in the hands of calculating itinerants; wresting images away from the institutionalized uses they have been put to is not an easy task but one with which these videomakers clearly grapple. Although a number of the films may appear conventional, they manage to imbue conventions with the particularities of time and place that jar the viewer into rereading of convention itself. Rather than simply employing conventions for their own sake, as part of a recognizable language of imagery, these tapes foreground the position and function of images or sequences within a larger social, political, and cultural context. When this method works best, the videomakers empower the viewer to reread and interrogate the accepted wisdom of images transmitted by the mass media as well as through a variety of social and cultural constructs of "others."

Rashid Mashrawi's *The Shelter* (1989), the only fictional work in the program, tells the story of Abu Samir, a middle-aged construction worker living in the basement of his building site, and his encounter with a younger worker who has no identification card and who spends the night at Abu Samir's place. The tape relies on many Egyptian cinematic conventions to depict the dignity of perseverance in the face of injustice. A worthy and sympathetic protagonist is challenged by forces beyond his or her control; the cinematic unveiling of the protagonist's character through long isolated shots connects the viewer to the story; the path the protagonist has chosen is clearly differentiated from events involving others, which are observed by the character and the audience but are outside the central narrative concerns of the story. Despite its clearly defined plot and restricted locale, the tape addresses a host of complex social and political issues. These arise from the tape's portrayal of Abu Samir's relationship to his Jewish boss and its inclusion of several incidents that Abu Samir and the younger worker witness while squinting through the cracks in the walls of their safe house, which itself is both confining cell and place of refuge. The closing shot, a slow zoom in of Abu Samir sitting in his cell with the voiceover of an exquisite lullaby lamenting the migrant worker's absence of family, may seem on one level like a hackneyed image; yet the tape's historical specificity restores to the image an eloquence and vitality that powerfully limn the painful circumstances of exile.

Mai Masri and Jean Chamoun's *War Generation: Beirut* (1988) differently but equally effectively revitalizes cinematic conventions. On the surface this videotape seems to follow the trajectory of a documentary, presenting a short, voiced-over historical introduction before leading in to the individual stories that make up the body of the tape. Yet the videomakers take the mystified and incredibly complex skein of relations comprising the conflict in Lebanon and render it quite sensible in the space of fifty minutes, through a combination of extremely lucid and well-edited personal testimony and dense political and social commentary.

At the opposite extreme, by virtue of their radical noncompliance with image conventions, are Mona Hatoum's two astonishing short videotapes. *Eyes Skinned* (1988) deals directly with the Lebanese experience. A veiled woman facing the camera circles and recircles her eyes with a long knife as various images of the war fade in and out of the frame behind her. *Measures of Distance* (1988) investigates the possibly futile attempt to reconstruct a certain state of intimacy. The tape addresses the relationship between the videomaker and her mother but extends its exploration into the realm of social life and the isolated, fragmented shards created by war. Images of Hatoum's mother form and reform themselves behind the veil of a letter whose Arabic script serves as a screen through which all other images are filtered. More than a map, the text becomes the body: starting from the fingers grasping the page, the film moves to her face, then to her naked back and breasts as she comes out of the shower and dresses; the images are all accompanied by a background of familial voices chatting in Arabic. In this jewel of a tape Hatoum creates her own language, one that accommodates the complicated nature of relations while questioning both the validity and possibility of simultaneously representing past life in Palestine and exile in Lebanon, the need for testimony and the fear that no image or art can do these issues justice.

The Stone Throwers (1989) by Georges Khleifi and Ziad Fahoum is a look behind the scenes of the standard news footage depicting a faceless mass of kids lobbing stones at Israeli soldiers. The videomakers go into homes, down alleys, and onto beaches, letting the young Palestinians do the talking. Although there is a certain lack of cohesion to the tape, this is due in part to the circumstances of its production in the midst of an ongoing conflict, and the makers have incoprorated a discussion of these difficulties into the narrative.

In contrast to the frank simplicity of this footage is *Nazareth in August* (1986) by Norman Cowies, Ahmed Damian, and Dan Walworth, the only tape shown made primarily by foreigners to the region. The tape's main thrust is a schematic, fact-finding mission; its inclusion in the series illustrates some of the liens partisanship places on form. By trying to present an antidote to works made from either an Israeli or Zionist point of view at the level of content only, the tape seldom moves beyond the one-dimensional quality of counterpropaganda. The tape's dry impersonality stands in contrast to the density and texture of testimonials that evidence personal cost depicted throughout the rest of the videotapes.

Jayce Salloum and Elia Suleiman's work in progress, *Intifada: Speaking for Oneself* (1989; titled "Introduction to the end of an argument" in Arabic), is quite unlike anything that has been done on the Palestinians or Arabs in general. The videomakers have taken the dominant and oppressive structures of colonialism to task by deploying the most blatantly racist and stereotypical imagery they could find in a new context. Made almost entirely from found materials (news clips taken from the mass media, shots from films and cartoons), the tape is a dizzying roller coaster of cuts and jumps—from Henry Kissinger and Ted Koppel to Elvis, Paul Newman, Ali Baba, Mister Rogers, and any number of stock Hollywood terrorists. The carefully constructed editing provides a confident and scathingly ironic commentary on the uses and power of imagery; the tape would function well as a preface to the viewing of most conventional imagery on the Middle East.

Taken as a whole, "Uprising" affords an all too rare look into the contested area of the Middle East, and more than some respite from the standard canon. Yet venues for such films remain exceedingly few, even within the realm of places generally sympathetic to independent film and video. Scheduled to run at the Institute of Contemporary Art (ICA) in Boston, "Uprising" met with staunch resistance and a concerted campaign to significantly alter its presentation. After trying various approaches to neutralize the political content of the series, including a panel discussion and presentations by speakers not associated with the program, the ICA went so far as to demand an Israeli wraparound program, including works like *The Hundred Years War: Personal Notes* (1983, by Ilan Ziv), *A Search for Solid Ground: The Intifada Through*

Israeli Eyes (1990, by Steven Brand), and *Talking to the Enemy* (1989, by Mira Hamermesh), the last two of which aired on PBS early this year. The ICA planned to present these on alternating nights, without identifying a different curator. At this point, according to Micki McGee, video curator at Artists Space, the ICA showing of "Uprising" has been postponed, but negotiations between Artists Space, the curators of the series, and the ICA continue.

Given the ICA's pressures to change the format of the tapes' showing, it seems unlikely that "Uprising" will be presented there. Ironically, too, in the ICA's attempt at "balance," no mention would have been made of the gross budgetary disproportion between the works the ICA wanted to present and those in the "Uprising" series. This incident demonstrates only the tip of the iceberg of the impediments to access encountered by Middle Easterners who seek to represent themselves in the United States. One hopes that the "Uprising" series will engage other institutions and individuals more willing to take risks and give viewers the chance to come to their own conclusions about the issues involved.

1990

Too Much Past

Sugar Street, by Naguib Mahfouz. Translated by William Maynard Hutchins and Angele Botros Saman. New York: Doubleday, 1992.

Placing the Nobel Prize–winning Egyptian writer Naguib Mahfouz in a comprehensible context is no small task. While Western critics never fail to point out his extensive readings of modern European novelists, as if only the influence of Proust, Tolstoy, Dostoyevsky, or Joyce would grant him the legitimacy of being considered a real writer, these influences are mainly superficial. Such a presentation of Mahfouz (through the use of descriptive terms that border on the patronizing) prepares readers to focus on the trappings and intrigues of the tales he so artfully weaves, while neglecting the deeper implications and acute sense of prescience in his work. It also obscures the rich and complex narrative traditions that Mahfouz is heir to. His family portrayals, for example, owe more to the Book of *Genesis* than to Flaubert, while his sense of structure emerges from a culture that assumes—as in *The Thousand and One Nights*—that telling stories is a matter of life and death.

Deeply affectionate and poignant as it is, *The Cairo Trilogy* (*Palace Walk, Palace of Desire* and *Sugar Street*) stands as a damning indictment of a way of life doomed to exhaustion and failure. This remarkable chronicle, focusing on the lives and fortunes of a middle-class family in Cairo through two world wars, begins and ends with reverberations that are evoked by tensions between the interior and the exterior: the home and the street, the solitary mind and the physical world of action and chance. The very titles of the books, based on street names in Cairo's old quarters, suggest this dichotomy.

Palace Walk, the first in the trilogy, cannot help being an ironic comment on the old saying that "a man's home is his castle" as it traces the slow disintegration of the ties that bind the ruthless patriarch al-Sayyid Ahmad Abd al-Jawad and his possessions—possessions that consist, first and foremost, of his wife and children. The "walks" out of the palace include that of al-Sayyid Ahmad's wife, Amina, who disobeys her husband's command and leaves the house without him, and that of one of his sons, Fahmy, who ventures into the turbulent streets, filled with students demonstrating against British rule. None of these excursions, naturally, are without consequence: Amina is hit by a car and banished from the house; Fahmy is martyred by a British bullet.

The title of the second book, *Palace of Desire,* highlights the failure of desire to find its true object. Here we witness the temptations and depravities of the flesh through al-Sayyid Ahmad's sexual escapades and experience the false sense of intimacy felt by his youngest son, Kamal, in his journey of attraction and repulsion through Egypt's upper class.

The most bitter of the three books is the last, *Sugar Street* (first published in Arabic in 1957), which reads almost like an extended dirge: there is little, if anything, sweet left for al-Sayyid Ahmad. Old age and infirmity restrict him to the house, while his wife pays daily visits to the beloved sites of pilgrimage she risked so much to see at the beginning of the trilogy. The radio, for which he had only contempt in his days of revelry with musicians, singers, and prostitutes, has become an irreplaceable comfort. One after another, the people around the patriarch die—children, husbands, wives, friends—and the sense of gloom is pervasive. Even the magnificent courtesans are utterly transformed; Zubayda, once the queen of the singers, now a mad beggar, is discovered in a coffeehouse by Kamal and his Coptic friend, Riyad.

Within this bleak atmosphere, a younger generation—the grandchildren of Amina and al-Sayyid Ahmad—represents the major forces that will be involved in the formation of an independent Egypt. They include nationalists, Communists, and members of the Muslim Brotherhood, but the central role, that of Kamal, is of an indecisive teacher and writer, the closest Mahfouz has yet come to an autobiographical character.

Throughout the trilogy, the subtle and not so subtle gains and losses in power between individual men and women—not to mention children and parents—parallel Egypt's struggle for political independence. But the shifts in behavior that are so minutely recorded in the first two books give way to internal shifts of perception in *Sugar Street*. The old order is certainly gone, but there is nothing with which to replace it. And with little to look forward to, the past itself is transformed and glorified; after the death of al-Sayyid Ahmad, even Amina looks back with longing to her days of confinement. It is in the creation of such paradoxes that Mahfouz reveals his essentially tragic view of life.

The enormous task of translating and presenting the major works of Naguib Mahfouz in this country is truly a commendable endeavor, and translators of the present volume, William Maynard Hutchins and Angele Botros Samaan, are to be applauded for producing a lively and readable text. However, as minor as it may seem, their use of quotation marks for what, in Mahfouz's original, are remarkably seamless transitions in and out of interior monologues is unfortunate. Whether this came about through an editor's overzealous hand or a decision by the translators is impossible to say. Nevertheless, since these passages are made to stand out, American readers may be left with the feeling that Mahfouz attempted to appropriate the methods of Joyce and Faulkner without great success. This certainly diminishes our sense of his enormous achievement, which consists precisely of adapting various literary methods and conventions in highly original ways within a specific and local context.

It is this sense of the local that, finally, distinguishes Naguib Mahfouz. His immense popularity has done nothing to alter his sense of himself or his art. With the contemporary cult of personality and the pressures of instant global communications, there are few artists of his stature for whom this can be said. The ordinary nature of Mahfouz's world, with its willingness to confront the complexities of human intentions, makes it an extraordinary exception in a marketplace of manufactured ideas and is, for that, all the more admirable.

1992

The State of the Gulf: Abdelrahman Munif and Hanan al-Shaykh

Cities of Salt, by Abdelrahman Munif. Translated by Peter Theroux, New York: Randon House, 1987.

Women of Sand and Myrrh, by Hanan al-Shaykh. Translated by Catherine Cobham. London: Quartet, 1989.

One of the first waves of American interest in Arabic writing came in 1988, after the Egyptian novelist Naguib Mahfouz won the Nobel Prize. Hackneyed approaches to his work, however, only proved how deep a chasm existed in providing any context for such writing in America. Even direct American involvement in the destruction of Iraqi civil society has barely managed to generate more than superficial interest in the Arab world. Only as the media discovers the Kurds (dispossessed for over sixty years), do we suddenly find the horrors of war deemed newsworthy. Although great stress is put upon the status of the Kurds as a "non-Arab" people, the comforting spectatcle of Middle Easterners killing each other finally lets all the media pundits off the hook for their scandalously complicitous behavior in cheering on the U.S. policy of wanton violence during the relentless bombing raids over Iraq. Meanwhile, business goes on as usual. Some self-righteous indignation can be vented and the "Arabs" can act according to everyone's expectations, an equation George Bush certainly calculated in his game plan.

Given this state of affairs, it is quite ironic that Abdelrahman Munif's *Cities of Salt* (in Peter Theroux's graceful translation), would have been picked up by a major American publisher. Banned in Saudi Arabia and the Gulf states, Munif's book—because it plays into, around, and with so many stereotypes—will present formidable obstacles to American readers who have received little else. Although modern Arabic literature is overwhelmingly urban, *Cities of Salt* presents a world seen through the eyes of, at least for the prevailing categories of European thought, the essentialized tribal Arab: the desert dwelling, nomadic beduin. Yet, it is not about that timeless construct, the "Arab." It is the story, rather, of a people's relationship to their land and the gradual, ultimately radical, transformation of both through the discovery of oil and foreign intervention. As such, it is history *and* allegory. Greeted with great acclaim when the first volume came out in Beirut in 1984 (the Palestinian writer Jabra Ibrahim Jabra, exiled in Iraq, for instance, said its epic quality had no equal in Arabic fiction, while the critic and scholar Issa Boullata considered it "a new beginning" for the Arabic narrative).[1] The English translation was received somewhat less graciously in North America. As John Updike wrote in *The New Yorker*: "It is unfortunate, given the epic potential of his topic, that Mr. Munif appears to be insufficiently Westernized to produce a narrative that feels much like what we call a novel."[2]

Born in Jordan, Munif's family was originally from Saudi Arabia. His experience (study in Baghdad, Cairo, and Belgrade; the stripping of his Saudi citizenship; a stay in France; and current residence in Damascus), is typical of the almost perpetual motion of many contemporary Arab writers. Moving from capital to capital, these writers dodge the false unity of repressive regimes only to enact, through language, their dreams against exile. One can only wonder what Syria's present alliance with the United States against Iraq might mean for someone like Munif. In this world of shifting alliances and constant vigilance, Munif slowly spins the tale of Wadi al-Uyoun (Oasis of Wells), and the new cities of the desert kingdom, Harran and Moran, built over its memory.

> Wadi al-Uyoun was an ordinary place to its inhabitants, and excited no strong emotions, for they were used to seeing the palm

trees filling the wadi and the gushing brooks surging forth in the winter and early spring, and felt protected by some blessed power that made their lives easy.[3]

A seeming wasteland to outsiders only interested in what might be underground, each part of the desert maintained a unique character, wedding the people to the land, "named not through desire or caprice but by nature itself, which had determined the importance, features and location of each hill."[4] Memories of place and particular events marking time—"She was sure because she had been wearing a new dress Saad brought her when she put Mugbel on her shoulder and he pissed on it."—stand against the calculated oblivion of official history.

When the Americans first arrive, Miteb al-Hathal, the patriarch closest to the mythic past, is certain "that something terrible was about to happen."[5] The chronicle of these events, the disintegration of the community of Wadi al-Uyoun and the transformation of the beduin (along with the huge influx of foreign workers) into a class society whose allegiences and privileges are based on a very different order, constitutes the central narrative. While the novel seems like nineteenth-century naturalism, the fact that it parallels the actual history of Saudi Arabia makes it, so to speak, unnatural, in the sense that Munif is acutely aware of how narratives are constructed and maintain significance. As the critic and scholar Muhammad Siddiq has pointed out, there is "an absence of recognizable plot" as the cast of characters simply changes several times "to sustain the novel's referential bearing to history."

By abandoning the "plot," Munif comes closer to history while subverting the official Saudi version. Controlling history, of course, is as important as maintaining control over the flow of oil itself. Given the fact that Munif has spent time as an oil professional—as director of planning and crude oil marketing in Syria, later as editor of *Oil and Development* in Baghdad—he can both understand and pose a threat to new and old clients and allies. With his caustic parody of the life of emirs, and his pointed reversal of subjects and objects (beduin and their researchers), no one is spared. We witness the "march of progress" as the new usurps the old through the development of "modern" institutions: traditional healers give way to quack doctors and hospitals; tribal henchmen to uniformed soldiers and armies; custom and justice are replaced by arbitrary decrees and the rule of "law." As less and less of the old life remains, a new sense of solidarity emerges.

> The people of Harran looked at their faces and then at each other,
> thinking how unhappy and oppressed they were and grew sad
> when they reflected that there must be terrible reasons for the
> depression. They felt afraid, but still dared to say things they
> would never have said had they not been so consumed with sor-
> row and anger. Why did they have to live like this, while the
> Americans lived so differently? Why were they barred from going
> near an American house, even from looking at the swimming pool
> or standing for a moment in the shade of one of their trees? Why
> did the Americans shout at them, telling them to move, to leave
> the place immediately, expelling them like dogs?[6]

This new class of people, now fingerprinted and segregated but ready
and willing to fight for rights that had never before been questioned or
usurped, begin the process of resistence. This journey toward redefining
the newly created social selves they have become includes, by definition,
reinterpreting their mythic past, an act that characters and readers must
perform together. As epic, chronicle, satire, commentary, and reflection
on the nature of historical truth and collective memory, *Cities of Salt* is
an ambitious and profound undertaking, a call to struggle against both
the new and the accepted order.

Faced with tenacious forms of both internal and external repression, contemporary Arab writers have shown great resourcefulness in
forging a distinct branch of what Barbara Harlow calls "resistance literature." Yet, much of this complex tale simply cannot be told to a wider
American audience: the books just aren't available. Language is only
part of the problem, for many translations are released in Britain but
never find American publishers. A striking example is the work of
Lebanese novelist Hanan al-Shaykh. Her 1986 *Story of Zahra,* a classic
by any standards, has yet to appear here. Banned, like *Cities of Salt,* in
Saudi Arabia and the Gulf, the novel traces Zahra's coming of age during the civil war in Lebanon as the war raging outside begins to illuminate the many wars she has already fought on the home front.

Her new book, *Women of Sand & Myrrh,* set in an unidentified country in the gulf that seems like Kuwait, offers an uncompromising vision
that, in many ways, complements Munif's oppositional history. In al-
Shaykh's case, however, the enormous terrain she has staked out cannot
be found on any map: it is simply the internal life of women, with its
vast and minute journeys of acquiescence and resistance to the social

constructs they have either been forced to accept or cannot help but perpetuate. One almost suspects that al-Shaykh's work has been hard to place here because her characters ultimately make choices that are not easily categorized and often contradictory. In other words, her work resists simplistic interpretations about women and, more particularly, about Arab women. At the same time, the complexity of her women is never gained at the cost of the men: both exist within a structure of roles and possibilities that, in radically different ways, are equally limiting.

Beautifully translated by Catherine Cobham, the novel tells the story of four women, each in separate sections: Suha, who has come to the gulf with her husband to escape the war in Lebanon, finds the desert suffocating and oppressive. Her descriptions of a landscape in which there is sand and wind but no old houses or garlic in the markets, sets the tone.

> In my discussions with women who hated it here, both Arabs and foreigners, I used to struggle to find objections to their arguments and take the discussions to absurd and trivial limits: I told them that the situation here was ideal in a way, and that they were lucky because they were seeing how cities were built, and witnessing the transformation of man from a beduin into a city-dweller. This was a great opportunity for them, I added: nothing was laid on for them as it was in other countries, and they would have to fight for what they really wanted. Despite what I said, I myself thought that time was wasted in searching for and constructing what existed and was recognized as normal or obvious anywhere else in the world.[7]

The second section, narrated by Tamr, a local girl taking English lessons from Suha, contains some of the novel's most powerful writing. Her relations with the children of her father's favorite wife, an amalgam of utter terror and despair, are presented only to the extent of her consciousness: we are left to decipher the shards: "I even began to long for us just to open our door because they used to leave their rubbish beside it, a dead rat, potato peelings, a gold paper crown, all of which, as far as I was concerned, formed part of a dialogue between me and them. How I wished I could explain to them how much I longed to know them."[8] Only in this section is there an extended flight into the past, in the form of the tale of Tamr's mother, taken as a concubine from a village in

Turkey. The very telling of it, despite her mother's bitter realization at the lack of control she has had over her life, binds mother and daughter in the kind of resistance that memory provides. Her mother's story serves Tamr as a testament against which she can hone her own survival skills.

The third character, Suzanne, is almost a reversal of Suha. "An ordinary American housewife," or so she says, Suzanne finds herself an object of endless and insatiable desire. Her affair with Maaz, a roller-coaster of abandon and fantasy that leads her to believe her expectations and images will always be fulfilled in random interludes, clashes with mortality. Yet, upon seeing Maaz (along with the newborn child of his wife Fatima) wasted by syphilis, Suzanne finds a paradoxical sense of resolve: "As I rode through the streets, protected from the burning sun outside, Maaz's house began to seem a continent away. I sensed the slow regular pulse of life, which was apparent even from the men and goats resting in the shade, and found that I loved this reality. I forgot the baby bit by bit and vowed not to leave here whatever happened."[9]

Wealthy and privileged, Nur, the fourth character, is at home everywhere and nowhere. Her mother serves her but imparts no memory, and Nur, estranged from her husband, is only left with the will to dominate. While some of al-Shaykh's characters pass in and out of each other's lives, the most significant connection is an affair between Suha and Nur. Deeply shocking and unexpected to Suha, the passion is intense but calculated for Nur. Yet, it is the human imbalance of their relationship, not its radical challenge to the patriarchal order, that propels Suha into a realization of her true desire: to take her son Umar and return to Lebanon. The split between "Suha of the desert and Suha the city dweller" can only be resolved through flight that is also a return, one of the great themes of Arabic literature.

Needless to say, *Women of Sand & Myrrh* has had its share of problems: copies were confiscated in Kuwait and reviews from the Gulf were hostile. While al-Shaykh does not consider herself particularly courageous or frank, Arab critics—particularly men—feel that she is. Despite the expected reaction from the Gulf, responses from most of the Arab world, particularly Jordan, Lebanon, Egypt, and Syria, were enthusiastic. Al-Shaykh has emphasized the fact that critics appreciated her ability to present such a wide range of women's experience without preaching about it. Given the general state of things, the fact that such a book dealing with such issues would get such a reception in such countries might come as a great surprise to many American readers.

One hopes an American publisher will realize what a following there would be for the powerful work of Hanan al-Shaykh and so many other Middle Eastern writers like her, lost in the cracks of ignorance and prejudice. As debates about multiculturalism continue, more connections need to be made. Our inheritance inludes a Europe formed in symbiosis and confrontation with Islamic civilization. The lack of contemporary Arabic writing available is only the smallest part of a gaping absence of things Arabic in this country. Still exoticized and left to the domain of experts, an inordinate amount of control is exerted over our access to knowledge about the Arab world, whether it be from the pre-Islamic, medieval, colonial, or contemporary period. As the effects of the bombing of Baghdad continue to reverberate, seizing some control over this knowledge will be essential in challenging the new world order.

1991

Our Memory Has No Future:
On Etel Adnan

Of Cities & Women (Letters to Fawwaz), by Etel Adnan.
Sausalito: The Post-Apollo Press, 1993.

Paris, When It's Naked, by Etel Adnan. Sausalito: The Post-Apollo Press, 1993.

Although she has lived in America more than thirty years, the pleasure and power of Etel Adnan's writing remains the privilege of far too few readers in this country. Born in Beirut to a Syrian Muslim father and a Greek Christian mother, Adnan began, even then, to negotiate what she has called the two poles, the two cultures that Beirut and Damascus, the landscape of her childhood represented. She attended a convent school until the age of sixteen when World War II, the first of many to interrupt and realign her life, broke out. It was then, just as later during the Lebanese civil war, that women began to find themselves in different places than they might have expected. In this case, after taking a clerical job with the French Information Bureau, Adnan soon found herself part of a unique adventure, as a participant in the French University's newly opened Beirut Institute for Literature and Linguistics. This institute, and its intimate circle of students, was led by Gabriel Bounoure, an enormously neglected literary figure who would later be an essential interlocutor to Edmond Jabès, another major francophone exile. After her studies at the institute, Adnan went on to pursue philosophy at the Sorbonne. From there, in the mid-1950s, she went to Berkeley and Harvard. Since then, she has taught at various places, returned to Beirut for a number of years, and divided her time between California, Europe, and the Middle East.

Adnan's work, almost by definition, cuts through many of the boundaries imposed on writers with such "interesting backgrounds." She presently writes in English, after having written in French for many years. At the same time, she is, unquestionably, an Arab writer. How, then, can one come to an easy definition of Adnan? Is she a Lebanese writer, a French writer, an American writer, a woman writer? Her example also throws into relief the narrowly defined and often exoticized category of Arab women's writing, a body of work that American readers are only beginning to familiarize themselves with through the work of more well-known writers like Nawal el-Saadawi, Hanan al-Shaykh, and Assia Djebar, as well as lesser-known writers such as Fadwa Tuqan, Alifa Rifaat, Salwa Bakr, and Sahar Khalifeh, among so many others. As always, part of the problem in seeing the larger picture has been availability. Since most American publishers are loath to take even minimal risks in order to introduce new writers in translation, American readers are left with only the most schematic vision of foreign literatures and little or no sense of the dense interconnected texture of relationships out of which particular writers emerge. The remarkably innovative and exhilarating artistic life of Beirut, for example (which forms such a central part of Etel Adnan's experience), remains a largely closed chapter of intellectual history to those who were not directly involved.

As well as being a novelist, essayist, and poet, Adnan is also a painter, a fact that constantly informs her work, particularly her two latest books, *Paris, When It's Naked,* and *Of Cities & Women (Letters to Fawwaz).* Of the connections between language, image, and origins, Adnan has written that she can only express herself in Arabic through painting. Despite the multiplicity of Adnan's cultures and endeavors, these books provide an excellent introduction to her unique blend of acute observation, emotional integrity, political clarity, and philosophical speculation.

Paris, When It's Naked, is the testimony of a lover whose conscience is stricken, whose awareness has been pierced by the fruit of other knowledge and experience. The lover is Adnan herself, the object of her desire is Paris, and the forbidden fruits are her past and present allegiences. Composed of short sections, each titled "Paris, When It's Naked," this gem of a book offers a very unconventional but crucial narrative. The relentless honesty, openness, and accumulated memory implicit in Adnan's writing probes the idea of Europe as margin and center in ways that are increasingly important for us to grasp. Describing an encounter with a Parisian friend, Adnan writes:

> Paris is beautiful. It aches to say so, one's arms are never big enough to hug such an immensity. Claude can say it innocently. It's harder for me to say so, it's also more poignant. It tears me apart. Paris is the heart of a lingering colonial power, and that knowledge goes to bed with me every night. When I walk in this city I plunge into an abyss, I lose myself in contemplation, I experience ecstasy, an ecstasy which I know to be also a defeat. Look, look how ugly are the Arab Quarter's pimps, how dehumanized the Algerians who squat in it, how destroyed their women, how degrading their prostitution to the very ones who vote for their expulsion. And I consider this monstrous being called Paris to be beautiful.[1]

At the same time, Adnan never assumes the role of victim. Her gaze penetrates the cityscape, the objects and people inhabiting it, but never at the cost of sparing herself, of abdicating responsibility. Having grown up "thinking the world was French. . . . And that everything that mattered, that was 'in books,' or had authority, did not concern our environment," Adnan "returns" to Paris, to French and everything that implies. She roams the sites that had been projected onto the now distant but ever-present soil of Lebanon, implanted within her through language, in order to interrogate herself through those very signs, cultural icons, and ways of life that once stood for both total liberation and utter defeat. But the relations are never simple, for this amalgam of the "implanted" has formed, as well, the deepest recesses of her own being. As she writes toward the end of the book:

> Dear Parents, why did you lie to me? You told me the sky was blue while we watched it together, in Beirut, by the sea, and the sunset

was a flame. You fooled a whole generation, then you destroyed it, the city is destroyed. The sky is not high either, as you taught me, it is so low, low, below my ceiling. I wonder if the rain will come in and spoil my books as it does my bones. I feel them, tonight, these bones you gave me. Neither one of you ever saw Paris, or intended to. Your trains never ended at Gare de Lyon. You thought of France as an intruder into the order of things as you knew them. Paris was a place of perdition, you said. Be reassured: I did not lose my soul in it. I only lost my illusions. And you.[2]

Adnan does not simply refer to aspects of a place, a culture or a people; rather, she partakes in and of them. And her range is exhilarating: from retracing the steps of Djuna Barnes, saying "hello to her at least once a day" and "dreaming of her," to recording the very same colonialized pain, aspirations, and defeats of the cogs that make the great machine of Paris operate so smoothly.

A lot of immigrants work in factories and create a major problem: how to make them work without having them breathe our air, live in our cities, or look at our wives and husbands? This equation has not been solved. They go on with their menial jobs, genuinely happy to make a living. They love rain, asphalt, warm bread, goat cheese, industrial oils, long grocery hours. They see work as energy and life. People think it's incongruous that they smile in traffic jams. Paris is the machine that eats them and could reject them. What would you say if you became spit? You wouldn't know it. Spit doesn't think; it evaporates pretty fast. I'm not going to spit carelessly anymore. Out of respect for the street.[3]

Of Cities & Women (Letters to Fawwaz), takes many of the issues aroused by Paris on through an extended itinerary, in letters written to Fawwaz Traboulsi, a Lebanese writer living in exile. Traboulsi had asked Adnan to contribute a piece on feminism for the special issue of a journal he was editing on Arab women. In lieu of the article, she began a correspondence with him and the book is made up of her letters to him over a two-year period, posted from Barcelona, Aix-en-Provence, Skopelos, Murcia, Amsterdam, Berlin, Rome, and Beirut. But where *Paris, When It's Naked* delves into the accumulated layers of the self, *Of Cities & Women* is more concerned with the nature of the race itself, its definition and redefinition, through philosophical speculation, observations on the relations between artists and their ostensible subjects, between women and cities, between women and men. As Adnan writes: "It is no longer a question of clarifying the distinction between the feminine and the masculine, but of redefining the human species."[4]

Adnan goes about thinking through this redefinition in many guises: through an incident in the red-light district of Barcelona; the tale of a "disturbed" single woman on the Greek island of Skopelos who had been taken to a mental asylum; the death of a close friend in Beirut; her obsession with "what Cézanne and Picasso can reveal about women, about the way women are looked at."[5] The passages on "these two sacred monsters,"[6] in addition to representing some of the most revelatory writing on Cézanne and Picasso, are also some of the most striking sections in the book. After traveling to see where Picasso spent the last twenty years of his life, Adnan comments:

> Picasso had enclosed himself in 30,000 acres of mountain land, of Cézanne's mountain, but on the side opposite to the one which Cézanne painted; he leaned back against this mountain as against Cézanne himself, as if against a wall, the chateau and the wall reminding one of the taut spiritual shadows of Barcelona's high palaces, inheritors of fanatical battles, the Crusades, and the Inquisition. At the bottom of a superb valley, on his rival's mountain, the old Andalusian master, who came through Catalonia, bought for himself an empty kingdom which he would people with his thoughts, and his canvases. That's where he locks himself up with the mystery of the woman . . . Picasso becomes voyeur, therefore witness, therefore woman. He depicts a primary sexuality, without culture, without decoration, which is neither bestial, nor angelic . . . In his exile he identifies with women, they who are exiled from Power, the place of origin.[7]

Weaving throughout the letters, as always in Adnan's writing, is the awareness of war as presence, companion, nightmare, yardstick, and fulcrum: "The cool breeze of early September awakes old memories. Of what? Of the sea rocks close to the Café Ajram in Beirut (long since destroyed), of the smell of the orange trees burnt fifty years later by napalm. Our memory is woven with war."[8] The imminence and eventual outbreak of the Gulf War also haunts these letters, as does Andalusia and the cultural genocide of the Arabs in Spain, followed by the slaughter of the Indians in the New World. Andalusia, Adnan laments, "the first loss, the death of the Mother, and of the orchards of which Lorca was the last tree."[9] An exquisite lyric sensibility (a cross between such great medieval mystics as Rabia or Hildegard of Bingen, and the American lucidity of Emily Dickinson or Lorine Niedecker), displayed in *The Spring Flowers Own & The Manifestations of the Voyage* (Post Apollo, 1990), generously infuses the spirit of Adnan's evocative prose. Here also, as in two other key works, *Sitt Marie Rose* (Post Apollo Press, 1982) and *The Arab Apocalypse* (Post Apollo Press, 1989), Adnan embodies the role of both visionary and chronicler, seeing what is to come by unveiling accepted ways of receiving and recording the past.

With what another Spaniard, Juan Goytisolo, has called the "memoricide" of cultural pluralism taking place in the heart of Europe, as fundamentalist warlords obliterate not only the people but the material, spiritual, and cultural inheritance of Bosnia, we would do well to take cognizance of Adnan's insistence on remembering, on her insistence that difference is memory, and this fact sustains the survival of the species:

> The Christian militias of East Beirut concentrated their attacks, as if to annihilate the essentially Muslim center of the city which was the beauty—and the memory. They behaved as if they believed that they had to destroy History in order to assert their specificity. But like a man who has murdered the woman he loved, the Lebanese will start and have started to become the mad lovers of old Beirut.[10]

By never losing sight of the primal and contradictory impulses that motivate human action, Adnan serves as an essential guide to a world bent on obliterating even the traces of unsanctioned existences, a world where, as a friend of hers in Beirut says, "Our memories don't have any future."[11]

1994

"The war was ending, the diasporas beginning"*: On the poetics of Juan Goytisolo

Like the quivering of the spear, then it shook. Now the time of its quivering is the same as that of its shaking. He says "then," although there is no lapse of time. Similarly with the renewal of creation by breaths, the moment of the nonexistence of a thing is the very moment of the existence of its like . . ."

IBN ARABI, *The Bezels of Wisdom*

Historical conditions work in all kinds of ways, depending on the degree to which you've been touched or made conscious by them. Various forms instruct, inform, or translate, historically and politically, as well as emotionally. As the Egyptian filmmaker Yousef Chahine has said: "Memory is confrontation, a confrontation with oneself. You must first confront yourself before confronting other people, or a whole country— that's also the political context of memory."[1] As I have written elsewhere, much of my work has involved the process of both finding and losing my "self" within the gaps I find in American discourse, gaps primarily having to do with either the lack or the suppression of any tangible political and historical space or consciousness, however these end up getting defined. Part of the difficulty of working through this is that I feel as if I have embarked upon an enormous journey only to come back to where I started from: in my case, a distinctly American language and American idiom, only to wonder what happened along the way. Every

---

Quarantine by Juan Goytisolo. Translated by Peter Bush. Normal, Illinois: The Dalky Archive Press, 1994.

now and then I wonder what it might have been like to just let myself work out of and through the language and the given circumstances without taking the actual physical and linguistic and cultural and political and experiential steps back and forth to other places that I did take. But when I encounter people who I think should know better, I realize that I *had* to traverse those territories: even if afterward the words I write remain identical, they would have to, at some level, be marked by knowledge picked up or shed along the way.

One of the writers who did know better, and who has marked my work deeply for the twenty-odd years I've been familiar with it, is Juan Goytisolo. My first encounter involved the odd experience of reading the trilogy backward: beginning with *Juan the Landless,* I moved on to *Count Julian* before finishing with *Marks of Identity.* From there I quickly went to his essays, as collected in *El furgón de cola* and *Disidencias,* as well as his work on Blanco White. Sometime after this, I wrote to Goytisolo with a request of one kind or another and, to my amazement and delight, he answered immediately, with great kindness. Since then, we have corresponded off and on, regarding a variety of things. Through involvement with the question of Palestine—and its direct relevance to many other things, both past and future—our concerns and attentions have often coincided. During the war in Bosnia, I often heard his name mentioned by friends as one of the sojourners whose visits there were truly appreciated. Most recently, I sent him materials on the imprisoned Israeli nuclear technician Mordechai Vanunu, a *mizrahi* Jew originally from Morocco. Before I knew it, I received articles from the Moroccan press about a campaign that Goytisolo had embarked upon to have Vanunu declared an honorary citizen of Marrakesh, his hometown. Since, at the time of my writing this, I am only anticipating our first meeting, I find it most ironic that while he is in New York, I will be in Jerusalem. Suffice it to say that I recount this brief itinerary of my encounter with Goytisolo only to realize how much his work opened up for me and, at the same time, how closed off American intellectual and literary discourse has been to the issues involved in the kinds of choices he has made as a writer and citizen of the world.

There are, of course, ostensible reasons for this: unquestionably, Goytisolo's early engagement in the Palestinian cause beginning in 1968 could do him no good among the mediocre arbiters of taste who largely succumbed to the triumphalist Zionist vision that followed the war of 1967 and have permeated American political and cultural discourse on the Middle East ever since. Nor, I think, did the complexity involved in reconciling Goytisolo's politics with his knowledge and intimacy of Sephardic Jewish culture help matters much. But I think the problem goes even deeper: by consistently refusing to commodify his language, Goytisolo has forged a poetics that serves to create a field of resistance preventing any facile assimilation of his work within familiar categories or uninformed cultural and historical assumptions. In an interview with Julio Ortega, Goytisolo points out that "When writers just starting out seek advice from me, the first thing I say is that they must give up the idea of making a living from their work and seek out parallel forms of sustenance. To a great extent, the monstrous proportion of redundant works and irresponsible writing that floods the literary marketplace can be explained through economics. . . . The writer must also maintain the right to remain silent and not produce."[2]

Like a poet, Goytisolo has chosen to situate his work within the historical context of language as it has been used, along with all the uses it has been put to; in the same interview, Goytisolo says: "the only kind of writing that interests me is that which is situated outside of canonized literary forms. . . . When I write, I don't invent situations, characters or actions, but rather discursive forms and structures, textual groupings that in combination take the shape of occult elective affinities, such as in architecture or the plastic arts. . . . Therefore, the kind of reading that I am partial to on the critical level is that which looks at the text itself in relation to the literary corpus of the language."[3]

In a curious way, the political consciousness and involvement, as well as the historical position on language from which Goytisolo initiates his art, place him well outside the scrutiny of most of the insular and self-reflexive modes of critical theory now practiced. In fact, when one looks at the depth and breadth, as well as the foundation in diverse languages, idioms, and cultures that nurture and sustain Goytisolo's work, one might conclude that the discourses mentioned above have largely involved themselves, literally, in nonissues. To state this more clearly, Goytisolo's writing can be called "inaugural"; in other words, it is the kind of writing that creates the conditions for the invention and emergence of its own idiosyncratic critical vocabulary, refusing at every twist and turn the imposition of a preordained discourse that cannot possibly take into account the particular circumstances of its generation. Goytisolo himself has called this kind of writing "critical practice." We are too often faced with a situation in which the writer is considered a native whose idiosyncracies must be contained or domesticated by the critic or theorist. The wholesale colonization of what I have here termed "inaugural" writing by derivative forms of theory or literary history within academic and what passes for intellectual discourse in this country, also has a basis in economic structures and equations. To put it simply: the long, continuing apprenticeship of writing—a vocation that might involve unpaid silence—cannot possibly be equated with or renumerated at the same rate as the hierarchical models of production that both academia and middle-brow journalistic literary criticism represent. But that is the topic for another conference.

To pursue the issue of language further I would like to follow two strands of thought: the first is a line of inquiry that emerges for us from the work of Emilé Benveniste but has deeper roots in early medieval Arabic and, later, Hebrew grammatical theory. The crucial difference between poetics and grammatical theory derived from Aristotle and Greek models and that of Arabic thought is that in Greek models the unit of significance is the word rather than the sentence. Given this, the weight of prepositions, pronouns, definite and indefinite articles—all the seemingly inconsequential words that glue nouns and verbs together to form sentences—assume a completely different significance. Moreover, unlike Aristotle who was intent on determining what was common among the imitative arts, Arabic philosophers were more concerned with finding out what was different and unique about poetic art. In another vein: the great medieval Hebrew poet and biblical commentator, Abraham Ibn Ezra, in a note on Chapter 4, verse 35 of Deuteronomy, wrote that: "The human element of speech is divine or partakes of divinity." Since one of the most important divine attributes is infinity, both text and talk, the letter and the voice, retain fluidity and remain limitless. This preoccupation with language as human access to the infinite also implies the possibility of representation through syntax itself, in the delineation of optative and prepositional states of being in relation to the unknowable: toward, away from, before, up to, if. Goytisolo notes that "As determined by Benveniste, the "I," the "you" and the "we" do not refer to an objective reality, like the majority of nominal signs, but to a discursive reality, to the mere process of enunciation. Neither the interrogative you nor the interrogative I possess a precise and concrete identity, and the reader cannot know with any certainty who is the transmitting subject and whom the receiver."[4] A determination of this kind brings us much closer to the poetics of epistemological and linguistic investigation in writers like Gertrude Stein and Jack Spicer or the reinvention of epic in the poet Alice Notley. While such figures might appear unlikely correspondents to Goytisolo, I would contend that they offer potentially more fertile avenues of investigation than the standard tools of reference brought to bear upon his work. But this too is a topic for another discussion.

In speaking about the movement of language within the trilogy, Goytisolo notes that "the writer cannot abandon himself to inspiration and feign innocence in the face of language for language itself is never innocent."[5] He has also indicated that the trilogy moves toward a potential closure or exhaustion of one kind of design or discursive form just as it opens up another—that is, the terms set up in *Marks of Identity* almost presuppose the need to go beyond them in *Count Julian;* likewise, the terms of *Count Julian* present the challenge that is met by *Juan the Landless.* The boldness of attacking grammar and syntax and actually ending the trilogy in Arabic is a signal sending at least two contradictory or paradoxical messages; for one thing, it tells us, literally, that the Spanish used until now must be unpeeled to reveal the texture of other membranes below the apparent surface. At the same time, this revelation is much more than a "mark" of "identity." While the trilogy clearly represents a massive and frontal attack on official Spanish culture, the movement into language represents an even broader and more comprehensive cultural critique questioning the whole notion of Europe's knowledge of itself. This "critical practice" comes to fruition in works like *The Virtues of the Solitary Bird* and *Quarantine.* In his meditation on Ibn 'Arabi, by his very engagement, Goytisolo asks a simple question that few—either before or after—seem to have asked so lucidly. If Ibn 'Arabi was born in Murcia, is he not also a "Spaniard"? That is, how many generations does it take for someone to be considered "European"? Isn't Goytisolo's interrogation both a condemnation and, at the same time, an attempt to recuperate the heart and soul of a Europe banished, even unto itself? Having earlier, in some sense, expelled himself from Spain, Goytisolo now propels himself through time and space in a continuing hejira written into the very fabric of his syntax and vocabulary as whole blocks of prose act like movements in a cosmic drama of restitution and recomposition. Indeed, these works confront crucial philosophical and ethical questions as, in the words of the Guyanese novelist Wilson Harris, they draw "upon unsuspected resources within an unfinished genesis of the Imagination."[6]

To clarify what Wilson Harris means, let me just mention two examples of "unfinished genesis." We might recall that in the Hebrew *Book of Genesis* itself, Hagar and Ishmael are left to die in the desert, without water. Yet, it is upon their legacy and names that the Prophet Muhammad creates new forms of worship and lines of sacred transmission that become a new religion. We might also remember that Aeneas, the central character of Virgil's *Aeneid* and the founder of the Roman Empire, had appeared in a very minor role in several stanzas of Homer's *Iliad* many centuries earlier. The juxtaposition and reappearance of such figures is not at all unlike Goytisolo's description of a long neglected aspect of the genius of Cervantes, that is, his ability to create a completely new reality by freeing a remarkably diverse range of existing characters from the strictures of their history and generic circumstances. Let us not, at this juncture, forget the etymology of the word genre and its relation to words like race, stock, family, origin, source, begetter, and ancestor. As the poet Jed Rasula points out: "Now we see genre distinction practiced as a kind of racism. The "characteristics" are learned (and what is worse, taught), strict demarcations are observed to a crippling extent [readers of novels can't read poetry, readers of poetry can't read philosophy. . . . All of this snaps back from the praxis into the shadow of an attitude: "poet" "novelist" "dramatist" "painter" "sculptor" "critic," i.e. submission to the sociological demand that everyone identify themself in the form of a racial obsession."[7]

Wilson Harris also speaks of an "imaginary constellation," where you can "steep yourself in a theater, so to speak, of plural masks that bear on the travail of humanity; in an orchestration of ancient and modern histories and characterisations and imageries as well revolving, so to speak, around a transitive principle or musical chord. . . . To arrive in a place where we are not, brings into play transitive chords within densities, transitive dimensionalities that unlock doors within the body of language itself."[8] Here, again, we are brought close to Goytisolo's sense of his evolving work, as it unfolds in space so that it must "be 'read' like a mobile by Calder."[9] But it is in the evolution of my second example, that of Aeneas and Virgil, that Wilson Harris's thought proves an essential guide to understanding the full significance of Goytisolo's work beyond the trilogy, particularly in *Quarantine.* Harris writes:

"Original epic in our age, I would hope, begins to move the enigma of resurrection into new dimensions that we need to nurse within the complex life of the Imagination; original epic may help us to take up afresh the burden of an uncertain but far-reaching rescue of the universal spouse . . . that death-dealing *ideologies and regimes* marry and imprison around the globe. . . . In other words the absolute commandment issued by a sovereign death-dealing regime is partial . . . and that partiality is threaded *into inequalities, into injustices,* harbored by one-sided traditions. You may recall how Virgil—who had labored for Dante in guiding him through the inferno and the purgatorio—was unjustly excluded from the paradiso. He was deemed a pagan because his address lay in a pre-Christian age. How one-sided is such a paradiso? Does it not need a profound, re-visionary momentum of the frame of language in which it is cast? Once such deep-seated inequalities remain within traditions, the Soul of tradition itself is orphaned. It suffers cosmic abandonment in that it appears *to nurture absolutes which polarise* humanity irreconcilably. Unless such absolutes can *yield their partialities within* plural masks that question themselves, the Soul is cut adrift and may lose its potency to arbitrate, with profoundest creativity, between divisions in humanity.[10]

Goytisolo understands only too well that these "deep-seated inequalities" that "nurture absolutes which polarise humanity irreconcilably" are the very fabric through which a "national" culture is woven, and this knowledge gives him the authority to ask the kinds of rhetorical questions that appear and reappear throughout his work. In *Quarantine,* for example, after taking Dante to task in a variety of unsettling contexts, Goytisolo writes: "Are the reprobates Dante ignored Kurds, Shi'ites, Palestinians, panic-stricken deserters, or simply children of fertile Mesopotamia clinging to the last of their instinct for life, the only solid truth that is beyond dispute?"[11] In a world rife with new crusades (some of which have resulted in genocide), by favoring the possibilities of life so clearly, Goytisolo emerges as one of our most articulate arbitrators attempting to negotiate the ever present "divisions in humanity." By probing suppressed chapters in his personal and our collective histories, Juan Goytisolo interrupts the lethargy of our received assumptions in the hope of charting new itineraries along which memories of our future can be routed.

1998

Dispatches

A Stitch in Time

The following text was written in 1987, in Jerusalem, following the arrest, abduction, and imprisonment of Mordechai Vanunu, an Israeli nuclear technician who "revealed" the "secrets" of Israel's nuclear capablities to the world. Vanunu remains in prison in Israel; far from being embraced by the liberal left, he has been abandoned, left to cope with conditions created to make him insane. When charged with "exposing state secrets," Vanunu said: "The individual can compel the establishment, can say to it, You are accountable to me. The individual can expose the dark machinations of any regime in the world, in any sphere, by means of civil disobedience. . . . An action like mine teaches citizens that their own reasoning, the reasoning of every individual, is no less important than that of the leaders. . . . They use force and sacrifice thousands of people on the altar of their megalomania. Don't follow them blindly." The specific politics still seem quite apt, even at the remove of these years, even despite the agreements reached between representatives of the Palestinian and Israeli people.

A few days after getting back from Cairo, I found myself in bed reading the paper and listening to the radio. I was recovering from a case of laryngitis the germ of which, I suspect, had been planted by a mean wind coming out of the Libyan desert in Saqqara; the germ was then nurtured by the bitter March cold of Jerusalem. Radio Jordan was on the tail end of a twelve-part series called "25 Years of Rock." After Lyndon Johnson's fateful words, "I regret the necessities of war have compelled us . . ." a song I remember well came on, "The Eve of Destruction," by Barry McGuire. The song reminded me of the strike my brother had helped organize to shut down our high school during the bombing of Cambodia in 1970; it reminded me of the older students we saw tear-gassed and beaten by the cops in the afternoons in Harvard Square or around the Boston Common, of the Black Panthers I used to talk to as they sold the Party paper on streetcorners. Everything that had been a way of life for kids from Roxbury or Dorchester slowly entered our lives. We didn't have to be black: having long hair or hanging around the park after dark was as good a reason as any for the cops to flip on their searchlights, invite you in for a ride, and start asking funny questions.

In the paper I was reading, under the bold headline, HE's NO TRAITOR, HE's MY BROTHER, two dark, resolute faces stood out against the silhouette of buildings and TV antennas. It must have been the end of another long day. Asher, who looked a little more like his older brother Mordechai, seemed a bit wearier than Meir Vanunu. Neither really had the time to shave. Whatever their worries, something else came through their eyes: a look that surfaced from a deeper source, the place where feeling and conscience unite in action. The caption under this stark image said it all. In Hebrew the literal phrase was, "He went in the light of day." "He came clean," I'd say, in good American. I was glad at least someone was their brother's keeper.

An Israeli paper had asked me for a contribution to a special issue devoted to twenty years of occupation. I must confess that my first reaction was one of extreme cynicism. Fine, I thought, they'll have a cock-tail party, maybe even a barbecue. Many Israelis and foreigners, myself included, seemed guilty of institutionalizing the terms of oppression through subsidizied research, ideas, and, finally, talk and more talk about a simple unadorned question of power that remained as clear as the light of day to any stonemason, prisoner, taxi driver, short-order cook, or right-wing politician. Meanwhile, olive trees continued to be ripped out of Palestinian earth and placed cosmetically along the flow-ered paths of Israeli institutions for the benefit of Hadassah ladies or vis-iting artists and academics. Land continued to be confiscated; houses blown up; people imprisoned, expelled, and tortured; families kept apart; students teargassed and shot. Daily. Weekly. Monthly. Like the rent. Or taxes. Just part of life. At least Vanunu had done something dramatic. Then I figured, why not write about him? After all, speaking your mind never hurts. Maybe there was more light in Meir and Asher's eyes than I'd bargained for. So I wrote something, but they didn't publish it.

I've never been one to subscribe to what I call the liberal "dream deferred" theory that once there was a pure Zionist dream that went askew: for some, in 1948; for others, in 1956, 1967, 1973, 1977, or even 1982. More like a rotten apple, I thought, or the fig of good and evil. A description of Albert Entebbi, one of the more important Palestinian Jewish leaders in the early 1900s, kept coming back to me during Vanunu's capture and the disclosure of his diaries. They called Entebbi an "arrogant, haughty, capricious, perverse, irascible, violent, despotic, ruthless," and, finally (in my mind, at least), the key word: "Asiatic."[1] Entebbi had repeatedly argued that Palestinian protest was generated by the practices of the new settlers and not the "violent" or "despotic" nature of anyone. Has anything really changed? Or were the slurs against Vanunu simply the same prejudices, with subtler methods? In remembering how he grew up in Marrakesh, Vanunu said: "The rich lived outside, but most of the people lived in the *mellah*. There were Jewish schools in the Quarter, but I studied at the Alliance School, which was outside, we studied half a day in French and the second half in Arabic, with about an hour a day in Hebrew. I used to go around quite a bit, I remember there was a place called the *Jamaa 'l-Fnaa*, people would come from all kinds of places outside the city and there were all kinds of performers there—snake charmers and acrobatic cyclists, someone reading from the Quran, musicians, and everyone used to sit there and I used to go there myself, a little kid, by myself, and wander around." Later on, after being bound and gagged in court, he managed to describe the way he was kidnapped in Italy and brought back to Israel: "They brought me here like Kunta Kinte, chained up like a slave."[2]

In contrast to the reigning rhetoric, I thought of a new year's sermon I had been studying, given in 1942 by Moise Ventura, the chief rabbi of Alexandria: "After the lamentable failure of Western civilization, the Orient is again called upon to play an important part in the cultural life of Nations. The Orient means Egypt, Palestine, Syria, Iraq; more specifically, the Semites—Jews and Arabs—are again called upon together to play a vital role within the scene of history. . . . Everyone whose mental

capacities are in free working order must recognize that today the enemies of the Jews are as well the enemies of the Arabs—that is, the
enemies of civilization."[3] In the long run, Jews will always remain a
minority in the world, and in the Middle East. The choice remains to
either keep building the ghetto walls higher and higher and thicker and
thicker, or to start picking and chipping and breaking them away—to
look at the light of day and see that there is no Palestinian problem but
an Israeli one; that "security" can only be measured by how one reacts
and acts against continuing oppression. The memory of a suffering people, as Jews know only too well, is long and both good and bad deeds
are inscribed in everyone's remembrance. Moreover, true relationships
are always reciprocal, and relations between people have always out-
lived those between states.

In 1945, Rabbi Ventura delivered another sermon in Alexandria,
entitled "An Echo of the Atomic Bomb." It began like this: "The state of
the discovery of the atomic bomb marks the historic moment of the
most spectacular explosion of materialism, that world system founded
on the principle of the eternity and indestructability of matter."[4] The
monotheistic concept of God, as delineated by both classical Islamic and
Jewish theologians, projects a spark of brilliance into the nuclear age.
Yet the authorites continue to act as if they were in the vanguard not of
the twenty-first, but of the nineteenth century—still living as if this
world will last forever, still thinking in colonial, positivist, materialist,
and determinist terms. Maybe the decision of Mordechai Vanunu's
brothers to initiate a public campaign on his behalf; to refuse the terms
and implications of his imprisonment, and to attempt to throw those
terms back in the face of his accusers as a challenge is part of a deeper
critique, a deeper revolt, part of the way back to another vision of things
that can break down the ghetto walls. The choice? To mix mortar and
cover the bricks that will seal our eyes from the light of day, or to
retrieve forgotten and buried chapters left out of official and received
history, alms against oblivion that can be turned to knowledge and used
in the present, the only place they might have any possible bearing on
the future.

1987

Court Report: Prolonging a Farce

The continuation of Faisal Husseini's hearing, prolonged due to failure in the judge's computer on 29 March 1988, was scheduled to commence at 11:00 A.M. today. At approximately 11:15, a clerk informed the waiting family members that the time of Husseini's arrival was uncertain. On several prior occasions, Husseini was either "forgotten" in prison for a scheduled hearing or simply not brought causing further postponements in reaching a verdict on his case. Of all the "occupational" hazards Palestinians are constantly subjected to, the blatant devaluation of their time must be considered one of the more subtle but undeniably provocative forms of oppression. Some minutes after this first announcement, another clerk informed the waiting group that Husseini had, in fact, left Ramle prison and was on his way to Jerusalem but apparently had been taken to the wrong courthouse. The new expected time of arrival was set at 12:00 noon. By this time some colleagues of Husseini's from the Arab Studies Society along with employees of the Palestine Human Rights Commission had arrived; they, along with the interpreter, went out of the courtroom and into the grounds of the Russian Compound to observe a demonstation (under the heading: FREE PALESTINIAN CHILDREN FROM ISRAELI PRISONS) taking place by the gates to the prison section. The Russian Compound, better known to Israelis and Palestinians as the "Moscobbiyya," remains one of West Jerusalem's best-kept tourist secrets. Yet, the scenes one can witness there daily, particulary in the last months since the beginning of the uprising, have come to resemble more and more the kinds of scenes familiar from news photos of less traveled and more "exotic" sites: Argentina, Central America, South Africa, Iran, etc. With indifferent regularity, prisoners handcuffed to policemen are led from the prison to the courthouse and back; paddy wagons pull in unloading new batches and mothers, sisters, brothers, and fathers—many in traditional dress from remote villages—gather off to the sides, hoping to catch a glimpse or have a word with one of the many missing or incarcerated. By 12:00 noon, the family members and colleagues were joined by several other people, among whom was Dr. Edy Kaufman of the Truman Center at Hebrew University. The interpreter was later informed that Robert Ruby, a reporter for the *Baltimore Sun,* had come to cover the hearing but, in a typical combination of inefficiency and willed misinformation, was told that the trial would be held on 11 May. By about 12:20, the prosecutor suggested to the defense counsel to begin proceedings and, along with Dr. Mahdi Abdul-Hadi, the witness for the defense, they all entered the courtroom. Here, new evidence was submitted: Dr. Abdul-Hadi displayed a Jordanian tourist map that had a depiction of the Jordanian flag in color on it. This flag had, as Dr. Abdul-Hadi explained in his testimony, the exact same design and color pattern as the Palestinian flag along with the addition of one star on the left-hand side in the middle of the triangle. Along with this Dr. Abdul-Hadi submitted an article from the Hebrew daily *HaAretz* by the former head of Israeli intelligence Professor Yehoshefat Harkabi; the article, dated 19 April 1988, was headed as follows: "The PLO Flag is the Flag of the Palestinian People." In the short article, consisting of approximately fifteen lines, Professor Harkabi made basically the same historical points as those made by Dr. Abdul-Hadi in his earlier testimony. The prosecutor and the judge differed somewhat on the relevancy of this piece of evidence and they discussed this issue for some time. By about 12:50, Faisal Husseini was led—in handcuffs and leg chains—down the hall outside the courtroom; all those who had been waiting for him—by now about twenty-five people—spontaneously went toward him and gathered around him; he first embraced his wife and children before turning to greet everyone else. He seemed to have a good rapport with his guard who simply stood off to the side watching. Dr. Edy Kaufman asked him if he had received a package of books on nonviolence by Gene Sharpe that he had sent in care of the prison; Husseini said that he did *not* receive the books but that the prison authorities had queried him about books of such a nature indicating that they had arrived but were simply confiscated. After about five minutes, the guard indicated that they had to leave. Husseini's wife pointed to her husband's hair while bringing out a comb; as she ran it through his hair to straighten it out, Husseini and the guard turned to be driven back to the wrong courtroom in East Jerusalem to which he had earlier been brought. Apparently, since he was brought to the wrong place, he now had to go back *there* in order to again be released so that he could return to his own hearing which, in fact, was in the process of finishing. Back in the courtroom, the judge had taken a recess in order to check certain sources regarding the new evidence that had been submitted. The prosecutor then asked the interpreter whom he was representing, upon which the interpreter told him that he was preparing a transcript for Amnesty International. The prosecutor then began to inquire about Amnesty, an organization he had obviously heard of but was not very familiar with. The defense counsel then spoke of his own experience as a former *client* of Amnesty, when he was under house arrest from 1980 to 1983 in Jerusalem. They then proceeded to talk about the various merits of various judges on the circuit that they had appeared before; the defense counsel spoke of the need for more judges to know Arabic well since many of the nuances regarding the intent of witnesses and defendants were lost in translation. By about 1:45 the judge returned from her chambers and a few minutes later Faisal Husseini was brought into the courtroom, with his handcuffs removed but still in leg-chains. The Hebrew/Arabic interpreter introduced himself to the lawyers and summarized for Husseini the prior proceedings. The judge first asked the defense before them, stating to the court that there were no further witnesses or evidence to be submitted in the case; she then noted that both sides would submit their conclusions and closing arguments in writing within two weeks and that after reviewing the material she herself would come to a decision no later than a month from the present date. She asked Husseini when he was scheduled to be released from Administrative Detention (9 June 1988) and said that, were he to be released before a decision was made, he would be informed by the court officially. Court was adjourned and Husseini was left some time, in the hall, to spend with his family. Later that same day, in the late evening, it became known that Mubarak Awad, the head of the Palestinian Center for the Study of Non-Violence, was arrested and taken to the Russian Compound for interrogation with the intention of issuing an order for his deportation within three days.

1988

The Trial: A Real Farce

The defendant, Faisal Husseini, was led into the courtroom by three guards; his feet were chained. Besides the officials in attendance, Faisal Husseini's family, a member of the Arab Studies Society, and the lawyer Henry Schwartzschild from the American Civil Liberties Union were also present. The primary purpose of the hearing was for the court to hear the defense's witness, Dr. Mahdi Abdul-Hadi (President of PASSIA; Palestinian Academic Society for the Study of International Affairs), and a fellow at the Harvard Center for International Affairs, regarding the prosecution's evidence. The hearing lasted approximately three hours and concentrated on three pieces of evidence: the letter opener, and two drawings done on cloth.

The first series of questions by the prosecution dealt with whether Dr. Abdul-Hadi thought the evidence before him was the work of amateurs or professionals and if so (in either case), what light that would shed on the case. Afterward the history of the flag and its color scheme as used in various other Arab countries was gone over; following that there was a series of questions on the Palestinian National Charter. The judge, at several points, requested that the prosecution clarify its questions; the defense offered a number of objections to questions on the grounds that they were leading or irrelevant; a number of these were sustained. The following is a sampling of the kind of exchanges that took place:

Prosecution: What difference would it make, in your opinion, whether we were dealing here with work done by professionals or amateurs?
Witness: First of all, to anyone familiar with Arab culture, the style of the work before us is clearly that of amateurs; by emphasizing this, my point is that the people doing this reflect the values of a popular culture, not a well-educated or an academic artistic culture. The work expresses the culture of the street, the local school, the family, the mosque or the church.
Prosecution: You said the colors used were not particularly "artistic," that they were unfulfilled . . .
Witness: Yes, the colors are vague, unclear.
Prosecution: Do you have any background in the arts?
Witness: Although my expertise is in history, I certainly do have enough understanding of the arts to say whether a work is connected to a particular tradition or not.
Prosecution: Could you tell us, in your opinion, what the significance of the vagueness of these colors is?
Witness: As I said, the people who painted these pictures are expressing things from a popular level, things that cannot come from an organized entity like a party, a club, an organization . . .
Prosecution: Is the PLO one of those organizations you refer to? Are these works not connected to that organization?
Witness: No, these works are not connected.
Prosecution: You've said that these colors [used in the flags depicted in the works] have been connected to the Palestinian National Movement since 1917?
Witness: Yes, since 1917. These colors were endorsed for a flag after the Arab revolt of 1916. The Palestinians participated in that revolt but shared the flag that was used by Sharif Ibn Ali in 1916.
Prosecution: Does this flag resemble the flag of any present Arab country?
Witness: Yes, the Jordanian flag, from 1921 until the present. On the Jordanian flag, however, there is a little white star which does not appear on this flag.
Prosecution: Besides this, is there another country that has such a flag?
Witness: From 1947 until the present, the Ba'ath Socialist Party of Syria has adopted this same flag.
Prosecution: We spoke of states, does Syria use this flag?

Witness: The Syrians use the colors of this flag in a different sequence. I have to add also that the Hashemite emblem uses the same sequence of colors but has no star.

Prosecution: I ask again: does the Hashemite Kingdom use this flag?

Witness: The seal, the symbol [Faisal Husseini points to the Israeli emblem hanging above the judge's desk] of the Hashemite kingdom has this same Arab flag which, I would like to reiterate, was adopted in 1917, except for the star. The flag does have a star, but the symbol does not. My emphasis here is on the *Arab* factor, evident in all the countries whose flags have the same colors but are used in different sequences and arrays. This is so because the *original source for all these flags is the flag used officially since 1916, adopted by the Palestinians in 1917!* These flags have been used at all kinds of inter and pan-Arab meetings and the form we see here is precisely the same one. So this flag is nothing new, it does not come out of nowhere nor was it invented recently: it has a long history dating back from 1917.

Prosecution: So, besides Jordan there is no other country in which the array of colors appears in the sequence of this one?

Witness: Yes, Iraq. From 1921 to 1958. On that Iraqi flag there were two stars since Iraq was the second Arab state to gain independence, after Syria.

Prosecution: [Displays copy of the Iraqi flag] So this is how the Iraqi flag looks?

Witness: Yes.

Prosecution: So you would say that today only Jordan uses such a similar flag?

Witness: Yes, but I would have to add, as I said earlier, that the Ba'ath Party uses the same flag.

Prosecution: Yes, but today, who else uses this flag?

Witness: The Palestinian Arab people, as they have been since 1917; this has not changed since then.

Prosecution: Do you mean the PLO?

Witness: Not necessarily.

Prosecution: What do you mean?

Judge: Here I would like a very clear answer.

Witness: Not necessarily because when a Palestinian Arab individual, a family or an institution raises this flag it does *not* mean that they are raising a PLO flag.

Prosecution: If the PLO raises a flag, do they raise *this* flag or another one?

Witness: The PLO presently raises the flag of the Palestinian people and not the other way around.

[A drawn-out discussion on particular details of the exhibits followed, with specifics of color, dimension, etc., being pored over in minute detail. The prosecution unfurled a flag confiscated from a demonstration and used it to compare the depictions drawn on the exhibits. The judge finally intervened.]

Judge: We're playing with words here and going in circles—let's just see a flag.

Prosecution: I can be of some help here. Now, here is a flag made by amateurs [unfurls flag with red triangle on the left, and three stripes in the sequence green, white and black]. Is this the flag used today by the PLO?

Witness: The colors used on this flag are the same colors as those used by the PLO. The correctness, the better likeness is gotten here by the higher professionalism of the work.

Prosecution: Couldn't you just say that this form, the red triangle, the three stripes and so on—IS THIS THE FLAG RAISED BY THE ORGANIZATION? I want a clear answer.

Witness: This is the flag of the Palestinian people that the PLO *also* raises.

[Further discussion on the amateur/professional issue follows; the judge intervenes].

Judge: I think we're going in circles. I think his answer is clear, that the flag *could* be used by the PLO but does not necessarily have to be.

[Prosecutor presses on about the likeness of the flags in the exhibits].

Witness: Yes, there is a likeness but not an absolute identity.

Prosecution: Could it be the flag of another organization?

Witness: Yes, as I said, the Ba'ath Party, for instance.

Prosecution: Is this more like the Ba'ath flag or this flag I showed you?

Judge: We all have eyes, we can come to our own conclusions.

[Drawings on cloth are exhibited before the court, witness is asked to describe them.]

Witness: There is a woman with a Palestinian shirt carrying her daughter and there is a sequence of colors from the Arab flag, very vague and unclear, with also a Palestinian head-covering and there are some shackles raising a torch.

Prosecution: The essence, I think, you've not pointed out. Isn't this the Land of Israel, Palestine?

Witness: The drawing is not really clear as to whether or not it's a depiction of the historical land of Palestine but someone looking at this could certainly give it more than one interpretation.

Prosecution: Do you see here Palestine, the Land of Israel?

Witness: Yes, in a very inexact manner.

Prosecution: Are the colors the same here?

Witness: Yes, there are colors, not artistically accurate, but yes, they do resemble the other colors.

Prosecution: But here there is not a message of peace, but rather a violent message, a Kalashnikov being clasped.

Witness: The average Palestinian does not have sufficient military knowledge to know whether or not this is a depiction of a Kalashnikov.

Prosecution: But do you know who drew this? If I told you that it was drawn by a Palestinian prisoner, would that change your opinion? [Defense objects].

Defense: We all know that the show centered around "The Day of the Palestinian Prisoner" but there were many other displays there as well which haven't been discussed; books and pamphlets from the non-violence center, for instance.

Prosecution: Here is another piece, with a flag.

Witness: The style of the flag is quite incomplete and doesn't really resemble that of any organization.

Prosecution: We all know this is an inexact drawing but does this triangle here resemble that triangle.

Witness: No, not really.

Prosecution: Doesn't this flag resemble the Land of Israel?

[Extended discussion over resemblance of color and shapes follows]

Prosecution: Are you an expert in history or in art?

Witness: I am an expert in history but I do have enough understanding of art to differentiate a bad rendering from a genuine one.

Prosecution: Do we not see a PLO flag here?

Witness: No.

Prosecution: Do we not see the Land of Israel?

Witness: There is some likeness to the coast of Palestine here but very inexact. Yes, one could say that this is a likeness of historical Palestine albeit a very innacurate one. Nor would I say that this here is a Palestinian flag but that the colors used here *resemble* those of the flag.

Judge: What is the significance of the words: "You have nothing to lose but your chains and your tent, Revolt!" [inscribed on one of the exhibits].

Prosecution: [Interjecting to the witness] So you didn't translate the first word ["revolt," coming as the last word in the translation and not the first word as in the Arabic original]. Meaning: make revolution, be violent! Arise and fight, meaning that if you do that you will have nothing to lose but the refugee camps [here there is a play on words in the original Arabic between tents and refugee camps].

Defense: First of all, this is inexact. This is a copy of a Western slogan that has been introduced into all kinds of Arab movements and resembles, both in history and usage, the slogan "Workers of the World Unite." What I mean is that the adoption of a slogan already fitting to the tone or mood of a people's movement doesn't mean that the movement itself either has to fit or be the originator of the ideology from which the slogan was adopted. What this means, in essence, is that not everybody who would draft or repeat this quotation is necessarily committed to the source or the ideology from which it was originally extracted but is simply copying or repeating a phrase with no deep knowledge of its context; nor does it mean that they will necessarily or are about to follow it through. To say "Workers of the World Unite" is not any indication of the truth of that statement at the time it is being said.

Prosecution: [examining letter opener] These colors at the top of this Palestine-shaped object—does this not suggest, along with the slogan, the need to fight in order to return to the land from the camps?

Witness: Again, I want to emphasize that these colors are those of the Palestinian Arab people. The saying written along the side there is taken from a standard Western slogan except the only word added here is TENT. No, the three things, the slogan, the map and the colors put together do not mean that you are calling for a revolt. The phrase, in fact, "you have nothing to lose," is also a phrase long used by Arab nationalists beginning from 1915 still during Turkish rule, through the Mandate and in the Jordanian period in open organizations and meetings. What we see here is simply a COPY and repetition of very common phrases. When people copy this it DOES NOT MEAN THEY ARE PART OF A SECRET ORGANIZATION.

Prosecution: In the context of "The Day of the Prisoner," with this combination and this map, that is, a map of the land prior to '67, before the occupation, don't you think that this then takes on a completely different significance: that of a full return to the land taken by force by the Jews?

Witness: As someone who has some sense of history, the first thing I would notice is that the Palestinian people are the first Arab people, historically, to demand independence from the Turks; in Syria there was also such a movement, involving both Arabs and Jews . . .

Prosecution: I am speaking of the Land of Israel, not the Turks, but of the Jews in the Land of Israel. Now, the same artist who painted this, would it be too far-fetched to think that he might have had, in his mind, the Palestinian return to his territory?

Witness: I still don't understand the question.

Defense: Wait a second [reaches for the letter opener], I don't see this at all like that. Where's the Dead Sea? Look, right here . . .

Prosecution: Right, well then, this does include, this is after '67.

Defense: I haven't intervened so far and I usually don't like to do that but I think that the questions should concentrate on the exhibits at hand because we've gotten pretty far from the point here.

Prosecution: I say that this represents the State of Israel with the territories, do you agree?

Witness: It is an inexact likeness of historical Palestine in the Mandate period.

Prosecution: Even though you're a historian, I want you then to speak about 1986 to the present . . .

Judge: Just a second, you know that a historian can also deal with the present . . .

Witness: In terms of what?

Prosecution: Do you agree that it is the Land of Israel with the territories?

Witness: I've already said that for me this represents an inexact likeness of historical Palestine, that is what I see TODAY [points]. I cannot really say with much certainty that this is that or that—

Prosecution: I am not arguing ideologically here; wouldn't it be clear to practically anyone that this is the Land of Israel with the territories?

Witness: I am not a geographical expert, I can speak of historical knowledge, in terms of what I see.

Judge: So let's talk about the present then.

Witness: In terms of what?

Judge: The prosecutor is not asking for political positions but geographical questions. The question was simple. Do you see this piece of wood as a likeness of the territories that would include the State of Israel and the territories under military control?

Witness: Yes, roughly.

Prosecution: Is it not true that one or even the central idea of the PLO is to return to the whole Land of Israel?

Defense: I have to object. We are talking about these exhibits here and whether or not they have any connection to the PLO [discussion on procedure follows].

Witness: There are a number of trends within the PLO that differ from each other. The PLO itself as a political infrastructure does not support this policy, there is a faction or trend within that does. In general, though, you would have to say that as a policy the PLO does not. The PLO as a whole accepts the 1947 partition principle. Arafat signed a document with McCloskey in Lebanon accepting *all* UN resolutions, starting with the '47 partition. In 1974, the PNC [Palestine National Council] accepted the two-state partition concept. This exhibit, for instance, would under no circumstances either represent or express the full range of the PLO spectrum, nor does this particular piece really demonstrate allegience to any particular movement or ideology.

Defense: I would object again here; there is actually no proof that this piece was created by a prisoner [reads label]. In fact, from this, it is obvious that it comes from some kind of student organization, from the Faculty of the Humanities, 1981.

Prosecution: But it was done for "Prisoner's Day."

Judge: Let's be clear here—how do you know that?

Prosecution: Alright, are you familiar with the Palestinian National Charter? [defense objects on the grounds of irrelevancy and asks which charter is referred to].

Prosecution: The one that expresses the idea of the return of the Palestinians to Palestine.

Defense: Look, I reject all inaccuracies; please, if you want to talk about it, please produce this document. I refuse to be party to a discussion in which we are not speaking of a specific document that we have before us, we cannot rely here on paraphrases or inaccurate quotations.

Judge: But he's a historian, if there is inexactitude, he should be able to correct it.

[A decision is made to search the chambers for a legal volume in which the Palestinian National Charter was quoted in a previous court case.]

Judge: Look, we're dealing with a few levels here; first of all the exhibit, and the defendant's relation to that exhibit.

Prosecution: Yes, but we are also talking about intent and the charge is whether or not the defendant, by his action, expressed identification with an illegal organization.

[Prosecutor reads Hebrew version of Article 19 of the Palestine National Charter.]

Defense: Look, if the argument is about the charter, then I can bring in as many experts as you like to discuss the subject, like Prof. Harkabi for instance, who would explain precisely the changes that have taken place since 1974.

Prosecution: That could prove quite interesting; the question, however, is whether or not—given the full context—the artist might have thought of the charter.

Judge: You'll have to state that some other way.

Prosecution: Alright, not the charter but the return of the Palestinians to Palestine.

[A long discussion follows about testing the expertise of the witness through questions about the charter.]

Judge: You will now be read the Hebrew version again and it will be translated, this is Article 19 as cited by an Israeli court.

Prosecution: [Reads] Now, earlier you said that the charter agreed to partition; obviously there is a discrepancy, which is right?

Witness: The Palestinian National Charter was written in 1964. The version of that charter related to the ideas of the people at that stage. Since the charter is not a sacred text but a political document, there have been *many* changes in it throughout the different periods of evolution. At the same time, even from the time it was written, it is not a document that is binding upon the Palestinian people. The officials dealing with the technical aspects did not see fit to keep correcting the charter during each period. Such a cumulative document would have to check every period and put in all the corrections, something that has not yet been done. New resolutions, rather, superceded the old basis. But, to repeat, the 1974 resolution clearly accepts partition.

Judge: What I would like to know now is if the last word of the PLO is to agree to concede to just the territories under occupation putting, for the moment, the question of Jerusalem aside?

Witness: Yes.

Judge: I just want to repeat this to you to make sure I've gotten it right [reads transcript].

Witness: I did not use the word "concession"; I said recognition of partition. When the PLO recognized all the UN resolutions, including 242, as a package deal, they were, in other words, also explicitly recognizing the partition of 1947, which means two states in Palestine.

Prosecution: Does that mean the borders of June 1967, or 1947?

Witness: I don't know.

Prosecution: So what you are saying is that the charter has been changed from the version read here?

Witness: Yes, '68 is not '88. The PLO of 1964 is not the PLO of 1988.

Prosecution: Maybe the PLO of 1988 has issued a new charter expressing these ideas?

Defense: Objection!

Judge: So you are saying that the decision of 1974 means a change in the charter?

Witness: Yes, naturally.

Judge: What the prosecution wants to know is whether there is a new document or an implied change; is there an updated version of the charter?

Witness: No.

Prosecution: So how exactly do you expect to convince us?

Judge: This seems to be going too far.

Prosecution: No, I mean then maybe the law isn't the law and we should just free the defendant [Faisal Husseini nods and everyone laughs].

Defense: Look, one can bring in Harkabi to check on all of these things.

Judge: I think that the witness's opinions on the charter have been quite thoroughly covered. I would call a recess here.

[Due to a failure in the judge's computer, the hearing was not continued and a postponement date was set for May 5, at 11:00 A.M.]

1988

"Ay, de mi aljama": Palestinians and Israelis Meet, in Spain!

I was asked to speak about a research project I was involved in a few years ago on the political attitudes of Jews from Arab countries. That study served to combat the racist stereotyping of *mizrahim* then prevalent in the Israeli media. It also hoped to provide a basis on which prominent *mizrahim* could strengthen their political positions to offer more daring initiatives toward reconciliation with Palestinians. Unfortunately, many were unwilling to take the risks needed even though it was clear, to anyone willing to listen, that such initiatives would have met with overwhelming popular support. At the same time, the great exclusionary machine of the Ashkenazi left went into high gear, ensuring that *mizrahim* would remain the subjects of studies and not the initiators of bold political actions. Once such dangers were quelled—after the public meetings between Israelis and the PLO in Rumania and Budapest—Israeli policymakers and technocrats themselves went into high gear, in a very different direction. This direction is what I would call the lowering of expectations among the majority of their own population, namely working-class *mizrahim*, something that could be seen as the Israeli power structure's own safety net against the day when a political resolution between Israel and the Palestinians would become inevitable. All of this came against a background of intense political activity among Palestinians, Rabin's Iron Fist policy, and large-scale public crises and scandals such as the abduction of Mordechai Vannunu, the Nafsu case, land scams, and bank frauds. But then December 9 came and fifteen-year-old Hatem al-Sissi became the first martyr of the Intifada, the number of which increases even as we speak. Here, once again, the Israeli powers that be found the ideal glue to hold a disintegrating social body together. Now, they could claim, the very fabric of the state was being threatened, not by distant armies but by those Palestinians who were supposed to have reaped such benefits from the enlightened rule of the region's only "democracy."

Two major elements were left out of my research: first is the institutionalization of the *mizrahim*—as a class—into the economy and social structure of the occupation after 1967. While the Ashkenazi left sees 1967 as the beginning of the end of their dream, we must not forget it was only after 1967 that the *mizrahim* managed to climb at least one notch up the social and economic ladder. Given the present rhetoric, peace as it is now envisioned cannot be perceived by a majority of *mizrahim* as being in their best interests: the massive cuts in health, welfare, and the privatization of the educational system seem like preliminary exercises for the day after a Palestinian state, when the *mizrahim* can take a twenty-one-year step backward and pick up the mop handles again. The lowering of expectations has become an almost complete erosion of expectations to the point where now a curfew in Gaza is celebrated in development towns because it means there is a little more work to go around. And the next generation is surely being fitted into the mold of factory work and manual labor. The ignorance in America as to the status of *mizrahi* Jews in Israel will only make it that much easier for foreign capital to dig its tentacles even deeper into the already unviable Israeli economy. Despite the utter brutality confronted daily by Palestinians, their lot at times almost seems enviable: Even though Palestinian trade unionists are banished and tortured, they at least express the will of their people; even though Palestinian universities are shut, students beaten and shot at, at least they know those are *their* universities. For a trade union, the *mizrahim* have the Histadrut, which is like someone condemned to die by hanging going to the executioner to buy the rope; as far as education goes, a *mizrahi*, with luck and many sacrifices, might actually get into an Israeli university, those finishing schools for the Ashkenazim, and make a valiant attempt to assimilate into the mainstream and forget where they came from.

There can be little doubt that the flames of the *Intifada* are fueled by the enormous amount of internalized rage borne of the injustice and frustration felt by the Israeli working class. And the powers that be may be afraid of a political solution precisely because it could mean the potential beginning of a *mizrahi Intifada* within Israel. After close to a hundred years (coinciding with the founding of the Zionist movement in Europe) in which *mizrahi* Jews have been locked out of the power structure, an agenda might be set that would demand both economic and social equality as well as a truer cultural recuperation, internally and throughout the region. Here, the Ashkenazi left—and even the more militant antioccupation groups that have sprung up since the *Intifada* began—play right into the hands of the ruling class, primarily because they themselves form part of it. It often seems as if the Israeli left's primary motive for—and notice the rhetoric—"solving" the Palestinian "problem" is so that they could have as little as possible to do with Arabs in the future and return to their garrisoned, pure, and beautiful little Israel, with its utter contempt for the peoples and cultures of the region. And their protests—because they ignore questions of social justice and cultural equality within Israel—only further entrenches and alienates the *mizrahi* majority.

Which brings me to the second element left out of my research: it is unquestionable that only a small minority of *mizrahi* Jews are ideologically Zionist in any way that is more than skin deep. What this means, concretely, is that there are often much greater and far-reaching points of access (on a political, cultural, and social level) that can be reached by a Palestinian in a supposedly "right" wing *mizrahi* than in a supposedly "left" wing Ashkenazi, whose basic outlook is still greatly indebted to certain Zionist assumptions. And this phenomenon should not be taken too lightly. No matter what anyone says about the past, it is simply a fact that Jews lived throughout the Mediterreanean and Arab world right up until the twentieth century and, as Yehuda Abrabanel put it in his great commentary, they were primarily "not the builders, but the inhabitants of great cities." Now the Arab and Mediterranean Jews are crowded into a tiny, claustrophobic space that knows no windows to its native terrain, and they are miserable because of it. Their nativity is like a time bomb, poised to shatter and make obsolete the hegemonic but ultimately more tenuous structures and forms that have served as models until now.

But the *mizrahim* are a long way off from the present revolutionary spirit that twenty-one years of occupation, forty-one years of exile, pan-

Arabism, betrayal at the hands of reactionary Arab regimes, and a hundred or so odd years of Zionism has prepared the Palestinians for: despite many truly heroic cultural and political workers (of whom some are here with us), and the development of new alternative institutions, there is apathy and despair. The erosion of expectations means that very little can be offered the *mizrahim* to pacify immediate needs. Yet, the rage smolders within, and it is this, more than anything, that the authorities manipulate as their last hand in a game that is looking more and more like Russian roulette every day. Absurd as it may seem, one would almost like to see the Unified Command in the territories address the Israeli working class directly, not with directives but with very difficult questions. Given the circumstances this may be too much to ask, but it would be a gesture of enormous magnanimity and one that, it seems, could have real repercussions.

Besides its more obvious expression of Palestinian nationalism, the *Intifada* can be seen as the collective explosion of all the suppressed progressive movements of the Middle East in this traumatic century. And the popular support, as well as the fear expressed by reactionary regimes throughout the region only proves this. Yet, it seems not only unfortunate but tragic that the example of Israel's own fervent nationalism has been taken up as the be-all and end-all of Palestinian aspirations. My personal hope is that we will one day reach a point in the Middle East where no one will be proud to be a nationalist of any kind, where the glorious impurities of the Levant will prevail, where we will all, in the words of Mahmoud Darwish, "guard the plot of the book against the prophets." And I wonder about such a world and what it would be like if, because of the Cuba/Palestine trade pact, there was a glut of Havana cigars on Salah el-Dinn Street; if the Central Bus Station in Tel Aviv was crowded with Moroccan and Algerian tourists who heard that rare cassettes of old singers like Reinette, Zohra al-Fasiya, and Raoul Journo could now only be found among the Jews; if people from Isfahan were seen cautiously asking directions to the *felude* stand in the HaTikva Quarter and, once enjoying the cold sweet drink, found themselves at a loss as to why the nice young Jewish owner only remembered a few words of Farsi; if Fairuz appeared at the Sultan's Pool to finally sing about the city of peace, since there isn't much left of Baalbek; if, because of the Yemen/Palestine alliance, Rabbi Kafih led pilgrimage tours to holy sites like the grave of the great poet and mystic Shalom Shabazi; if Jews again became native Arabic speakers and writers; if people could live wherever they wanted—refugees from Jabalya and Dehaishe could build new villages and everyone could lend a hand in taking sledge-hammers to the camps and the housing projects; if Israelis moved to Cairo, Algiers, or Damascus to be closer to their Palestinian partners and handle Middle East Common Market tasks more efficiently. . . . Communication, good relations, new places to go and see, new people and cultures to get to know, hopes for a better world. I guess I must be completely nuts.

1989

Israel/Palestine 101: A Letter to Robert Creeley

Invitations to Jerusalem, particularly international festivals or gatherings of one kind or another, can serve multiple purposes, depending primarily on the kinds of information one arrives with or, more accurately, what kinds of things one is alerted to pay attention to. For a certain kind of Israeli elite, these festivals promote the perpetuation of a particular take on reality while globalizing it through subtle recruitment of other information recorders and bearers' (such as writers and artists), who leave with very distinct impressions. This, naturally, makes it more and more difficult to find the right leverage to create a wedge into which alternative realities might fit. To this end, I felt very strongly—having been back in the United States for little over a year—about presenting alternatives to friends invited to such gatherings. I found, and continue to find, true distinctions between people prepared to grasp and absorb new information as simply another aspect of their kinds of knowledge about the world and those finding it a burden. At a time when, with some "networking" and "modification" of my positions, I might have been able to turn to a kind of writing that would "reach" a wider "public" in the form of articles for larger-circulation magazines, I thought my efforts were better spent on reaching people for whom I knew the information would not become an expendable commodity, tossed—in the best case scenario—into the recycling bin at the end of the week. Here is one such effort, in the form of a letter to Robert Creeley, not exactly a beginner in any sense of the word, and someone whose subtlety of thought and keen intellect made the task a pleasure, since I knew I could present things in a kind of shorthand that would be caught by analogy on the other end:

29 January 1990

Dear Bob,

Alright, here's my missionary quotient, propaganda bit, information binge package: I had planned something more ambitious and organized/coherent but this is as far as I got. . . . And since you really asked for what could be useful, I've put some thought into the kinds of discourse you're likely to encounter & how you might identify it rather than present you with the comprehensive solution to the ME conflict & human rights in the West Bank & Gaza Strip, etc., etc. I've also gathered up some stuff, more of a paradigmatic nature than anything else since much has been superceded & there is also certainly no dearth of further cases (i.e. quantity) involved, but simply to illustrate how some of the information (or lack thereof) fits (or doesn't) into many of the kinds of discourse you're most likely to encounter.

To backtrack somewhat: modern Jewish dogma has accepted persecution as the canonical form of religious identification and belonging—to question this is anathema. Zionism & the Israeli structure of things was created / creates itself in the face (reverse) of this image: Offense as a means of defense. The Israeli army is called the IDF (Israeli Defense Forces). Without going into the whole hullabaloo of who did what when, it is a remarkable fact that over 400 Palestinian villages were literally wiped off the face of the map in 1948/9, yet this has rarely—if ever—been used as a primary propaganda point on the Palestinian side. More interesting is the fact that Israelis always claim to fear that Palestinians want to return to Jaffa and Lod and Ramla, etc., places they only left forty-two years ago (i.e., in this lifetime), also saying that such wishes are totally unrealistic, while at the same time themselves laying claim to lands and places "they" claim to have lived in over 2,000 years ago!

That is how some of the internal wires are set: the bells ring and the lights light up at the mention of: in other words, I always find it (and during the uprising even more powerfully so) absolutely astounding how much self-control Palestinians exert in meetings, debates, etc., when they are presented with an Israeli who speaks like a victim. This victimization is like gender, an entirely acquired social construct. The usual scenario is that the Palestinian (whose parents might have had a house on the land that the anguished Israeli's kibbutz now happens to be on), will not even mention that fact. You can see some of the communication problems that might develop. What appears self-evident in the eyes of a Palestinian as simply a gesture of acknowledgment, of reciprocity, is already *in the subconscious* as well as conscious social makeup of the Israeli an admission of guilt and, in fact, a complete reversal of the whole value system hierarchy that he/she has been brought up to accept & believe in.

To skip some stages: on a collective level, Israelis have only begun to approach even the possibility of addressing the fact of their active involvement in the destruction of Palestine; naturally, the right wing, as is usual in such cases, has a much easier time dealing with this: in fact, they know precisely what they did and are not afraid to admit it. But here is where things get tricky: Israel's whole culture, both internally & what gets dispatched out has been built on Labor Zionist liberal mythology. This mythology pitted the perfect blend of stereotypes to achieve their goals: the once weak but now strong & heroic Jews defend themselves against the barbaric masses of fanatical Arabs who, in any case, were too stupid to realize that the coming of the Jews was a blessing since the Jews would bring them houses and water and a higher standard of living etc. Suffice it to say that the "Jaffa" orange had been a Palestinian staple for quite some years before the coming of the Jews. . . . The persistence of this ethos can be seen in the whole development of Peace Now, which began as a select group of officers addressing "their" minister of defence & prime minister. The amount of time it has taken them to move toward the possibility of expressing solidarity with Palestinians is remarkable in terms of any other kind of protest movement I am familiar with. Their elitist & exclusionary tactics I won't even go into (of course I will: we were invited to Hebron once—a group of "Oriental" peace activists—and one of our members prepared to address the gathering in Arabic. A riot almost ensued as the Peace Now organizers of the gathering expressly forbid any Jews from addressing the crowd in Arabic. . . . Nor is this an isolated incident—the history of the conflict, from the 1870s to the present—and I've documented it quite well—has always had its quotient of tourist versus native).

I'm losing the thread. The point is this, to get us into the present. The first real challenge to Labor hegemony, both in its ideology & practice, came about with Menahem Begin's victory in 1977. Despite everything, Begin was quite a figure (it was he who vehemently opposed the awarding of German reparation money to victims of the Holocaust in Israel, something Ben Gurion championed and the essential element in soldifying and finally freezing the Israeli class structure into place; Begin was also for the abolition of the British Mandate Emergency rules used so often now because he said a point would come when they could be used against anybody, such as in the Warschawski case I've included material on). Not to mention (and this is also well documented) that human rights abuses under the Likud government have generally been lower than under Labor (this is expressed in the numbers of deportations, houses blown up, demolished, or sealed, censorship, the extent and particular types of tortures used, etc.). Now, I'm beginning to get to my point about one of the prevalent kinds of discourse you're going to hear. For liberal Israelis, everything was fine before 1967; "we" lived in our beautiful little country with all its attendant problems but life was simpler and better, people were more honest, there was greater equity, etc., etc. These people are generally Ashkenazi and form part of the elite in one way or another; i.e., there are very few garbage men or textile workers among them. For these other people, the so-called second Israel (Jews from Arab countries, the Levant, Iran, & other such places beyond the pale), 1967 and the occupation represents something completely different: it represents, first and foremost, some possibility of economic escalation due to the expanded economy & the new lines of business opening up in the territories, particularly in the construction field. Next, it represents some return to the Arab world from which they were so abruptly and hermetically excised. Ironically, for the Ashkenazi / Western oriented elites, 1967 really does present a crisis since it becomes clear just how marginal they are in the complex of this world they inhabit & just how tenuous a hold on power they have. Thus, the need to become a superpower, nuclear development, etc. (Please note the material on Mordechai Vannunu here, mention of whom will bring paroxysms of horror from the most liberal figures: also ask Allen [Ginsberg] about his reading at the Jerusalem Cinemateque, a bastion, actually a shrine of liberal secularism, in which Steve Taylor sang a song by Tuli Kupferberg about Vanunu and got a standing ovation from three of us in the packed auditorium—catcalls and hisses followed and I thought we would, literally, get lynched after what had been an audience enthralled with Allen the whole evening, awaiting every syllable and move.) Am I moving too fast???

At any rate, besides all the racism engendered by such divisions, keep in mind that "Peace" for the Israeli liberal means getting rid of the Palestinian "problem"—in precisely those terms; it means "us" living nicely in our highly defended & secure state and them doing whatever the hell they want with themselves in their own state. This kind of arrangement clearly precludes reality of any kind & it is interesting to note that there is a completely different rhetoric of "arrangement" among even the most right-wing of Arab Jews. Naturally, the liberals feel that the Oriental Jews should be back where they were twenty-five years ago since there will be a dearth of Arab labor, one of the true inconveniences of the two-state solution but an entirely soluble one. All of this gets played out on the literary / cultural plane as well. I could tell you stories of my own experiences of trying to get published or of trying to publish translations of little known people. And this is me, who can certainly, and more so, pass for white. A prominent Israeli poet, for all his professed Palestinophilia, wrote a series of columns toward the beginning of the uprising that were remarkable in the openness and extent of their anti-Oriental Jewish feeling; they even prompted a debate of sorts & exchange of letters. There is nothing unusual in this, it's simply the norm. What is unusual is that there is very seldom anyone there to call these people on these things *to a foreign audience* (I did what I could when I was there, which was something), so they continue to get away with murder. It is unimaginable to me to think of figures of similar stature in the States making remarks about Jews or Latinos or Blacks or Asians or Gays or any single block of people (except maybe Arabs!) and not being drummed out of the business or made a laughingstock.

Is this what I really wanted to tell you? I'm not sure. . . . On the practical level: there are the university closings, the question of academic freedom and censorship, issues which a group of writers are certainly qualified to comment on. Beware (as I'm sure you will be) of the blanket statements: two people living side by side, etc., la de da. The system is oppressive to everyone & will silence whomever, Palestinian or Jew, it chooses to. This has become more than evident in the trials of Jewish activists, as well as the imprisonment of a number of Jewish journalists. I've included material on a case close to me (since I used to work at the Alternative Information Center); this is an important one & the harshness of the sentencing only shows how scared the authorities are of the populace getting out of control & thinking; in this, I find it encouraging.

Another odd issue: the Russian Jews are Israel's last great white hope & are being encouraged to come specifically to maintain the present ethnic/class structure of the country. This issue will be completely buried except on the most local level. The statistic to add to this equation (and the misplaced rage found amongst eighteen-year-old working-class Israelis sent to beat up kids and old ladies in the territories), is that there are now more Israeli Palestinian citizens of Israel attending and finishing Israeli universities than Oriental Jewish Israelis, who constitute over 60 percent of the population, maybe even more so in that age bracket. So, when a working-class Israeli getting several hundred dollars a *Month* working in a sweatshop in the middle of the desert with four or five kids at home hears how nice it would be to go back to the good old days so he/she can pick up a mop/broom again. . . . In other words, in the so-called peace camp, you will hardly ever hear of global solutions (i.e., peace = social justice), only anguish, misplaced guilt, fear, exhaustion, etc. Not hearing any such rhetoric from any quarter remotely connected to "peace," this not unenlightened & hardworking citizen will naturally put two & two together and vote, if not *for* something, at least against *that*: thus, Israel's famous and ominous "turn to the right" among the "popular classes."

Keep in mind that the torture sequences in my *cairo notebooks* were mostly taken from testimony of prisoners held at a place called the Russian Compound or in local parlance, the Moscobiyya. This is the local torture chamber, not on tourist maps as such, but well worth a visit (i.e., a walk by if there's a vigil or protest taking place). It's in the heart of town, only a hundred yards or so from the Central Post Office. Also, the Women in Black, Friday afternoon at 1 P.M. in Paris Square (about a ten-minute walk from where you'll be staying at Mishkenot) can be quite impressive. But, more important, it would be significant for people to have a look (not in a "deeper" way which is impossible given the timing of such things), but in an *active* way that could level the stigmas of addressing these issues in a pragmatic fashion. This is why I think the academic freedom / university closure issue is important because it could provide something for people to take a bite into and digest back home, wherever that may be. And, naturally, once the universities are reopened & there are exchange programs with Palestine, there will be some acquaintances in place. . . .

I obviously feel frustrated & wish we were still living there so all this could be peripatetic. For what it's worth, this is my grab bag & I do hope you'll find it of use—also, please feel free to spread/share the material if you think it can be of use. Some of the particular cases I included (the one-page kind of appeals, like the case of Dr. Riad Malki), have been resolved and are way out of date. It's just to give you an idea of how these things look since they won't be on the newsstands. Also the institutional information would still be valid and I'll go on to list a number of places & people whom you could get in touch with should such a need arise. I've included some odds & ends from *News From Within* simply because I used to work there & feel rather proud of it as a truly lively alternative source. The nuclear piece is in the old style, before the office equipment was confiscated for the trial; other articles are in the latter, more haphazard modes we had to use. Other things really are odds & ends that for one reason or another I put in; the Arab Studies Society material would relate to issues of academic freedom, etc. Also, the little piece by Gabriel Bensimhon (which I hope I'll have typed) is one of the talks given at a meeting I went to last summer in Toledo, Spain, where about forty Israelis (all of "Oriental" extraction) convened with very senior PLO people, including Mahmoud Darwish.

As far as people & places go. Should nothing be set up, you or someone else might want to try & get in touch with Dr. Hannan Mikhail Ashrawi who is a poet as well as the Dean of Humanities at Bir Zeit University. She might be miffed at the late notice, but beyond that I'm sure she would be open to meeting or at least explaining the university situation to people. The El Hakawati theater (like the Arab Studies Society) is an open & shut case; i.e., they might be open, or they might be shut. Both would be worthy places to look into. The head of the Arab Studies

Society, Faisal Husseini, may or may not be in prison. People there (at the society), who could also be contacted would be Mahmoud Hawari or Ghada al-Shammali. Great people who could also facilitate any contacts that need to be made (though their days are filled with cataloging broken bones & spontaneously aborted fetuses through tear gas inhalation, etc.) are Samir & Jan Abu Shakrah at the Palestine Human Rights Commission. Also Tikva Parnas at the Alternative Information Center. I've put phone numbers and addresses at the end of this letter. Again, some of these instances might be more along the lines of arranging a solidarity visit or something of that sort. Things don't always move quickly because there are so many foreign groups coming in but should the magnitude of the thing be made known (along, hopefully, with the will), then the idea of arranging something like a meeting of writers or academics in solidarity with the closing of institutions or something like that might prove to be an interesting or possible activity. Let me hear how it went . . .

1990 / 1999

Quality Control

Living in Jerusalem in the 1980s I became very involved in the kinds of public discourse and debate that have almost ceased to exist in America. Much of it not taking place on the streets or through political activity came through in the Hebrew press and literary and cultural magazines or supplements. At the same time, those segments of the Israeli press aimed at external audiences and appearing in English, represented a very timid and pale reflection of the kinds of controversies actually taking place, whether culturally or politically. I expended much effort in trying to expand the parameters available in places like *The Jerusalem Post* or the magazine *Modern Hebrew Literature*, with varying degrees of success. While I was able to publish book reviews in *the Post* consistently, I didn't fare as well in publishing translations of writers eventually included in *Keys to the Garden*, or in opening up the pages of *the Post* to the kinds of lively and heated exchanges that characterized the Hebrew press.

The first exchange of letters below concerns an invitation I got to guest edit a section of poetry in *Modern Hebrew Literature*:

> As you probably know, the poetry editor of our publication *Modern Hebrew Literature* is now in Boston for a year. He suggested that

perhaps you would be willing to act as guest poetry editor for the next issue (Spring 1990).

This would mean selecting and translating the poetry and introducing the poets. I understand that he discussed with you publishing your translations of Shlomo Avayou and Erez Bitton's poetry and had intended to feature those poets in the next issue. To this end we received from you translations of the poems "Wild Weed" and "Odalisque of the Levant" by Shlomo Avayou. . . . Finally, I would like to bring to your attention that the magazine is now being edited by Prof. Gershon Shaked.

In a query on some details regarding space, payment, and copyright, I also sent a list of poets I thought of including, to which I got the following reply:

> With regard to the choice of poets, we are committed to Shlomo Avayou, but not to Erez Bitton. I have consulted with the editor of MHL, Prof. Gershon Shaked. He is keen on the idea of giving space to Shelley Elkayam, but feels that the poetry of Sami Shalom Chetrit and Tikva Levi is less important. However, the choice is up to you. I would like to suggest that to do justice to each poet, it is probably necessary to choose a selection of three or four poems.That is the situation. I hope you will still be willing to take over the preparation of the issue. . . . Awaiting your reply.

After sending my selection, I got this letter:

> Thank you for the poems. Prof. Gershon Shaked, editor of MHL, has gone over the selection and has grave reservations re the standard of poetry of Tikva Levi and Samir Chetrit. There also seems to be the problem of squeezing too many poets into too small a space, meaning none of them are explored in any depth. We would prefer to return to the original plan of Erez Bitton and Shlomo Arayon, with Shelley Elkayam.

To which I responded:

> I must say that I was quite dismayed (though not completely surprised) by your letter stating Prof. Shaked's objections regarding

the poetry of Sami Chetrit and Tikva Levi. I was, however, surprised by the idea of sticking to the "original" plan. I had assumed,
perhaps naively or mistakenly, that being a guest editor also
entailed a minimum of authority: i.e., that I could more or less
choose works that I wanted to. I had said that I only had one poem
of Erez Bitton's available (one that, at any rate, has been published
often—in addition, I believe you also published one of his poems
in the last issue); you had *already* requested the Avayou poems
(which you are certainly welcome to use)—that doesn't leave me
with much of a plan! I had thought that it would be important to
publish some younger, lesser known poets whose work emerges
from a social and political context quite unknown to most readers
of contemporary Hebrew literature in English translation. I suspect that what is in question here is not quality (particularly since
Sami Chetrit is a literary prize winner and Tikva Levi's work has
been accepted by Hebrew literary magazines; rather, it seems that
some kind of nerve has been hit and I now feel that I must stand
on principle. In other words, feel free to use the poems you
requested (of Shlomo Avayou), but I cannot, in all clear conscience, be a participant to what seems to me a not so subtle form
of censorship. That is, if you are unwilling to publish my selection
as it stands (give or take some particular poems), I would really
rather withdraw from the project since I am quite insistent and
adverse to such forms of coercion that refer to poetic "standards"
regarding work that is obviously powerful and of merit. At any
rate, the role of guest editor needs to be better defined in future if
you expect to find cooperative participants.

This was followed by an apology:

We too are sorry about the turn of events. While the editor who
holds ultimate, overall responsibility for the contents of the magazine respects your choice, he does not feel that these two poets
match up to the level of the publication. The objections do not
relate to the contents of the poems; first and foremost the criterion
of quality must be met, and that is the sole source of disagreement
in this case. We will be very sorry if you decide not to continue
with the project, but would still very much like to publish your
translations of Avayou and Elkayam. . . . Again, I am sorry that

things have worked out like this and certainly hope that it won't get in the way of future cooperation.

The correspondence, and the project, ended with this:

> I regret having received the answer I more or less expected regarding the work of Sami Chetrit and Tikva Levi. I am sorry to say, but I do not want to continue with the project as is; I feel that the issue of "quality" is an issue of taste and, I daresay, in this case a rather arbitrary and coercive one at that. As far as future cooperation goes, I don't see how anyone will want to cooperate given the lack of definition: as I said earlier, insofar as my experience goes, a guest editor does have final say on selections. I do hope, however, to write about this experience (as well as numerous others) to illustrate the murkier caverns of certain more genteel forms of suppression. I also would *not* like the Shelley Elkayam poems to appear in this disputed context; you, however, have my blessings on the Avayou poems since those were what you requested in the first place . . . My best wishes to you and Prof. Shaked.

At the time, I simply filed this as another episode in the continuing saga of attempting to publish Israeli poets whose last names do not happen to end in "man," "stein," "baum," or some newly minted Hebrew consonant, but rather *begin* in "Al" or "El" or some other barbaric, Arabic-sounding syllable. Of the poets they had requested for the issue, Erez Bitton was one of, if not *the,* first Israeli poet of Arab Jewish origin to explicitly address this thematic in his work. After being shunned, ignored, and even ridiculed, he came to be both popular and quite respected in the literary community. At the same time, whenever the literary establishment is in need of a token "Oriental" poet to display some of Israel's exotic flavoring, it is Bitton who is most likely to be turned to. While this certainly is not his fault, I had thought it might be more interesting to present some younger poets whose work also came out of the *mizrahi* Israeli context. To this end I queried the *Review* only to be reassured that: "the choice is up to you."

Most interestingly, though, both Sami Shalom Chetrit and Shlomo Avayou's names underwent transformation during the correspondence. At one point, Avayou became Arayon. In the social/semantic codes at work here, this means he was "Israelified." Even more astonishingly,

Sami became Samir, that is, an Arab. Regardless of the editorial decision, I found the spelling errors, on reflection, even more telling. Perhaps, given the strength of Chetrit's poetry, and the obvious political and human allegiances it forges, the poet himself had turned into an enemy of the Jews; naturally, in such a context, this would mean an Arab. So his name could go from Sami to Samir completely unnoticed: he was out of the picture, no longer a concern of ours, excommunicated, unedited, out of the mag. Although such an exchange—or even such orthographic innacuracies—might seem completely ordinary or innocent, I was grabbing at straws, well into my *ninth* year of attempting to get some of the *mizrahi* Israeli writers I had become familiar with published. It was only in 1992 that some of these translations began to appear; they continued to appear sporadically until an earlier version of *Keys to the Garden* came out in 1994 as a special issue of *The Literary Review,* followed in 1996 by the expanded version.

This incident, though, brought me back to an earlier, even more pointed exchange with the expatriate British poet Dennis Silk, a longtime resident of Jerusalem and then editor of a page in *The Jerusalem Post* called "Poets Cornered." My letter to the editor of *The Jerusalem Post* magazine explains the circumstances:

As editor of the magazine, I wanted to bring the enclosed correspondence between Dennis Silk and myself to your attention for a number of reasons, none of them (honestly) vindictive. A number of people (along with Dennis himself) suggested I submit some poems and translations for "Poets Cornered," which I subsequently did. As I recall about ten or twelve poems along with two or three translations of work by Shlomo Avayou, an Israeli poet. My complaint is not even, at this point, with Dennis's rejection of my work. This is certainly his prerogative as an editor—the difference of opinions on that score expressed in my letter are purely methodological and have nothing to do with the dictates of taste. Nevertheless, his reference to feeling "envy of my Sephardic background" certainly came out of the blue and seemed quite odd until I received information regarding a scandal over a literary prize that was supposed to have been awarded to young Israeli poets of Sephardi origin. This was a number of years back and involved some very prestigious Israeli writers. This also is not my central concern nor the reason I decided to send you this material. What bothered me most about the exchange of letters is the fact that Dennis rejected out of hand translations that I hadn't even sent him while at the same time not even mentioning the translations that I did send him. For an editor to do this is not only absolutely unprofessional but also extremely insulting. Given such treatment, as a writer and translator, one really begins to wonder what the use of sending things out at all is . . . Beyond the specifics of this particular case which, I would again reiterate, doesn't at all bother me as me but simply rather depresses me regarding any possibilities of some level of literary discourse in English in this city, the point I would like to make is about the *Post* itself. Despite the enormous improvement in things, the literary section remains remarkably erratic. At a time when the literary supplements of the Israeli papers are in stiff competition to publish both original work as well as a wide range of reviews, the *Post* seems to lag behind in a very clubby atmosphere—this exchange with Dennis remaining for me an indication of that. This seems to me a real pity for *The Post* remains a vital source of information about Israel all over the world, particularly in the Arab world. Yet, one would be hard put to get a cohesive sense of anything going on here from the *Post's* literary page, which remains a hodgepodge of excellence and mediocrity. The point I was trying to make to Dennis in my letter (using the analogy of Simon Lichman's reading series, as well as the possibility of publishing our exchange), is that a literary page (as it certainly is in the Hebrew press) should be an open space for controversy, debate, opinion, and information rather than the "preserve bounded by a prickly pear hedge" that Dennis describes. That is exactly what this whole country is and to reproduce that situation in a literary page seems to me truly depressing. This, again, at a time when the Hebrew papers finally seem to be opening up to both the world around them (the recent attention given the translation of Tahar Ben Jelloun, the Moroccan writer who just won the Prix Goncourt, for example) and the world beyond—Latin America, postmodern American writing, etc. Part of the problem still seems to be some sense of being outsiders that English and other non-Hebrew language writers feel in Israel; it is almost as if they have delegitimized their own presence by not allowing themselves to be engaged in any debates or controversies or opinions, by leaving those things to the Israelis. In this sense, at least, I was gratified that a review of mine (on *Arabesques* by Anton Shammas) was able to provoke a rather sharp letter to the *Post* by A. B. Yehoshua. This was, of course, pale in comparison to the debate between Shammas and Yehoshua in *Kol Ha'Ir* and then the follow-ups by Sami Michael and others. It was, however, a sign of life, giving an Israeli writer some sense that American or English language responses to Israeli writing can go beyond the smug and self-congratulatory to touch the very real issues that are now at stake.

The exchange that I sent this editor consisted of my letter to Dennis Silk along with a Xerox of a postcard that he had sent to me in response to the work I submitted. The postcard featured an uncomfortably close, almost fish-eye shot of a cactus now known as the "sabra." The caption on the back of the card read: "Sharp but sweet—the Israeli Sabra," while Dennis's message read: "You're right, Ammiel. 'Poets Cornered' is a preserve, and bound by a prickly pear hedge. It's for anyone—*anyone*—who fights off his fuzz to get there." In a previous letter, he had written: "I'm sympathetic to your viewpoint. I rather envy you your Sephardic heritage and knowledge, and I hope you'll train yourself and ground it in the sensuous and precise." Having a "Sephardic background" to be envious of, I suppose, is kind of like having a natural sense of rhythm. Looking back on it, I think my response in this instance is as precise a statement of my poetics as I've ever been able to articulate:

> Without intending to be ironic, I must say that I read your letter with some puzzlement and, ultimately, disappointment. The disappointment was not at not having my poems accepted (though the retort of a young poet whose "pride" has been wounded is a distinction almost inevitable in such cases and even fulfills the criteria of many mistaken assumptions about the why of writing). The disappointment went further than that, extending to a collectivity or rather a field of diversity that might not yet exist in formalized terms but easily could. Let me explain: Simon Lichman [also a British poet] for example, had the chance to organize a year-long series of readings at the Ticho House. What he did was to simply open the field up, letting as many people who are writing seriously in English into the game (insofar as circumstances allowed). Now you or I or anyone else might have completely different criteria with which we might measure the respective weight of each of these people and for each of us those criteria are perfectly legitimate. I'm not advocating a free-for-all here, but I must say that while you envy me my "Sephardi background" (it was just part of the package and I don't see what on earth it might have to do with mine or anyone else's poetry), I envy you the sureness of

judgment your letter indicated. You may even be right, but that isn't the point. . . . What Simon's series tried to do is formalize—through the convention of a reading series—a contingent field of possibilities in which some kind of discourse might take shape. What I'm saying is that I truly don't give a damn about my poems insofar as they're mine: I do care very much about having their intention/language/form engage, participate, adjust, and/or affect the possible range of discourse of the place in which they were written. I don't think poems have "subjects" or "viewpoints" so much as choices, words, and lives of their own. But they certainly do get written within a certain milieu before going on to form their own alliances or misalliances as well as reiterate, crystallize, condense, or eliminate certain stages of the "arguments" generally occurring in other kinds of discourse besides and including the poetic one. To do this, of course, it helps if they see the light of day. The social consciousness or function of writing has much less to do with any subject or viewpoint or with the writer being engaged than with its practice and the range of questions that a writing context proposes and allows itself to address. Xeroxing is fine (Robert Duncan made a vow to Gestetner for ten years before publishing his last book), but printing (particularly in a weekly or monthly space) is much more efficient. In fact, in most places, any self-respecting editor interested in the continued state of writing would find it fit to open or continue a debate by printing a letter such as this.

There are lots of reasons why I don't think Jerusalem is a real city under its present circumstances, particularly among its English-speaking constituents, but it seems to me that it doesn't really ever stand the chance of becoming one so long as things are "judged" or channeled like this, so long as a page such as you have the privilege of editing remains a preserve and not a meeting place, forum, or source of news (i.e., in the sense that poetry is news that stays, etc.). I simply don't think anyone can afford such a luxury in what remains, for all intents and purposes, a rather provincial and limited space and where there are no similar outlets. And believe me, none of this has anything to do with my poems or your reflections on them. It just seems to me too bad for there to be yet another limited access road adorning an already quite restricted landscape.

P.S. I must say that I'm even more puzzled by your reference to Shelley Elkayam: she certainly doesn't write in English but in Hebrew. . . . I can accept judgments but prejudgments are a little harder to take, particularly due to the fact that you never even received my translations! What's more, you didn't even so much as mention the translations that I *did* send you: Elkayam, Avayou, Alcalay, I guess all these names sound pretty much the same anyhow. . . .

1987 / 1990 / 1999

Ushering in the New Order

My first encounter with the recently imprisoned Palestinian scholar and activist Sari Nusseibeh was as a student in his medieval philosophy class at Hebrew University over ten years ago. As his mind scanned the astounding logic of Ibn Rushd, Ibn Sina, and Musa Ibn Maimun (known to Westerners as Averroes, Avicenna, and Maimonides), we would stare in amazement as he continuously rolled and flipped a lit cigarette back and forth between the fingers of his left hand. That kind of tightly reined-in daring precisely characterized the way Sari thought and acted. Even then, his will to work within the political and institutional borders of Israel met resistance from many quarters. When I returned to Jerusalem some years later, we saw each other quite often, whether at lectures, meetings, vigils, demonstrations, or trials. Although the news of his arrest was not surprising, it is certainly ominous, given the fact that he was so well protected. This safety net consisted of many strands: the class privileges that went with being born into one of Jerusalem's oldest and most prominent families; his education at Oxford and Harvard; his high visibility among foreign journalists, diplomats, and statespeople; and, perhaps even more significant, his participation in the Israeli debate itself. These are all things he was often resented for—not without some justification—from the grassroots base of the *Intifada:* the people on the streets, in the villages, the refugee camps, and the prisons. It is the very issues such antagonism raises that lie at the heart of a deeper understanding of the conflicts in the Middle East and the accepted discourses about them that prevail in the West.

On January 28, a day before Nusseibeh's arrest, a prominent group of Israeli intellectuals usually associated with the Peace Now movement called a press conference to send an open statement to the antiwar movement around the world. The group included Amos Oz, A. B. Yehoshua, Yael Dayan, Yoram Kaniuk, Amos Elon, and Yehuda Amichai. The thrust of their message was summed up by Yael Dayan (who only last year toured the United States with Faisal Husseini), when she said: "Peace now in Israel really means war now."[1] Such a group, themselves part of a privileged elite in Israel, has never been able to fathom the perception that other countries of the region might have about America's role, and by extension that of its closest ally Israel, as an imperial power. Naturally, the role of an imperial power is to control resources as well as the existing hierarchies of power that make those resources "accessible." Of course, the role of a native ruler or a regional power, no matter how benign or despicable, is certainly *not* to act autonomously: policies or solutions to problems can only be imposed from without. Thus, attempts by an Arab coalition to deal with Iraq's invasion of Kuwait, at a time when the Iraqis were actually pulling their troops back, not only had to be dismissed out of hand but sabotaged. As Bush prepared the world for the "inevitability" of war, it is remarkable to what extent Saddam's various proposals (no matter how tainted by self-interest they might have been and, indeed, what politician's words and deeds are not), for a comprehensive settlement of regional problems were both villified and ridiculed.

As far as the Israeli peace movement is concerned, particularly Peace Now, the total inability to step outside the role of victim and examine political realities and possibilities is also the result of a certain racism that has characterized mainstream Israeli views about the Arab world. The peace envisioned was always one of retreat, never of involvement: Israel should simply pull back to the 1967 borders and distance itself as far as possible from any contact with the world surrounding it. Thus the heavy investment in alliances with non-Arab countries, such as Turkey and Iran, or American clients such as Morocco. Only one of the many pitfalls of such an approach, however, is the fact that most of

Israel's population are themselves native Middle Easterners: over 50 percent of the Jewish population comes from the Arab world, along with the approximately 20 percent Palestinian Israeli population. The vast difference in attitude between those with roots in the Arab world and the predominantly Eastern European or Sabra elites, can be seen in a remarkable interview recently given in the Hebrew daily *Hadashot*.[2] Three Iraqi-born Israeli Jewish members of Knesset, former minister of energy Moshe Shahal, Binyamin (Fuad) Ben Eliezer (an ex-general), and Ran Cohen, were asked their opinions on Saddam, Iraq, and the current crisis. Their views reflect only the most recent instance of a way of thinking so suppressed it can only seem shocking to an American audience weaned on the usual drivel about "the Arabs" emerging from the "peace" camp.

Throughout the interview, Shahal, Eliezer, and Cohen spoke of Western arrogance as a prime component in the current crisis. As Cohen put it: "I speak not out of admiration for Saddam, but out of disparagement for the frivolity and arrogance of those who sincerely and naively believed that an Iraqi would be unable to aim a missile accurately and hit a target simply because he's an Arab degenerate. The media portrayed the Iraqis as if they were still in the stone age. It is precisely because of this picture that the arrogant West had of the Iraqis that they now find themselves where they are today: the war has turned into a series of surprises. What wasn't said in Israel and the United States at the beginning of the war! We would wipe them out in less than twenty-four hours! Maybe the Iraqi people are degenerate Arabs but those who relentlessly bombed camouflaged decoys for three days without even noticing it were actually the Americans." Seemingly exasperated by this line of reasoning, the interviewer stopped to say, "But after all, Saddam is a madman." Responses to this were unequivocal; as Fuad commented: "Again, Western disinformation. Saddam is not a madman, nor he is out of touch with reality. Those who were really out of touch were the Americans. Saddam prepared very well for this war and took into account his limitations." Moshe Shahal added: "A madman would lose all his planes by going right into direct battle, face to face. This is just further proof that we're talking of a cunning and strategic leader leading a wise people."

They went on to discuss their efforts during the Iran / Iraq war to open a debate in the Knesset on ceasing Israeli support for Iran in exchange for recognition by Iraq of the Camp David accords. As Shahal said, "I almost made it to Baghdad." Their clandestine meetings in Europe with high-ranking Iraqi officials were laughed off as ploys at self-importance for what was then called the "Iraqi lobby" in the Knesset. Well aware of Iraq's emergence as a regional superpower, Shahal ironically recounted how a sneeze in the Soviet Union would engage serious debate among dozens of Sovietologists, "but when things happen in Iraq, nobody listens." Again and again, the talk turned to culture and feelings of allegiance. When Shahal spoke of the high educational standards of Iraq and the knowledge Iraqis have of their own contributions to civilization, the interviewer, with some degree of surprise, asked, "Like what, for example?" "Like what, for example?" Shahal retorted, in a moment between the sublime and the ridiculous, "Like Hamurabi's Code, for example." Finally, they spoke of the past, and their disillusionment with how much of that past remained alien to their children. As Fuad said: "We're very proud of what we had in the past, what we created in Iraq. As far as our children go, this whole past has just been wiped out." Both the feelings of such native Jews and their earnest attempts to open a true political debate in Israel on its role in the Arab world are part and parcel of an alternative history that remains quite unfamiliar to most observers of the Israeli scene, whether they fall to the right or the left of the political spectrum.

Meanwhile, it is indeed ironic that the same draconian laws that the Israelis chose to maintain in their inheritance from the British Mandate—and which have been applied to Sari Nusseibeh, among so many others—have recently been put to use by the British themselves, America's strongest ally in the very calculated and well-thought-out campaign to destroy Iraq's military and civilian infrastructure. On January 17, only one day after the American and allied attacks on Iraq, 174 Iraqi, Palestinian, Lebanese, and Yemeni residents of the United Kingdom were rounded up and slated for deportation. Almost half of the 174 decided to leave the country without appeal. Another 35, students but former Iraqi conscripts or reserves, were made prisoners of war. The over 50 remaining people decided to appeal their cases since they wished to stay in England. A number, in fact, were longtime residents whose children had been born in England. The most prominent of these was Abbas Shiblak, a Palestinian scholar and human rights activist. When I first heard of the arrests, I simply assumed that Abbas might have been a prime target: he was simply too honest and even-handed to be tolerated during such times of knee-jerk hysteria.

My first encounter with Abbas Shiblak came through his small masterpiece, *The Lure of Zion: The Case of the Iraqi Jews,* published in 1986 by al-Saqi Books in London. I found Shiblak's book unique in the field: he managed to tell a remarkably complex story—that of the demise and transfer of the world's most ancient and important Jewish community—with a rare mixture of clarity, understanding, and sympathy. In fact, by concentrating on the minute details of one particular historical juncture, his work shed new light on the tangle of forces that went into shaping the Middle East as we now know it: the role of the colonial powers, the emergence of Zionism and Arab nationalism, the question of Palestine, and the fate of minorities in the postcolonial Arab world. When we finally met, he conveyed the same qualities present in his work. Both gentle and inquisitive, I grew to admire him more and more as I found out about his other activities. As one of the founding members of the Arab Human Rights Committee, Abbas pointed his finger at abuses wherever they appeared. One of his primary targets, for which he was persecuted, was the regime of Saddam Hussein. Throughout, and never as a matter of convenience, he remained outspoken on the need for peace between Palestinians and Israelis.

While the American press maintained a complicitous or indifferent silence to these outrageous events, a large public campaign—particularly on behalf of Abbas—mounted in Britain. Martin Amis, Nina Bawden, Angela Carter, Margaret Drabble, Antonia Fraser, David Hare, Hanif Kureishi, Simon Louvish, Ian McEwan, and Harold Pinter were among those to come to his defense while questioning the legal grounds under which the others were being held. Under British law, however, people such as these, detained as "risks to national security," have very little legal recourse. They can neither know the charges against them nor be represented by a lawyer. Luckily, due to public pressure, both Abbas Shiblak and Ali el-Salah (a Palestinian computer salesman whose major crime seems to have been his involvement in the General Union of Palestinian Students some twenty years ago), along with three others, were released on February 6. The others, however, still remain in prison, still slated for deportation.

Like everything having to do with the Middle East, the events recounted here are also linked. Both Sari Nusseibeh and Abbas Shiblak have managed to retain a historical sense of the commonality of Islamic and Jewish culture, and a human sense of the deep bonds that connect all the peoples of the Middle East to each other. If truth is the first casualty of war, certainly this truth will die a long and painful death as the war continues and their vision, shared by so many but so often suppressed, becomes harder and harder to attain. The passion and fear struck, for instance, by even the mention of granting Palestinians a right to return has always seemed to me both inane and insulting: Sari Nusseibeh, whose very Muslim family holds the keys to one of Christianity's most sacred sites, the Holy Sepulchre in Jerusalem, is being held hostage to the whims of a government that, should the circumstances seem auspicious, could easily deport him. Born in Haifa only forty-seven years ago, the dream of someone like Abbas Shiblak, to return even for a visit, is considered completely unreasonable. The interest of Iraqi Jews like Fuad Ben Eliezer, Moshe Shahal, or Ran Cohen toward the country of their birth are met with suspicion or scorn. At the same time, Russian Jews and Israeli settlers are being conditioned, through what Yusuf al-Kabir, an Iraqi Jewish lawyer, termed, back in 1938, the dictates of "militant archaeology," to live in places once inhabited by Jews several thousand years ago. While there is nothing inherently wrong with such an impulse, it posits a static view of the world that has nothing to do with the dynamic, interactive, and transformative nature of Middle Eastern life and culture, not to mention the present land-owners. Alternative visions, deeply rooted in the space and memory of the region (like the feelings of the Baghdad-born Israeli Jew Ran Cohen when he speaks with envy of Moroccan Jews who can go back while he cannot return to the scenes of his own ancestral memories in Iraq), remain light-years away from what generally passes as "dialogue" in the liberal discourse about Israel we have become so accustomed to in the United States.

From this vantage point, it seems almost unquestionable that American involvement in the Middle East will be long and bitter. As the geographic boundaries of the future are redrawn, so will maps to the past be rewritten. With 1992 looming ahead, and the enormous range of events planned to commemorate 500 years of the expulsion of the Jews from Spain, the deeper history of that encounter will either be marked "forbidden territory," "no trespassing," or, even more ominously, left off the map altogether. Attempts will be made to finally sever the common fates of Jews and Muslims (who were expelled from Spain in even greater numbers), and alienate both peoples from allegiances and elements of each other in themselves through mutual recrimination, ignorance, and an acceptance of the status quo. It is essential for active

Americans now becoming more attuned to a region of the world that has remained cloaked in the shrouds of facile assumptions to scratch below the surface of the stereotypes and examine some of the choices and options that have been distorted and suppressed for so long. As the planet finds itself depleted, as George Bush exorcises the demons within by bombing the site of the Garden of Eden to kingdom come, and the only means of solving a conflict in the new world order is through confrontation and violence, we would do well to remember that the "natives," too, have something to say.

1991

Reflections at the End of 1992

I am happy that my first and only participation in one of the big Sephardic events of 1992 is coming so close to the end of the year. It is a year that, I must confess, I am also most happy to see coming to a close. While many have been glad to see the proliferation of conferences, festivals, publications, tours, exhibits, and other general hoopla, I feel that—with only a few rare exceptions—this has been a year of missed opportunities, a year when the real message of Sepharad, of al-Andalus, has been obscured to the point of obliteration. 1492 has become a kind of theme park, with Spain (in the words of Juan Goytisolo) "the Euro-Capital of instant culture"; with Turkish officials lobbying Israelis lobbying Americans to hush up any mention of Armenians as they promote junkets around the Sephardic world in eighty days or less; with Sephardic Jews finally entering the curriculum, but only to join the interminable martyrology of the Jew as eternal victim, this time of the Inquisition. Hardly anywhere has the common fate of Muslims and Jews been spoken of, the massive expulsions of the Moors and eventual banishment of almost all traces of the 800-year presence of Islam in the heart of Europe. Rather than finding a symbol in Spain's partial, belated, and self-serving recognition of only some of the children of Shem, I find the destruction of Sarajevo a much more fitting sign of the times. In a recent article, John F. Burns has written of a Muslim family, the Džirlos, that traces its roots back to the last of the Spanish Moors—Sakir Džirlo, a forty-four-year-old electrical engineer, comments: "Here is a tragic situation, like in Spain, when Ferdinand and Isabella said to Muslims and Jews—Get out."[1] More recently, Burns wrote of Mirta Kamhi, a twenty-four-year-old Sephardic student of literature at the University of Sarajevo who risked her life to join a Muslim friend at a Mass on Christmas eve. It is these transcendent but very real moments which I have found conspicuously absent in the public discourse on Sephardic Jews that has taken place in this year of our Lord, 1992.

Like these valiant citizens of Sarajevo, Hebrew thought and traditional Jewish practice have always remained zealous in their affirmation of life. In this tradition, the passage into death is ripe with the possibilities of living memory. Yet, as I look back on 1992 I haven't felt that our collective past has been linked or brought to bear upon the present and the future. I have felt, rather, like someone watching a team of skilled technicians most resembling grave robbers as they pore over the remains of my ancestors—describing, cataloging, filing, categorizing, but rarely, if ever, connecting them to the living and those not yet born. Despite massive outbursts of activity, not to mention the budgets allocated to these activities, our creators—our rabbis, writers, artists, and musicians—remain unavailable, illegitimate, or under academic lock and key. In this year of the quincentenary, the works of our greatest poets cannot be found outside specialized library collections, the works of our greatest composers are not considered a part of classical music but pejoratively referred to—if at all—as folklore. Meanwhile, in Israel all the standard socioeconomic markers show that the majority of living *mizrahi* Jews are further than ever from access to the powers of self-representation within the existing structures; many of the great names of our illustrious past—Alfassi, Algazi, Abulafia—are now prisoners *in* Zion, in Israeli jails like Tel Mond or Beersheva. Many of our truest living creators, heirs to the legacy of Ibn Gabirol, Samuel HaNagid, Israel Najara, Shalom Shabazi, or Osnath Bat Barazani, operate under desperate conditions. Yehezkel Hai Albeg, one of our greatest repositories of ancient musical traditions, sells insurance in Encino, California; Brahim Souri, the great oud player, sells shoelaces and razor blades at the Mahane Yehuda marketplace in Jerusalem. And there are many, many more. Worse yet, in the diaspora most *mizrahim* are unwilling to rock

the boat, remaining only too happy to toe the party line and erect institutions that only pay lip service to the very real crisis we face, locally
and globally.

We can conclude and begin again with these resonant and allusive
words of Yehezkel Kedmi, the homeless poet of Jerusalem who has—
against the battle lines of poverty and coercion, against acquiescing to
accept the naming of one's enemy—almost literally made of his lines
and stanzas a house, a covering, a place of refuge:

> The lone house—my soul's yearning—was like a wonder the
> interpretation of which I knew not. I knew no wonder like the
> wonder of the house as we would see it from a distance. The sight
> of the lone house at nightfall, it is and will remain in my heart as
> I lament it. The lone house at dusk, which no one has yet nor ever
> will go back to. Inverted the lone house will turn back into the
> wonder of all wonders, in times at times, evenings and nights, and
> each person will come back. Until there is no man or man.
>
> Over and above this the knowledge and over and above this my
> people. And the chasm is unbreachable. In this I am.[2]

1992

Why Israel?

For a number of years I have been quite vocal and, I daresay, even articulate, on issues that are a concern to all of us. Yet, because my way of seeing things has generally gone against the grain, my voice has been marginalized to the point that my opinions on Israel, the diaspora, Jewish/Arab relations, and Middle Eastern culture have not appeared in places where they might have done more good. Since the fiasco of 1992 when the quincentenary circuses commemorating the expulsion of the Jews from Spain erected only more borders between Jews and Arabs, I have mostly chosen the ancient rabbinic practice of strategically placed and emphatic silence. That is, I have spent more time talking about Bosnia than the Middle East. But since the PLO's progressive acceptance of the premises of Zionism and the subsequent accords with Israel, I have been getting invitations to speak or write from Jews who wanted nothing to do with me or even actively promoted silencing me for years. So I find myself in an unenviable position, asked to speak briefly about complex issues that are of great concern to me but of which I have largely chosen to remain silent.

At an evening sponsored by the Israeli consulate in New York a few months ago, I asked the Israeli novelist Meir Shalev where he thought

Israel's culture was heading, in relationship to the other cultures of the region. With immediate defensiveness, he snapped: "What do you want, for me to write in Arabic?" I said that I thought he might have a hard time switching languages at his age but that there would be no reason for his children, for example, not to consider writing in Arabic. After all, since Palestinians like Anton Shammas have decided to use Hebrew in order to express certain things to a certain audience, why wouldn't Israeli Jews also decide to write in Arabic, in order to reach another, much larger audience? In fact, some already do. I thought of a friend that I had visited recently in Petah Tikva, the Iraqi-born Jewish novelist Samir Naqqash. Although he is largely unknown in Israel, his plays, stories and novels, all written in Arabic, are well known throughout the Arab world. He had just returned from a six-week trip to Egypt with his family, where he was making arrangements for the publication of some of his new books that were to appear both in Egypt and Lebanon. I spent some time talking to his three kids, Eli, Tsion, and Miriam, ranging in age from five to ten, all attending ultra-Orthodox Shas schools. I wondered how they would convey their memories of Egypt to their teachers and classmates, of riding horses across the Libyan desert by the pyramids, of walking through the streets speaking Arabic with their mother Vicky, herself of Egyptian origin, while Samir hung around with his friends at the theater or the offices of al-Ahram, waiting to see if Naguib Mahfouz would be well enough to receive a visit from an old friend.

Middle Eastern Jews have come of age in the last 100 years between the push and pull of competing nationalisms (Arab and Jewish); universalism (in the form of communism); colonialism (as the minority of preference); and the world of the law (through rabbis desperately struggling to maintain viable communities under duress from every quarter). It is in this context that the traumatic encounter between Eastern European Zionists, ideological heirs to the most retrograde nineteenth-century assumptions about the "Orient," and Middle Eastern Jews took place. The scars of this encounter still remain open wounds and can be traced not only through all the usual statistical factors of class, income, education, and cultural and political representation in Israel but through even deeper, structural distortions and imbalances that hold implications for us all. The last truly authentic Sephardic leader, Eliyahu Eliachar, summed it up cogently twenty-five years ago, at a time when he actively spoke in favor of negotiating with the Palestinian leadership:

The biggest mistake of the Zionist movement was that we disregarded the fact that our country does not exist on a solitary, unsettled and uninhabited island, with other peoples—primarily Arabs—in its environs. The further I went into investigating the issue, as well as being a full participant in the events taking place in the Land of Israel for over fifty years following the "numbered" immigrations—as well as those prior—a film of errors passes before me, filled with the inability to take into account the inhabitants that have lived in our land for hundreds of years—not just the Arabs but, to my regret, the Jews as well. . . . In particular, one must point out, with great sorrow, the contempt held for our neighbors by a good portion of Israeli citizens. This contempt is a result, primarily, from Jewish-Israeli arrogance whose roots can be found in misleading information, lack of knowledge, lack of contact, and a lack of cultural familiarity. Certainly there are exceptions to the rule, but they only prove the rule. Anything that has been done by institutions relating to this issue—whether governmental, the Jewish Agency, or on a private level—to inform public opinion regarding our neighbors, is worthless when looked at against the obligation and necessity that should be imposed upon every Israeli citizen to become familiar with the surroundings we have planted ourselves in. Alienation will take its vengeance on us.[1]

This last sentence, "Alienation will take its vengeance on us," comes to mind so often: at every new suburban settlement obliterating Jerusalem, at every cosmetic olive tree uprooted from a Palestinian orchard to adorn an Israeli park or museum, at every deadly attack that kills either soldiers or civilians.

Most pertinent to our concerns here today is the fact that a continued surge of creativity inspired by the emergence of a Middle Eastern, *mizrahi* consciousness in Israeli culture—in the form of music, theater, writing, and art—has forced Israel as a whole—however unwillingly—to confront its suppression, misrepresentation, and willed obliteration of diaspora life. First treated as mere folklore or nostalgia, it has become quite clear that the *mizrahi* return to its past in the 1970s and 1980s signified a sea change for Israeli society as a whole. But what is significant here is not only an embrace of the past but the fact that this past is *there,* in the Middle East, within Islamic culture, among Muslims and Arabs.

This is why a seemingly unimportant act like the publication of books written by Jews in Arabic, for example, is more than a quixotic gesture but the reeling out of a life-raft in a void of desperation.

The crisis we have been brought to demands that we use our past to re-create new memories of our future, to reject versions of history that banish Arabs and Jews, Israelis and Palestinians, to separate realms, where there will be no intimacy or ambivalence, no love or jealousy, no respect or common destiny, where the full range of complex emotions, intentions, conscious and subconscious traces inherited through a long life lived in common will either simply be shelved in the name of some impersonal and polite forms of "cooperation" or, perhaps even worse, just deemed unimaginable. Any relationship to Israel must include a relationship to the Middle East, to Arabs, to Islam, to unemployment in Algeria, censorship and torture in Egypt, the abandonment of Muslims in Bosnia, to efforts at rebuilding Beirut, to the effect of sanctions against Iraqi children. We cannot continue traveling back and forth from Jerusalem and pretend that Damascus, Tripoli, Sidon, Fez, and Baghdad do not exist. If our existence as Jews in the diaspora is linked to Israel, then surely we cannot divorce Israel and its inhabitants from the world they live in. To make enemies of Arabs and Jews, to build layers of hatred through false assumptions, misrepresentations, propaganda presented as history, is to commit the most atrocious acts of self-destruction for we are all multiple and cannot pretend to be exclusively this or that. My Arabic last name tells me as much. Nor can we continue pretending that our texts and the inherited wisdom of our sages are blueprints and not parables. As the words of a popular Palestinian song go: "He who says 'the homeland is only land' is a traitor—the homeland's human."

1995

The Return: Variations on a Theme

Understanding Revolution

8 December 1989

Dear Ammiel / Klara & Walad,

Best Christmas / Hanukkah greetings.
The intifadah has become so
institutionalized by now it's
difficult to know what to say
to you except revolution until Victory!

Best regards,

Ray

1.

Understanding revolution: to get what is going on, to get what is being gotten. Genet, in "Four Hours in Shatila": "Perhaps we should also recognize that revolutions or liberations aim—obscurely—at discovering or rediscovering beauty, that is the intangible, unnameable except by this word."[1] But time certainly plays a part: for a revolution not to latch on to an inner cycle is to remain forever removed from any turn. I have institutionalized truths struggled for with great labor. In order to get on with it, "I mean living."[2] And so have you.

We were in Belgrade that summer, without, or rather, before the *walad*. (Unaware. Ashamed now. I was part of someone else's scheme. Thousands converged on the square: many gave blood, others just came for the music. On TV, the relentless bombing, the sky lit up over Beirut, but without even the faintest semblance of the sheer velocity, the otherworldly but entirely human violence that is speeding machinery: "The other day I saw you sticking up posters of new martyrs. Who's going to put up yours when you're gone? Tell you what: You should choose your own picture. Enlarge it and frame it. Make yourself 100 copies, with roses and all and hang them up high for everyone to see and then die, get it?")[3] Genet again: "Her face was pink, baby pink, the same color all over, very soft, tender, but without eyelashes or eyebrows, and what I thought was pink was not the top layer of skin but an under layer edged in gray skin. Her whole face was burned. I don't know why, but I understood by whom."[4]

It takes a long time to learn, not just with the head but with the head and the heart, just how false the models of sophistication and complexity we have been given are. Of beauty. And understanding. The enormous amount of work ("one method is the restoration of memory's remembering on its own terms, organizing along the lines of experience's trace, a reconstruction released from the pressures of uniform exposition—"the only true moments" the ones we have lost, which, in returning to them, come to life in a way that now reveals what they had previously concealed—the social forces that gave shape to them")[5] needed to reach what seem, once finally arrived at, the most obvious conclusions: "One does not write in order to say something, but to define a place where no one will be able to declare what hasn't taken place."[6] Back "home" for just a little over a year (PUBLIC OPINION: "I think he's a slimebag: kill him"),[7] I am trying to reconstruct some sense of our time elsewhere. Because here (in that ritualized disengagement from the world that is the fetish of consumption: lonely at dusk "the monologue of objects, as if they are to ricochet, requiring an anesthesia which skirts this morbidity, at least for now, in this America which one would occupy,"[8] guessing at models and license plates, waiting) and there ("As I left the house behind, I left my childhood behind too. I realized that our life ceased to be pleasant, and it was no longer easy for us to live in peace. Things had reached the point where the only solution was a bullet in the head of each one of us."),[9] inside and out, are two absolutely different places. There is always somewhere else, but here is where this takes place.

2.

Just an average day, many months before the uprising "officially" began. On the other side of the page further details fill in the picture: massive demonstrations of solidarity with hunger-striking prisoners; towns, villages, and refugee camps under curfew; students tear-gassed, wounded, and killed. Events before and after come spinning into focus, like in old movies: the abduction and trial of the nuclear technician Mordechai Vanunu, charged with exposing state secrets ("The individual can compel the establishment, can say to it, You are accountable to me. The individual can expose the dark machinations of any regime in the world, in any sphere, by means of civil disobedience. . . . An action like mine teaches citizens that their own reasoning, the reasoning of every individual, is no less important than that of the leaders. . . . They use force and sacrifice thousands of people on the altar of their megalomania. Don't follow them blindly."[10] His palm, facing out of the tiny window of the paddy wagon, with the name and date of the flight on which he was taken, tied to a stretcher: "They brought me here like Kunta Kinte, chained up like a slave."[11] Bound and gagged in court, a motorcycle helmet strapped over his head: the *Jerusalem Post* byline: "Yes, the law does allow for people to 'disappear.'" Locked up in a cell no bigger than himself, the lights on twenty-four hours a day, a video camera constantly pointed directly at him: "What kind of justice is there in this state and where are all the defenders of human rights? How did the authorities manage to gag them all without putting them in prison or holding them in solitary confinement?"[12] The stories he told, about growing up in Marrakesh: "The rich lived outside, but most of the people lived in the *mellah*. There were Jewish schools in the Quarter, but I studied at the Alliance School, which was outside, we studied half a day in French and the second half in Arabic, with about an hour a day of Hebrew. I used to go around quite a bit, I remember there was a place called the *Jamaa 'l-Fnaa,* people would come from all kinds of places outside the city and there were all kinds of performers there—snake charmers and acrobatic cyclists, someone reading from the Quran, musicians, and everyone used to sit there and I used to go there myself, a little kid, by myself, and wander around.";[13] Taking testimony, the press conference on children tortured in detention (Riad Faraj, fourteen: "Each time they arrested me, they beat up the other members of my family. The last time I was arrested, they broke two bones in my father's chest and back. They also smashed furniture and threw things about. They handcuffed me and beat me during the journey to Fara'a. Before they began interrogation, they asked me if I was ready to confess. They then hanged me by my wrists, naked, outside in the cold, and gave me hot and cold showers alternatively. A hood covered in manure was put over my head.");[14] Naila Ayesh's miscarriage during interrogation ("Naila told the court that the police had beaten her head against the wall and that she had not been allowed to sleep for nine days. She was also kept outside in the cold with few clothes on and a sack over her head, then taken inside to a room her attorney described as a "refrigerator." Although she told her male interrogators that she was pregnant, it appeared to make no difference to them. When her husband Jamal, later expelled ["MY WONDERFUL FATHER, MY BELOVED MOTHER, MY WIFE, ALL OF MY BROTHERS AND SISTERS, THESE ARE THE LAST WORDS I WILL WRITE TO YOU FROM WITHIN MY HOMELAND, IN THE LAST MOMENTS WE ARE LIVING WITHIN OUR LAND. I HAD HOPED TO SEE YOU FOR A FINAL VISIT, BUT THIS IS HOW THE ENEMY IS: IT'S ABOUT TIME THEY WOKE UP AND UNDERSTOOD THE VALUE OF THE RELATIONSHIP BETWEEN FATHER AND SON, BETWEEN HUSBAND AND WIFE. MY BELOVEDS, OUR HOPE INCREASES; THE JOY OF VICTORY IS CERTAIN. WE WILL RETURN. MY GREETINGS AND KISSES FOR EVERYONE. MAY I FIND YOU ALWAYS LIVING IN DIGNITY AND RESPECT. YOUR SON"], was asked if he knew why this had happened to his wife, he said, 'It could be because we studied abroad. Or it could be that Naila cared about the welfare of women and attended meetings of the Union of Women's Work Committees.'");[15] the assassination attempt against the cartoonist Naji el-Ali in London, his death a month later in hospital ("I learned drawing in prison. Some prisoners learn manual work, but I studied cartoon drawing. I used to draw on the prison walls.");[16] Rabin inspecting the blood-stained walls at Manara

Square in Ramallah ("No beating for beating's sake.");[17] Faisal Husseini's trial, the evidence two pieces of prisoner art exhibited at a research center headed by him; one, a wooden letter opener in the shape of Palestine, the other a scene of a mother defending her child painted on a piece of cloth (Prosecution: What difference would it make, in your opinion, whether we were dealing here with work done by professionals or amateurs? Witness: First of all, to anyone familiar with Arab culture, the style of the work before us is clearly that of amateurs; by emphasizing this, my point is that the people doing this reflect the values of a popular culture, not a formally-educated or an academic-artistic culture. The work expresses the culture of the street, the local school, the family, the mosque or the church. Prosecution: You said the colors were not particularly "artistic," that they were unfulfilled. Witness: Yes, the colors are vague, unclear. Prosecution: Could you tell us, in your opinion, what the significance of the vagueness of these colors is? Witness: As I said, the people who painted these pictures are expressing things from a popular level, things that cannot come from an organized entity like a party, a club, an organization. Prosecution: Is the PLO one of those organizations you refer to? Are these works not connected to that organization? Witness: No, these works are not connected. . . . Prosecution: You've said that these colors have been connected to the Palestinian National Movement since 1917. Witness: Yes, since 1917. These colors were endorsed for a flag after the Arab revolt of 1916. The Palestinians participated in that revolt but shared the flag that was used by Sharif Ibn Ali in 1916. . . . Prosecution: Yes, but today, who else uses this flag? Witness: The Palestinian Arab people, as they have since 1917; this has not changed since then. Prosecution: Do you mean the PLO? Witness: Not necessarily. Prosecution: What do you mean? Judge: Here I would like a very clear answer. Witness: Not necessarily because when a Palestinian Arab individual, a family, or an institution raises this flag it does not mean that they are raising a PLO flag. Prosecution: If the PLO raises a flag, do they raise this flag or another one? Witness: The PLO presently raises the flag of the Palestinian people and not the other way around.);[18] the research project on State Terrorism at Sea (after being released, and before being imprisoned again, Faisal related the stories of prisoners captured off the coast, in international waters, particularly during the siege of the camps around Beirut when, due to the famine, religious authorities had given residents permission to eat flesh: "I spoke extensively with four people from the *MARIA R* and briefly with perhaps fifteen others. The ship had an Egyptian crew and fifty young Palestinian men going from Cyprus to Lebanon to join and help protect their families there. All were in civilian clothing and none were carrying any weapons; their purpose was mainly to join and help protect their families there, to transfer money, food, medicine, or blood." One, describing the attack on the ship he was on, made this statement: "I don't know how to swim but I had the opportunity to put on a life jacket. The sea was very rough and my friends helped me. From the moment the ship sank, we were in the sea for two or three hours. I remember the time exactly because one of my friends had a watch. I was with eight other people hanging onto a light piece of wood which was floating in the sea. The two who were wounded and did not have life jackets sank immediately.");[19] the closing of the Alternative Information Center, the confiscation of equipment, the arrest of Mikado, the periodic beating of Ali, the endless phone calls, meetings, translations, groups forming and reforming, disputes, petitions, solidarity visits, marches, the Committee Confronting the Iron Fist, East for Peace, the Oriental Front, Rumania, Budapest, Geneva, Toledo, Bir Zeit, East Jerusalem, the search for decent yogurt, more or less presentable leaders, street theater, the women in black, communiqués from the Unified Command ("In the name of God the Merciful and Compassionate: Appeal . . . Appeal . . . Appeal: To our sacrificing people . . . to the mothers of the martyrs and, to the mothers of the detainees and the injured . . . We want to assure the Kings and rulers that we don't want their money, because we are willing to starve and go naked but will never kneel . . .");[20] the liberal use, the normal route, the prime task, the higher incidence, the continued functioning, the wonders of, to avoid using the word truth machine to press the point, in its power, even if an obviously assured, cherished thing, nation, last, blindfold, the public eye. And the camps war, the camps war, when it finally became clear just how easy it is to choose not to know (The doctor was quoted as saying six people died, and she amputated the legs of seven others gunned down when they rushed to meet the food trucks trying to get in. After all the cats, dogs, mules, and other animals in the camp were eaten, a mother and her five children comitted suicide to avoid having to turn to cannibalism.[21] Most of the people at the vigil had relatives up there. The nurses we met from Sabra and Shatilla were happy to be in Gaza. In Geneva, all the revolutionaries stayed in five star hotels).

3.

Albert, the barber from Bukhara on Jaffa Street: "In America, with three languages, you're a professor; here, with fifteen, you're lucky if you've got a barbershop." Land. Paper. Independance Day: the unbearable sadness of Ruthie, David, and Anna, our neighbor's three kids, walking back home hand in hand, clutching small flags. Silent aleatory vowels. A tight-lipped people speak like ants. Trying to obliterate the lines. Face to face with the prey taken lusting after your favors, you sustain the battle and in the abandoned ashes inflame the fire of love: "If I were leaving for Zion, I wouldn't wait but a minute more" of this, of the same, the time of. In other words, then: I could have gotten the word across—flapping in the wind, in the blue, in the white, in the green and the black, in the red wind. Marching to pretend but always striking first. Firing and tired and weak and hungry and fed up with it. Fed up to the point of satiety. Past laughter, past breaking, past the breaking up of the circumscribed: the dictated, described as no virgin nor oil nor olive nor spit of sand nor plot of earth untended. Come what may, the fire is expected, not about to be but underneath, indolent (no signs from glorious dreams, neither ladder nor rolling barley bread attended him in repose or perambulation, the rising and setting of the sun only confirmed his acceptance of the quotidian. Cut off from any continuity or need to disrupt, never to be lost in a sea of words, like a rope pulled taut, he knows only the sudden snap of a thing abruptly at its end. Trying to obliterate the lines, he learned about olives). But the sight of that rock across the street, jagged, the grass and weeds sticking out of it, the neighborhood waking up or finishing lunch. Not a point frozen in time, but a doorway: my own door broken down, the total enmeshment and involvement of everyone in everyone else's business, the only refuge to create other refuges—in myself, the city, the encounters I pursued. Never initiating or truly questioning but building within silence as protest and defense, letting things go until they had no further to go ("Anger fuels memory, keeps it alive. Without this fuel, you give up even the right to assert the truth. You let others write your history for you, and this is the ultimate capitulation.").[22] Pushed into a corner, crushed at some point, uncomfortable, never knowing quite when to leave, awe before the unspeakable conviction ("You abandon the past when you write a history of it. Make amends with your past, date your wounds and your estrangement . . .")[23] that harm inflicted on the innocent, allowed to *be* inflicted, is, ultimately, unforgivable.

4.

To want to retrieve or recuperate memory (kids with schoolbags running after a trolley in Cairo, late afternoon; cutting curves on the way to eat at Abu George's in Bethlehem, past midnight; Easter in Athens) would be to concede defeat: "There is no hope in returning to a traditional faith after it has once been abandoned, since the essential condition for holders of a traditional faith is not to know they are traditionalists."[24] An old story: if those who can only grasp things (the masses, the crowd, the people of the land) through the imaginative faculties (not the "intellect" and "reason") are given an argument that leads to a loss of faith, it's nevertheless obvious that they've understood the argument. Such thinking (or not thinking), assumes "progress," so the philosophers (and other custodians of order) exert "caution," usually by creating hierarchical systems, withholding information and mystifying terms of relation and description: "You had imagined that people would be more worn out. . . . You would have expected to see the signs of rebellion and of anger marked on the face of each one of life's disinherited. In fact, you notice nothing like that. You find the same good nature, the same smile ready to flower, the same lively emotions expressed on each face. Fatalism? Cultural temperament? There's a little of that. But you feel convinced that this is not the essential element. . . . So you tell yourself that it's so much the better that they show this enigmatic endurance, so much the better that they do not allow their oppressors to see the image of their defeat or weakness, and so much the better that they hide beneath their skin the yeast of future awakenings."[25]

5.

My father took a Greyhound cross-country. Newly arrived, and hungry to catalog another set of images, he went from the steel mills (sound bite: "The danger, of course, has to do with the hostile environment . . . the Middle East is nothing like the Middle West . . . with Damascus, Syria, near Youngstown, Ohio, Baghdad, Iraq would be close to New York City") to the Grand Canyon and the West Coast. I got a postcard from the Enchanted Castle at Disneyland and one from Lombard Street in San Francisco. My brother got some reddish chunks of petrified forest. It seemed a happy time, before the summer of high fever, dreams of the pit with prehistoric birds hovering over it, fainting in the bathroom, the stillness of playing alone on the abandoned tractor, the terror of seeing someone dragged away in a straitjacket at a night game.

6.

Not sympathy, never pity, but gesture, movement "raising the threshold of the urgent."[26] Public discourse admits a breach grinding off to a halting start. ("Given this sense of a "hidden" community of workers such as myself, I replaced "the story of the Revolution" with "the story of turning to words." This is not quite the same as saying that my writing became a substitute for political action, or that it is something I'll do in between periods of political activism. Rather, I think that I format my writing to go in and out of narrative to coincide with the way I respond to any worlded activity . . .").[27] In the dusty thicket intrepid liberty traps light. The discourse AD HOC, active and unfossilized, connected to the actual situation of people put away, assumes and adumbrates a poetics of the real, a politics intensely felt. Tomorrow it will be someone even closer. Submerged in a return that had begun when. And the intention of that desire carried by a language that grows out of itself and is the magic of fully living within the mother tongue: anyone from someplace can feel it, the brutal anonymity. The ripe the ready the soft the naked flesh. Memory of another time. This crowd, these vistas. Not enough noise. Excessively punctual. We are going (CLIPPETY) to the good (CLOP) people of Zamalek: "Saddika puts down her doll and goes to paddle in the canal. Suddenly a cart dragged by an infuriated mule emerges onto the road. The wheels turn rapidly, madly, with a creaking sound. Before Saddika can climb up the slope again, the cart sweeps round, bowls along, passes her, has passed by. . . . There is nothing left on the ground but a few rags, a little straw, and some tiny splinters.

'I will make you another one,' says Nabila, her elder sister.

'Never, never. . . . This is the doll I want.'

'I'll make you another one just like it, with these same rags, this same straw, these same sticks.'

'No, no . . . I want mine.'

With nothing but this little heap of mud and stuff in her hands, Saddika sobs. She will never be comforted.

However, by the middle of the night she has already come to the end of her tears. Astonished and disappointed that her tears should so soon be used up, she returns to the canal and ceremoniously lays the remains of her doll on the water. It floats away, rolled up in a damp winding-sheet. . . ."[28]

7.

Today's episode deals with the story behind: I would rather have it perish than be brought back by ———. It is only in leaving that something is given off. Frost on England's rooftops, a brick wall: SEND THE BLACKS BACK. Learn to draw blurry lines going away from them. Back home, the D train down off the bridge. Chinese billboard, like leafing through the bookstalls in Ezbekiya Gardens: empire of dreams, dreaming of empire and a night at the opera, burning. Pretty soon the first statistics of winter will turn up: "hypothermia." Translate: greed, lack of a roof, what am I supposed to do about it ("A woman puts two chairs together and tries to lay down but a guard immediately rousts her. The regulations state that everyone must sleep sitting upright in a single chair all night.").[29] And we'll go on using diapers assembled in Guatemala ("when a country tries to escape, our first effort is to bludgeon them back into the fold, and if that fails, then the fallback is to starve them out, to create economic chaos so that they will not be a positive example to anyone else who might want to break free"),[30] because they're cheaper, and more absorbent. I am here now (*"here—in the whirlpool of the city, in the incessant noise of masses of refugees and exiles from different lands and of different races, among sad displaced peasants in broad blue gowns who had left a homeland not their own to oppressors and bloodsucking landlords to escape emptyhanded to the distant and enchanting city of promise and to try their fortune there as porters and street-cleaners, doormen and pickpockets"*).[31] Here, now: these are the innocents. Over and over, they claim they have no one to talk to. I can touch the clouds, the trees, my window. Light all over, fast, under: love's body rocks the child to sleep. The staff of youth. A wooden figurehead: skeletal hands holding a small globe. Columbus. Cement tower of Pisa behind on a hill, streetlight to the right: David, Machiavelli, Atahualpa, a pope, Pissarro. Naked women holding a fish. Going from the Grand Canal to Lido and seeing St. Mark's Square for the first time, the line "I hear Arabia calling" kept repeating itself over and over again to me, like some long-lost amulet whose coolness I could finally feel against my chest: "The final page of my notes is about deception, a tree falls. There is the blank face of indifference in the afternoon of staring happily and thoughtlessly into your child, the ultimate learning, there is the face of hardheartedness, the adorned face of the confusion of having been taken by storm before thought could leap up, take you higher, and there is the face of wickedness, again the face of my education upon which I walk backwards like a devil on a moral precipice to cast off."[32]

1989

Exploding Identities: Notes on Ethnicity and Literary History

Every notion in vogue, including the retrieval of "roots" values, is necessarily exploited and recuperated. The invention of needs always goes hand in hand with the compulsion to help the needy, a noble and self-gratifying task that also renders the helper's service indispensable. The part of the savior has to be filled as long as the belief in the problem of "endangered species" lasts. To persuade you that your past and cultural heritage are doomed to eventual extinction and thereby keeping you occupied with the Savior's concern, inauthenticity is condemned as a loss of origins and a whitening (or faking) of non-Western values. Being easily offended in your elusive identity and reviving readily an old, racial charge, you immediately react when such guilt-instilling accusations are leveled at you and are thus led to stand in need of defending that very ethnic part of yourself that for years has made you and your ancestors the objects of execration. Today, planned authenticity is rife; as a product of hegemony and a remarkable counterpart of universal standardization, it constitutes an efficacious means of silencing the cry of racial oppression. We no longer wish to erase your difference, we demand, on the contrary, that you remember and assert it. At least, to a certain extent.

TRINH T. MINH-HA, *Woman, Native, Other*

1.

As 1992 came and went, with its proliferation of quincentennial Sephardic or Arab / Jewish conferences, festivals, publications, tours, exhibits, and commemorations, I felt some relief at not having been called in as a "native informant" until the very end of December. Throughout the year, I yearned for a transcendent moment of the kind described by Edmond Jabès as "a moment we do not manage to classify, whose consequences we do not manage to exhaust and whose effects we do not manage to neutralize."[2] Yet, with rare exceptions, it seemed a year of missed opportunities, a year when the deeper implications of the common fate of European Muslims and Jews faced with consecutive edicts of expulsion from Spain were obscured to the point of oblivion. For those edicts of expulsion affected not only the hundreds and thousands of Muslims and Jews forced into exile; they also forced over 800 years of "Euro-Semitic" culture underground, forever marking Europe's own self-conception by excising references to its tainted, impure past. This suppressed chapter in European history returned with a vengeance in what has come to be our own legacy, during the enlightenment and colonial periods when an imperial curriculum successfully managed to ethnically cleanse any references to Semites—Jews or Muslims—that might indicate them to be both possessors of an autonomous history and inextricable partners in the creation of "European" civilization. It is this very legacy that continues to affect not only our discipline but the way we think of ourselves and the world we inhabit.

In the context of Jewish studies, particular questions and issues that have already been debated in other fields remain largely unexamined or even unformulated as possibilities. The idea that Spanish culture might, for instance, be the result of an intense struggle, for, between and against the memory and reality of its Arabic and Hebrew past, rather than the "self-evident" "national" outgrowth of a particular ethnic group, is rarely taken as an initial assumption. Rather than hold conferences, for example, questioning the very term "European" or pondering just how many generations of nativity in a particular place is needed in order for "blood" and ethnicity to turn into accurate, geographical description, the activities of 1992 only buttressed the impermeability of the very categories themselves. Whichever myth one subscribes to—an idealized "multicultural" garden of coexistence or the precarious existence of a minority allowed its few moments of brilliance by the tyrannical rule of the majority, along with all the more or less subtle gradations in between—the terms of discussion have remained the same: Arab Muslim, Sephardic Jew, and Spanish Christian, with only the latter being granted the magical status of "European," despite the residence of the former on European soil for close to a millennium. The containers of identity remain fixed and iconic, regardless of the qualities their contents might possess.

The quincentennial also conveniently provided the finger in the proverbial dike that would shore up any leaks contaminating one arbitrarily constructed historical period from another. The construction of a "glorious" past (even when that "glory" is contested), is often, as in this case, more a concession dedicated to fending off the present and more recent past than a means of coming to terms with the continuing significance of the materials themselves. In this sense, the discourse of historical Jewish/Muslim relations in Spain has generally been constructed with certain assumptions or silences regarding present political realities. The very terms of debate (as seen, for example in an exchange between the prominent Jewish historians Norman A. Stillman and Mark R. Cohen)[3] range over an extremely limited spectrum of possibilities. The very terms "Jew" and "Arab" remain mutually exclusive and are rarely problematized by particular historical, economic, political, or cultural circumstances.

Perhaps even more significantly, at least as far as Jewish studies (however it may be construed) is concerned, this discourse has almost categorically refused to take into account the present political, social, and cultural status of Sephardi, Arab, or *mizrahi* Jews in historical and non-ideological or apologetic terms as a focal point through which different interpretations of the past can be filtered. One typical assumption is that since Arab Jews came from less "developed" countries, they could not compete with Ashkenazi Jews in the "open" market Israel presented; here, for example, is a quote from Jane Gerber's *The Jews of Spain* on the status of the *mizrahim* in the Israel of the 1960s: "Coming from Muslim countries with less advanced economies, their skills were often limited and their per-capita income and educational attainment were typically and strikingly inferior to Ashkenazi levels."[4]

The perpetuation of one narrative (or at least one set of constituent terms through which versions of that narrative are told), replete with experts armed with all the "required" data, only serves to police the borders of a policy of separate development. This move away from the multiply-constructed contexts of textuality and more toward entrenchment into narrowly defined territories, small fiefdoms of power composed of self-serving and "self-evident" truths, obscures the ways we have come to accept the "infallibility" of those very "truths." Moreover, it pre-empts even the possibility of raising precisely the kinds of issues that not only need to be raised but which the very materials under scrutiny demand be raised. For example, one can look at the unquestioned canonical status of Golden Age Hebrew poetry in Spain as a way of detaching it from the incredibly varied and rich tradition of Levantine Jewish culture that follows it over the next millennium. Ghettoizing "accomplishment" in one discrete period, with only flashes of glory to follow, leaves little room for a cohesive narrative that can be presented as an alternative to the centrality of the "European" Jewish narrative.

This pattern is made all the more resilient by the fact that far too few texts are easily available outside a highly specialized academic context. While many nations have standardized editions of premodern texts, this is not the case for Hebrew. As things stand now, only selections of some major writers (Ibn Gabirol, Shmuel HaNagid, Yehuda Ha-Levi, for example) are available and many others simply have not entered into the vocabulary. The classic rhymed verse narratives of Yehuda al-Harizi, for example, are out of print. From the tenth to the twentieth century, one can point to, literally, hundreds of writers whose influence on the present has hardly been felt due to the difficulty of gaining access to their work. Although substantial "readings" exist there is, for example, no radical rereading of the Hebrew poetic tradition, no text such as *An Introduction to Arabic Poetics* by Adonis; one could make a good case that the lack of such an endeavor is the result of the contemporary unavailability of the tradition itself. Ironically, many of the writers in question—for a variety of reasons too complex to delineate here but having to do with place, spheres of influence, usage, and intent—could have a lot to say to younger Israeli writers who are again fully inhabiting a Levantine space but are still looking for a language to do it in. In addition to this, the aura of prerequisite expertise that keeps such texts in a highly sheltered but largely inaccessible domain makes them unavailable for translation. Thus, the gaps existing in Levantine Jewish texts available for use in teaching outside of Israel, for example, are truly enormous. The complex set of issues that such a situation presents should be of vital concern not only to Israeli writers, literary historians, educators, and the general public but to scholars of medieval, renaissance, postrenaissance, and modern Jewish life, in all its aspects. Yet, for reasons that are certainly as intriguing as those causing the problem in the first place, open debate over a topic as crucial as this never surfaces.

2.

What can, for want of a better term, be called "Zionist discourse" (with its hybrid enlightenment, romantic, revolutionary, and colonialist legacy, as well as its attendant assumptions regarding Jewish history and the diaspora), has permeated every aspect of modern Jewish culture. The earnest critique of this legacy and these assumptions has only begun. In some fields, such as history, revisionist work has gained a foothold. Other fields, such as sociology, anthropology, and literary studies, are still dominated by modes of discourse that can only be called paternalistic, ahistorical, and inadequate. In literary studies, the field that most concerns me here, we can see this expressed on all levels. On the one hand, completely vulgar and almost comical assertions not only abound, but go unquestioned in purportedly academic contexts. Two of my favorite instances of this are as follows; the first is from a preface to a book of interviews with contemporary Israeli writers:

> Equally remarkable, I am abashed to point out that every one of the 18 writers who appear in this collection is of Northern European or North American, *Ashkenazi* background. Not a one can point to roots in the *Sephardi* Jewish communities of Southern Europe or the Arab countries. And yet such is the literary culture of contemporary Israel that, though of course exceptions could be cited—novelists Amnon Shamosh and Sammy [sic] Michael, poet Ronnie Someck, a number of others—my claim to being representative can justly stand. To all intents and purposes, Israeli literary culture today is not only predominantly leftist but wholly dominated by *Ashkenazim*.[5]

After being "honest" about his quandary, this author goes on to exonerate himself of any culpable judgment; he has, after all, mentioned some Sephardi Jewish writers so he knows that they exist. However, since there are no others, his "claim to being representative can justly stand." Thus, Q.E.D., "Israeli literary culture today . . . is wholly dominated by Ashkenazim." The next example reaches much greater heights of absurdity, purely on logical grounds:

> Israel is geographically part of the Middle East—and indeed is a major factor in contemporary Middle Eastern consciousness. Yet as astute an Israeli intellectual as Shulamit Hareven defines literary Israel as a territory whose borders skirt present-day Manhattan and nineteenth-century Odessa, with Czernowitz somewhere in between. She would prefer a more Mediterranean Israel, though

she surely knows that such an Israel is, in literary as well as political terms, still very much within the realm of utopian fantasy. Yoram Bronowski, too, is clear on this point: that Israeli literature moves willy-nilly on paths determined by European literature. It does seem that, for literary purposes, the Israeli sensibility is incontrovertibly a Euro-American sensibility. Very little about Israeli belles lettres can be called Levantine, even though a sizable proportion of the Israeli population (a segment that includes such authors as A.B. Yehoshua, Nissim Aloni, and Erez Bitoun [*sic*]) has Levantine or Oriental antecedents. From a Middle Eastern perspective, then, all Israelis, even those of Moroccan or Persian or Yemenite origin, are European; their literature is European; their outlook is alien or external to the Middle East.[6]

This speaks for itself and, though, the temptation is great, one does not, in the end, even feel compelled to add any typographical emphases. On the other hand, it is remarkable to observe just how deeply ingrained similar attitudes are, to varying degrees, in mainstream scholarship. These less blatant instances are often harder to contend with since they form the very building blocks of commonplace assumptions in practically all modern Hebrew literary criticism and literary history, whether written in Hebrew, English, or other languages. More insidious, embedded in gaps and silences, this discourse relies on exclusion or partial accommodation as a means of asserting truth and maintaining control. A few examples chosen from the work of Gershon Shaked, Benjamin Harshav, and Robert Alter, three dominant figures in modern Hebrew literary studies, can serve as an introduction to the problematic involved.

In the fourth and last volume of Gershon Shaked's *Hebrew Literature 1880–1980,* Shaked looks at writers (particularly Shimon Ballas and Sami Michael) that, as one of the primary arbiters of "taste" in the Israeli literary establishment, he had consistently chosen to ignore. He describes the work of these and other *mizrahi* writers as an expression of "socialist realism (though it is really more social than socialist)." In addition, Shaked describes their work simply as a reaction; writing about Ballas and Michael, he states: "Their immigration to Israel exposed them to social and ethnic humiliation. The Ashkenazi community turned them from a social elite into a second class. When they were able to express themselves in Hebrew, they set out to accuse those who had humiliated them."[7] Other writers that he discusses (such as Amnon

Shamosh and Yitzhaq Gormezano Goren), "prefer the folklore and customs that were to the Zionist lifestyle."[8] Shaked also takes pains to find "precedents" in mainstream Israeli writing to anything that might be construed as "innovative" in work by *mizrahim*. Again, writing about Ballas and Michael, he points out that "these two realistic writers "dared" to raise the Jewish-Arab question—caustically, and while identifying to one degree or another with the Arab position—only after this issue had been raised in a complex, camouflaged, and ambiguous way by the members of the new, modern-grotesque school as represented by A. B. Yehoshua."[9] In every instance, the judgmental language implies superiority and inferiority: the "Oriental" is barely capable of socialist realism, only "social" realism; the "Oriental" is incapable of independent agency, but can only express him, or herself in reaction to dominance; the "Oriental" is only capable of folklore and customs, not an ideology or a lifestyle; the "Oriental" is incapable of innovation and can only crudely imitate more complex and ambiguous literary works through direct representation and identification.

In one of a series of exchanges following the appearance of excerpts from Shaked's book, Shimon Ballas stated:

> In other words, there is no reason to relate to me—as a writer or as a human being—as to someone having principles or a worldview. One should only see my political positions as a reaction to the humiliation that I supposedly suffered. But what about the pure Ashkenazis who also felt solidarity with the Arabs and fought along with me? They didn't struggle because of degradation but because they had principles. But I, at least according to Shaked, couldn't possibly develop any principles but only react as a result of my humiliation. Such a claim is not only perverse, but racist.[10]

In Benjamin Harshav's new book, *Language in Time of Revolution,* Shaked's more openly polemical assumptions are woven into the realm of scientific authority and historical objectivity. In his preface, "the Jews" remain unqualified; thus, when he speaks of the numbered immigrations to Israel (the first through fifth), he can conveniently exclude the people who do not fit into Zionist historiography. If such people are excluded (the waves of Yemenites, brought in as a more "practical" alternative to Palestinian labor; the Bukharians and Moroccans who established early urban presences in Jerusalem, for example), then their linguistic influence can also be eliminated. In fact, outside of one mention of the educator Nissim Bechar, absolutely no role or presence is accorded to "non-European" Jews in the Hebrew revolution.

Harshav assumes the destiny of Jews to be universal: "In this sense, Jewish history is a staggered history: what happened to one Jewish group earlier happened to another group later."[11] This "universalization" of Jewish destiny, however, in addition to being completely ahistorical, cuts off areas of inquiry that demand attention, eliminating not only the need or the desire but even the possibility of beginning to think about modern Hebrew literature and its complex development in a *truly* comparative sense, alongside so many other cultures and literatures that underwent similar processes (Arabic, Persian, Turkish, Greek, Urdu, Japanese, or Bosnian, to mention only a few).

The revival of Hebrew and the creation of a new society, according to Harshav, "gave its users a vehicle for expressing a totality of twentieth-century experience in a language of their own."[12] The assumption here, of course, is that without such a vehicle, one could *not* express a totality of twentieth-century experience. Reading more carefully, one can build on the nature of Harshav's distinctions:

> But unlike other ancient civilizations that were modernized and gained independence at about the same time in their own traditional space, Hebrew came back to its ancestral land from a long absence, from the outside, and from the world of Europe and modernity. It was not an ancient language of a great ancient civilization, stagnant for hundreds of years (as Arabic or Indian cultures were), that is now gradually growing into the twentieth century, but rather a new language, recreated in the very heart of the transitions of modernity, in the context of the intellectual ferments in Russia, which itself underwent an earthquake, trying to embrace abstract, idealized forms of the culture of the modern West.[13]

In this passage there are subtle, yet clearly identifiable judgments being made: other ancient civilizations "were modernized"—passively acted upon, they did not modernize themselves; the world of Europe and modernity presumably never fully touched the "traditional space" of these ancient civilizations; unlike Hebrew, at the very "heart" of modernity, the ancient civilizations only "gradually grew" into the twentieth century. Later on, these prejudices are made explicit in such journalistic clichés as "backward, Ottoman-ruled Palestine";[14] "backward and despotic Ottoman Empire, in that desolate and hot land, amid the hostile Arabs";[15] and "orderly British Mandatory rule that recognized Hebrew as one of the three official languages in Palestine."[16]

In "Ashkenazi or Sephardi Dialect?" Harshav accomplishes a remarkably erudite leap of faith. After endowing the Ashkenazi dialect with richness, subtleties of nuance, musicality, and flexibility (as opposed to the artificiality of the "so-called" Sephardi stress which, nevertheless, became the official pronunciation), we are told that variations in "correct" pronunciation (where Ashkenazi overrules Sephardi stress positions), entail more than "just a phonetic issue." They give "a specific character to Israeli speech and its speakers. And beyond that, *this is the basic mode of the whole revival in Eretz-Israel:* an ideological decision and a drastic imposition of a new model of behavior, radically different from the Diaspora past, is accompanied by *a subtext of old behavior,* which reemerges with time: the Jew comes out from under the Hebrew."[17] Thus we come full circle; since non-European Jews have been excluded from the narrative, this Jew, (like "the Jews" mentioned in the preface), we are made to understand, is clearly an Ashkenazi Jew.

Finally, in Robert Alter's new collection, *Hebrew & Modernity,* we can see further manifestations of some of the problematic issues described above. Yet again, we learn, inexplicably, that "Hebrew literature, though now created preponderantly in the Middle East, resolutely remains a Western literature, looking to formal and even sometimes stylistic models in English, German, and, to a lesser degree, Russian, French, and Spanish."[18] The fact that novelists like Shimon Ballas or poets like Moshe Sartel might look to Lebanese, Iraqi, Palestinian, Egyptian, Turkish, or Greek models, is a nonissue. Although Alter remains resolutely sensitive to the nuances and resonances of Hebrew literature in its Eastern and Western European contexts, his informed readings in the diversity of premodern Mediterranean and Levantine Hebrew writing are tainted by his own qualifications. Modernity proper remains a European enterprise:

> That is to say, by the late eighteenth century, European Jewry was launching the radical historical transformation we call modernization, and what was at issue now in the act of writing Hebrew was not just an aesthetic pursuit but a programmatic renegotiation of the terms of Jewish collective identity. . . . To write, let us say, a sonnet

or a poetic epigram in Hebrew was an act of competitive cultural imitation, but one carried out within the confines of a highly conventionalized formal structure, and as such chiefly an aesthetic exercise, however deep the feeling behind some of the individual poems.[19]

In slightly more elevated terms, we again encounter the crucial and truer difference of *European* agency; the novel becomes an idealized form representing consciousness itself while "premodern" poetry can only aspire to be an "aesthetic excercise."

In other words, there can be no "modernity" before "modernity" proper. The crisis facing Judaism during the Inquisition, for example, in the "age of discovery," when new parts of the self were interrogated, discovered, and charted, is not "modern" enough to fit such criteria. Within the domain of such exclusive terms, the fertile field of analogy and inquiry between *marrano* and nineteenth-century Jewish experience remains cordoned off. Yet, as Shmuel Trigano has written, "The Marrano Sephardic Jews served, paradoxically, as the prototypes and the anguished laboratory of modernity, the 'political animal' divided into the fantasizing private person, and the universal citizen, abstract and theoretical. The citizen is 'free' but subject to law and the coercion of power. The private individual is 'free,' but that liberty can only be exercised between the four walls of 'cellular' rooms."[20]

Alter's proprietary relationship to the past is accompanied by a good deal of mystification, both about the status of modern Israeli writers and the particularities of the Hebrew language itself (one might almost even say: *'al 'ijaz al'ibrani* / "the inimitability of Hebrew," to paraphrase the Arabic dictum *'al 'ijaz al'-quran* / "the inimitability of the Quran," such a central idea to both classical Arabic and Hebrew literature). Regarding contemporary Israeli writers, we are given to accept the fact that translation of more popular writers such as David Grossman, Amos Oz, or A. B. Yehoshua somehow already implies or guarantees the importance of their work. The idea that contemporary Israeli writing might be a highly contested field, a place where social and political struggles occur, is never even broached as a possibility. The "Israeli literature which has become abundantly available in English translation"[21] has become so, presumably, only because of its quality. There is no intimation that this availability might have something to do with the creation of a receptive space affected by the political and economic relationship that exists between the United States and Israel, and everything that goes along with that, including the politics of publishing. Why aren't Iranian, Lebanese, Turkish, or Moroccan novels available with such immediacy? And even more to the point, why are only some Israelis translated and published abroad?

Although Alter links some Israeli writers with their Yiddish antecedents and apparent American or European contemporaries, these links are made to appear so seamless and natural that one finds it hard to even imagine that there might be parallel worlds, worlds where writers like Yitzhaq Gormezano Goren would find antecedents in Albert Cohen or Jacqueline Kahanof; where the work of Albert Memmi or Clarisse Nikoidski could exist alongside that of Albert Swissa or Amira Hess; where the work of Samir Naqqash and Shimon Ballas would find antecedents in Taha Hussein and contemporaries in Edwar el-Kharrat, Ghassan Kanafani, Yahya Taher Abdullah, or Hannan al-Shaykh. One could go on and on: while the abundance of Yiddish literature is assumed, we are never given, for example, even a cursory description of the massive production of literature in Judeo-Spanish and what *its* significance might be for the growth of a whole other branch of modern Jewish writing as seen in the work of Haim Davičo, Isak Samokovlija, Laura Bohoreta Papo, Elissa Rhais, Catulle Mendes, Ryvel, Albert Adès, Albert Josepovici, Mony de Boully, Veza Canetti, or so many others whose names are neither mentioned nor known in practically all studies purportedly meant to cover Jewish modernity.

Without belaboring a point that already seems belabored to the point of tediousness: my aim here is not to engage in accusations, to expose the "sins" of ignorance (no matter how egregious), or put the "blame" for the state of things as they are on this or that person. I am not writing as a victim, reaching, as Trinh Minh-ha puts it, to defend "that very ethnic part of" myself. Nor is it my aim to "struggle for my rightful share," to impose—along with the policy of separate development—a policy of *equally* separate development. The idea here is not to vie for a bigger slice of the pie but redefine the nature of the pie itself. Other areas have seen remarkable achievements in the past decades, combining theoretical erudition with a true scholarly zeal to produce authoritative and easily available editions of both classical and non-canonical texts. On the American scene, for example, African-American and women's studies have presented new paradigms, standards, and challenges.

The study of Hebrew literature and the writings of Jews in other languages stands at a crucial juncture. A combination of chauvinism, ideological blinders, political blindness, and the lack of a true comparative perspective have severely tested the abilities of students to emerge intact from most of the contexts now available in which such studies can be pursued. We can either expect more of the same, or strive to open the field up to new directions and new definitions. Entire periods are waiting to be defined and examined. No intellectual history of nineteenth- and early twentieth-century Jewry in the Levant, with its relationship to European thought, currently exists. Who, for example, has studied the correspondence between the great Orientalist A. S. Yahuda and Saul Tschernikovski, or Yahuda's remarkable critique of Freud's *Moses and Monotheism*? A literary scholar attuned to the complexities of contemporary Israeli and Jewish writing in other languages, could open up the whole issue of writing in an acquired language, moving across different cultures and periods. These are only suggestions hinting at the enormous range of unexplored material available, material whose unveiling would unquestionably dislodge and make obsolete the kind of facile, unfounded generalizations that presently dictate what can and cannot be studied, known or imagined. The amount of writing that remains "unread," in the largest sense of that term, is staggering, And the questions that this writing engenders, particularly when viewed through the lens of the complex amalgam of Israeli culture in *all* its aspects, are the questions that many literatures are or should be asking themselves.

3.

The works of Ivo Andrić, winner of the Nobel Prize in what was then Yugoslavia, have resurfaced lately as a source of anti-Muslim prejudice in Serbian cultural discourse. In particular, his thesis, "The Development of Spiritual Life in Bosnia under the Influence of Turkish Rule" (originally written in 1924 and published in English in 1990), has been cited in various texts on Bosnia. Andrić, though adopted as part of the Serbian literary canon (often as an "antidote" or in direct opposition to the Croatian writer Miroslav Krleža), was himself a Croat. It is in this context, in an essay called "Ivo Andrić's Place in Croatian Literature," that the Bosnian Croat novelist and critic Ivan Lovrenović discusses the absolute resistance to even speaking of Croatia's three towering, modern literary figures, Tin Ujević, Ivo Andrić, and Miroslav Krleža, in the same breath:

What model does this phenomenon present for a culture's internal relationship? Just this, that such a culture has a serious problem with the *recognition* of its own contents and their worth, with the realization of its own creative energies; in other words, in the final analysis, it has a problem with *self-recognition*. Furthermore, it means that this culture has a serious problem with the *integration of its own differences*. And this, in itself, contains within it a more burdensome and global diagnosis: such problems all derive from an *insecure identity*.[22]

Lovrenović goes on to make an analogy between the way Croatian literary history and literary politics abandoned not only Ivo Andrić but everything having to do with Bosnia:

The essence of this relationship resulted from an optical illusion in which, *looking at everything from the center,* the Bosnian Croat problematic was always and in its entirety viewed as an *appendage,* and a *second-class* appendage at that. . . . And we are speaking here of a full body of work stretching over half a millenium; the literary and linguistic continuity and memory of a whole world that had always been a vital element of Croatian history and the Croatian people. What does the tenacity and continuity of this optical deformation tell us? It tells us that the only model given legitimacy, the *metropolitan paradigm* of center and periphery, is inadequate. Putting it simply, this culture, as well as its literature, have had a different historical formation, polycentric and polymorphous. . . .[23]

One does not have to stretch the imagination far to see the remarkably fertile analogies present in this seemingly distant and highly localized example.

Lovrenović also speaks of those forces that have the means at their disposal—in the form of a state, an army, and a police force—to exert and maintain control over a writer, a work, or an event. This bitter knowledge of defeat and subjugation, so long a Jewish instinct, can be contrasted with Harshav's almost chilling tone of triumphalism: "But in place of the Hebraized terms, new "foreign words" and concepts were introduced, within the proportions of good taste allowed in a given genre. This was—and is—the *cosmopolitan openness* (as well as the

Yiddish and Russian background) of modern Hebrew. It was this openness that constructed a modern State with universities, literature, and an
air force."[24] This, in turn, can be contrasted to the wise irony of Isaac
Bashevis Singer; when asked what the difference between Hebrew and
Yiddish was, he replied: "Hebrew is Yiddish with an army."

The very imprecisions I have pointed to are what Erica Hunt
describes in her highly cogent essay, "Notes Towards an Oppositional
Poetics," as "codes and mediations that sustain the status quo" and
"abbreviate the human in order to fit us into structures of production."[25]
In this case, we are meant to fit into the structures that produce meaning and significance—as writers, scholars, critics, students, and consumers of cultural artifacts. But such structures and strictures contradict
our experience, no matter how casual or urgent it might be. To be
"abbreviated" in the multiplicity of our possible range of identities is a
form of oppression. In a context of extreme violence, the contemporary
Bosnian writer Nedžad Ibrišimović was asked if he should be spoken to
as a writer, a fighter in the army of Bosnia-Hercegovina, or just as a plain
Bosnian suffering with everyone else. He answered: "You can't talk to me
as a writer because I can't talk while I'm writing and when I stop writing, I'm not a writer." This answer, ironic and playful as it might seem
under the circumstances, embodies an insistence on the autonomous
nature of plurality, and a steadfast refusal to be pinned down into one
category or another. It is the categorical assertion and acceptance of difference *beyond* "a certain extent." Without losing sight of the possibility
of universal desires, claims, and responsibilities, what remains crucial is
precisely this ability to maintain a diversity of selves and roles that can
act locally in many places at once.

1995

Speaking with Forked Tongues, or Parables of Equilibrium

Our Street in the Promised Land

At the end of the street, our neighbor Shlomi served as a lookout for the local coke dealer. His sister worked for the police, as an "administrative assistant." Once, when I was serving as an interpreter at the trial of a political prisoner, I saw Shlomi being taken down through the halls in handcuffs. At the *Moscobiyya*, downtown Jerusalem, the torture chamber fifty yards from the Main Post Office. Naphtali Reubeni, who lived across the street from us, went to the synagogue at the other end of the street twice a day. He had a son in the army and a son-in-law who came back and forth from jail every couple of months in a paddy-wagon. His daughter and his daughter-in-law both had kids named Rachel. Zohar Argov, the great singer, used to come down the street very late at night in his BMW to buy coke from the guy who kept Esther and the kids up all hours. Not to mention Yehezkel, playing *sheshbesh* on his unfinished balcony, surrounded by cement blocks and twisted steel struts, cursing every bone in Eveline's body and every hair on her head as the sun came up and went down. Now I'm on the F train and someone is asking for money again. It snowed yesterday in Jerusalem and the horses keep galloping away, trying to defy gravity as they take the turn over the graveyards from McDonald Avenue to the Mount of Olives.

Rivers

Last August, less than three years since leaving Jerusalem, we moved to Brooklyn. The manic pace of Manhattan gave way to a different, more familiar chaos: we got our refrigerator off a guy from Nablus who grew up in Kuwait; I bought jeans and shirts from Isaac, a Jerusalemite who grew up on King George, right by the old Knesset; Hillal, also known as Jimmy, from the grocery store, gave me a calendar from home, with magnificent shots of the mud brick skyscrapers of Hadramout and the golden beach in Aden; up a few blocks at the grocery from Alexandria, I could rent any one of about 2,000 Egyptian movies. And there was Atlantic Avenue and Stanley Rashid, where I got the six-cassette remastered sets of Abdel-Wahab and Umm Kulthoum, 1920 to 1935. On my way back from work I could always stop at Albert "Pikanti" for nuts roasted just like at Bahari's (not the one at the top of the alley, but down by Jaffa Road), or Zahava's latest tape. Being here or there we speak the same language and going over the Manhattan Bridge always brings me to Cairo, to rivers, and back to Langston Hughes: "rivers ancient as the world and older than the flow of human blood in human veins."[1] The East River, the Nile, the Tigris, and the Euphrates. But this year the pictures have become a jumble, "rubble without a cause," as a friend's sixteen-year-old cousin put it. Vukovar or Tyre, Beirut or East New York, Basra or Mogadishu. The indelible image, dwelt on only because of our distance from it, conveyed by my mother-in-law through phone lines we can't always rely on, of streams of refugees walking over the mountains *into* Sarajevo. More "Lebanons," more disruptions, more routes canceled. In the words of Michael Abyad (or maybe it was Anton Shammas?): "The world did not return to its previous state, for the order of things was disturbed." And in Jerusalem, the Crusader Man keeps chopping off the tops of hills, building fortresses to lock himself into, raping the land, and leaving its lovers to burn tires and simmer in the fumes of their own rage.

Ghosts

Rather than present a brilliant and detailed analysis, full of theoretical pyrotechnics leading to conclusions most of us already agree with, I choose to reveal and conceal myself within the jurisdiction of poetic license. There are forks in the road: we are here and they (whoever and wherever they may be) are not. The inherent push and pull of a process that includes the struggle to redefine different space—personal, cultural, geographic, social, political—too often leaves language by the wayside, as if the work that needs to be done were that easy and you could simply rely on hand-me-downs. Yosef Ibn Chikitilla, a Jewish mystic born in Castille in 1248, wrote: "A person must understand and know that from the earth unto the firmament there is no free space, but it is all filled by a multitude of hosts; those that are pure, possessing kindness and mercy, and below them the impure beings, harmful and accusing, but all of them contingent, about to materialize. And there is no free space from the earth unto the firmament, but it is all filled with multitudes, those for peace and those for war, those for good and those for evil, those for life and those for death."[2] As unfashionable as it might be to pronounce, language is substance, the very thread and texture of historical material. Not only does it fill space as "a multitude of hosts" (in the language of "then"), but these very multitudes make up the roads not taken, the antithetical, oppositional, and alternative readings that are the unexorcised ghosts of contingent meaning.

The Return

In the end, Brer Rabbit always outsmarts Brer Wolf. In one of my son's favorite bedtime stories, Brer Rabbit tricks Brer Wolf into thinking that houses talk. Once he rousts Brer Wolf out of his hiding place and safely reinstalls his family into the house, Brer Rabbit triumphantly proclaims: "Houses don't talk, you know that."[3] But no matter how hard we try, our words stick to places and those places hold our words, our way of being in the world. By now I've almost lost the sound of colored vowels I overheard uttered by the women of Bukhara and Kurdistan while waiting for buses in the Katamonim. The qualities of those vowels, nurtured by time, the particular timbre of sky and clarity of air in which they were imbibed and transmitted, are fading too. People *can* be transformed, for better or worse, memories distorted and rechanneled. Nothing proves the spirit indomitable. Defeat is entirely possible. As Etel Adnan writes:

> They teach the children to obey: it is a castration. They teach the children the names of cities that have disappeared: they make them love death. There should only be one school, the one where you learn the future . . . without even any students. Located in the guts of the species. Where you would say:
> "If you could step out of your mind and walk in the fields, what would you do?"

"Nothing."

"What do you mean? If you could step out of your mind and walk in the fields, where would you go?"

"Nowhere."

"What do you mean?"

"I myself would like to know."[4]

I am in awe of journeys that stay their course, that breach no concession to roles that are so readily made to be filled, that resonate against the echo chamber. Like the *Mountainous Journey* taken by the Palestinian poet Fadwa Tuqan:

Enough for me to die on her earth
be buried in her
to melt and vanish into her soil
then sprout forth as a flower
played with by a child from my country
Enough for me to remain
in my country's embrace
to be in her close as a handful of dust
a sprig of grass
a flower.[5]

The layers such a poem traverses are almost unfathomable, given the simplicity of utterance and the use of a language that can be taken so many ways, once removed then reconnected to the context of the poet's life and the role prepared for her even before birth. Such language is a shield against opportunism of all kinds, against the nationalism of hotel rooms or the intellectual production of conferences, where what the Algerian writer Assia Djebar has called "the rebuilding of ancestral barriers"[6] keeps taking place. Posing as absolute submission, the "enough" of this poem is a record of bitter determination to sow the seeds of a new resistance, one that embellishes the courage of perseverance with the raw material of the body, given over to the earth in final union, just as some terraced olive groves blend imperceptibly into the hills before slowly fading off into the desert, just as a house stands sentry against the outside world while re-creating a paradise that absorbs all the shocks of cruelty and tenderness exchanged between men and women, parents and children, brothers and sisters, within its very walls. Insisting on the logic of a language and poetry that "makes judgment on judgment itself"[7] remains central to human existence and reason; it has to do with what waiting means and how we occupy time rather than space, what we do while we wait during the greater migration that is life itself in this world as we witness the effects of absence, the gaping wounds sutured over so readily by histories produced and consumed as governing realities. But houses still stand and even if we know they don't talk, we still try to speak to them, to speak for them, to speak for ourselves, and those no longer with us, fixed steadfast in our memory of the future.

1993

Diasporas / Exiles

The roots of the word *galut*, in the verb *gala*, can be found in the Phoenician language, where it means "to uncover"; in Ugaritic it means "to betake oneself, to go, to set out," and in Akkadian *galu* means "to go into exile." As we know, Hebrew incorporates all these meanings: "to discover, reveal, disclose, appear, expose, uncover, unveil, to wander, go into exile, depart, emigrate."

The resonance of this word, and its implications, are enormous, sometimes even humorous, in a Jewish way. When we hear a long and boring speech in Hebrew, it is fitting to say the speech is as long as the diaspora—*k'orekh haGalut*. But have no fear, I only have a few minutes to try and introduce this long and intricate narrative.

In many ways the central story, the central narrative of The Book of Books has to do with God's relationship to humans, beginning with Adam and Eve and then moving on to the people who become *'am Yisrael*, the Hebrews, the people of Israel.

The will to know and eat the forbidden fruit leads to the expulsion from the Garden of Eden and the pains of childbirth—the central human story of exile from the womb and birth into the world, uncovered, revealed, and exposed, our first diaspora, singular but part of the race's collective experience. Of the division between Cain and Abel, the story of the Flood, the Tower of Babel, and the wanderings of Abraham, we are all well aware. Nor should we forget that the narrator of this text, of the *Torah*, Moses himself remains in exile, never reaching the promised land, even though he is the single mortal who has had the closest encounter with the great union, the abolition of exile that the Holy Dwelling Place of the Lord represents.

Then as now collective punishment was a staple of political life and exile is also another term for captivity or forced deportation. In *The Book of Kings* we hear of the first deportations in the eighth century B.C., then the more significant conquest of Jerusalem by Nebuchadnezzar, which begins the Babylonian Exile, dated—according to the calculations of the prophet Yehezkel, in 597. Thus begins the long, historical story of Jewish diasporas and the very complex relationship between communities in exile and the idea of return, whether to a promised land or a state of spiritual union. In this history we also have the unique idea of an expulsion from exile, *girush Sefarad*, the expulsion from Spain, which—like Babylonia before it—came as close as it could to being *another* promised land.

And throughout this period of close to three millennia, we have the perpetual tension—sometimes creative and sometimes destructive, between the centrality of arrival, the idea of the promised land of Israel and Palestine—and its displacement to the margins through the dominance of Babylonia, Alexandria, Rome, Baghdad, Cairo, Cordoba, Fez, The Rhineland, Amsterdam, Istanbul, Salonica, Sana'a, Warsaw, Berlin, Budapest, Moscow, and New York, to mention only some. In this predominance of the diaspora, one can echo the words of Mony de Boully, a Sephardic surrealist poet of this century, when he wrote: "What utter folly to wish to name the promised land."[1]

Nor has the establishment of the state of Israel eased these tensions; in fact, the most striking feature of Israeli society and culture of the last several decades has been its struggle to come to terms with its own suppression of diaspora history, diaspora presence, and diaspora realities, both outside of Israel and among the ingathered themselves. In a novel by the Moroccan-born writer Albert Swissa, one of his many displaced characters, a certain Mr. Pazuelo, comments on the lapse in behavior and morals that he sees all around him in the promised land: "The world turned upside down. Some of them even get hit by their kids, still stretching out in bed at this hour. He didn't see them at synagogue, woe unto them, desecrators of the Sabbath. A fading generation, and the one after is destroying itself beneath it. Exile! There is no other path. Exile in the Holy Land itself. At a time of dispersion one must congregate."[2]

So exile too is a state of mind, a striving toward, a constant dissatisfaction with the smugness of having arrived. But though Jews, in many ways, symbolize the prototype of the diaspora, the Jewish people have no exclusive hold on either the pain or hope that diaspora represents and offers to the scattered remnants of any homeland. We do not have to look far for examples: the annihilation and forced displacement of native peoples in America; the African diaspora through enslavement; the destruction and expulsion of the Armenians and Greeks of Asia Minor; the tales of Ireland, Palestine, Kurdistan, Vietnam, Haiti, Bosnia, and so many others.

Throughout, there is a tension between the inside and the outside. This, in fact, has framed the hopes and dreams, the politics and discourse of Israel's twin twentieth-century diaspora, that of the Palestinians. Regarding that resonant Arabic word *"awdah"*—return—Edward Said has written: "do we mean that literally, or do we mean 'we must restore ourselves to ourselves?'"[3] In an incredibly moving and very radical passage—not just for its politics but for its insistence on the personal—the Palestinian poet Mahmoud Darwish writes: "I came to Beirut thirty-four years ago. I was six years old then. They put a cap on my head and left me in Al-Burj Square. It had a streetcar, and I rode the streetcar. It ran on two parallel lines made of iron. The streetcar went up I didn't know where. It ran on two iron lines. It moved forward. I couldn't tell what made this big, noisy toy move: the lines of iron laid on the ground or the wheels that rolled. I looked out the window of the streetcar. I saw many buildings and many windows, with many eyes peering out. I saw many trees. The streetcar was moving, the buildings were moving, and the trees were moving. Everything around the streetcar was moving as it moved. The streetcar came back to where they'd put the cap on my head. My grandfather took me up eagerly. He put me in a car, and we went to Damur. Damur was smaller, and more beautiful than Beirut because the sea there was grander. But it didn't have a streetcar. Take me to the streetcar! So they took me to the streetcar. I don't remember anything of Damur except the sea and the banana plantations. How big the banana leaves were! How big they were! And the red flowers climbing the walls of the houses.

When I came back to Beirut ten years ago, the first thing I did was stop a taxi and say to the driver: "Take me to Damur." I had come from Cairo and was searching for the small footsteps of a boy who had taken steps larger than himself, not in keeping with his age and greater than his stride. What was I searching for? The footsteps, or the boy? Or the folks who had crossed a rocky wilderness, only to reach that which they didn't find, just as Cavafy never found his Ithaca? The sea was in place, pushing against Damur to make it bigger. And I had grown up. I had become a poet searching for the boy that used to be in him, whom he had left behind some place and forgotten. The poet had grown older and didn't permit the forgotten boy to grow up. Here I had harvested my first impressions, and here I had learned the first lessons. Here the lady who owned the orchard had kissed me. And here I had stolen the first roses. Here my grandfather had waited for the return to be announced in the newspaper, but it never was."[4]

The diaspora makes you ask questions you might never have needed to ask in the homeland for, as the great modern Arab poet Adonis has written: "In migration you forget as if you are remembering and you remember as if you are forgetting."[5] You become doubly conscious of everything and, once expelled not only from the womb but everything that is familiar or assumed, you learn to see again, as Nazim Hikmet the Turkish poet exiled from his homeland wrote: "I didn't know I loved so many things and I had to wait until sixty / to find it out sitting by the window on the Prague-Berlin train / watching the world disappear as if on a journey of no return."[6]

These questions are central to human existence and reason and have to do with what waiting means and how we occupy time rather than space, what we do while we wait during the greater migration that is life itself in this world; finally, these questions also touch the core of our sense of wounded justice and our need to record those wounds, which is such an essential part of our chore here on earth. As Dževad Karahasan, a writer exiled from his native and beloved city of Sarajevo writes:

Late at night, the day we saw the Jews off, I felt, with a pain that cut off my breath, that my City had already actually migrated into that ideal where, for two thousand years, like the center of the world itself, the Jewish, my friend Albert Goldstein's Jerusalem had dwelt. Through shut eyelids I saw how Sarajevo, surrounded and loved, loved like never before, ascends from the earth, alighting and taking off towards somewhere, flying off to where everything is light and tranquil, flying into the innermost depth of things, there where it can be loved and dreamt of, there from where it can illuminate us with the feeling of meaning, like a beckoning destination.

Does this mean, my Lord, that I have already renounced my Sarajevo within myself? Does this mean that she no longer exists in this world the way I know and love her? Does this mean, if it be your will that this happen, that she was too good and beautiful for this world which seems not yet worthy of you, its Creator, in everything? Shall we really, my fellow citizens and I, for the next five thousand years on the eve of every holiday, on the eve of every day we hope will be beautiful, utter like a dream, an oath and a prayer: "Next year in Sarajevo"? And it, our Sarajevo, illuminates us with significance and hope, further and further from us and this world.[7]

1995

Stops Along the Way: Selected Interviews

The Alcalay Dictionary of Levantine Culture: Interview with Ammiel Alcalay by Shalom Kish

Shoshannah Shababo, Simha Zaramati-Asta, Tikva Levi, Nissim Rejwan, Samir Naqqash, Avi Shmuelian. Anyone who identifies even a few of these names scores high in their expertise of Israeli literature. You can be sure the clerks in Steimatsky's never heard of them and that they can't get any space in edgewise on shelves adorned with more well-known names like Shalev, Gur, Grossman, Oz and Yehoshua. But the partial list above is not simply composed of names taken at random—in fact, all the names included in it are worthy of full presence within the canon of our local literature, at least according to how it is presented in *Keys to the Garden,* an anthology containing over 200 pages of "Israeli writing," edited and translated by Ammiel Alcalay.

Alcalay's journey to collecting the forgotten names of Hebrew literature actually began in Boston where he was born a "first-generation American" forty years ago, to parents of Yugoslav origin. The house he grew up in was neither religious nor Zionist, but there was a sense of Sephardic pride, "perhaps even a hint of Sephardic snobbery in face of the surrounding Ashkenazi community." This conflict with the surroundings and what he calls "my discomfort as an American with European culture," brought Alcalay to investigate his family's cultural origins at a young age.

Against the wealth of information available to any young American Jew on the Holocaust or Eastern European Jewish culture, he encountered an absolute void regarding anything having to do with the heritage of Sephardic Jewry. The same curiosity that compelled Alcalay to study Latin, Ancient Greek, Spanish, and Italian swept him into that vacuum until he discovered—in that supposed emptiness—"a whole unknown world, with no readily available sources. This drew me in even more."

This initial pull was realized in 1978 when Alcalay won a literary prize for poetry and prose and he used the prize money to travel abroad. His first encounter with Israeli society came right after the "revolution" of 1977, a period in which *mizrahi* consciousness flourished and the search for roots became fashionable. "There are Americans who've lived here for twenty years and Israelis who were born here that really don't know Israeli society and have no understanding of the forces actually at work here," he says. "I had the good luck of acclimatizing myself to Israeli society through people who had been active in the Black Panthers and other *mizrahi* movements. This enabled me to see things quite clearly right from the start, and because of this I never went through the process of disillusionment." Alcalay used his first three-year visit to Israel to learn Hebrew and Arabic; it was then he developed his very meticulous guttural pronunciation of "ayin" and "het ("When I got to Israel I immediately figured out the significance of correct pronunciation. As opposed to how things are in most of the rest of the world, a correct pronunciation of the language here is a code for cultural "backwardness." It's quite something to realize that workers in the marketplace and taxi drivers speak Hebrew more correctly than most academics"). He finished his BA in Hebrew literature and continued making connections to *mizrahi* activists and cultural figures. "The connection to this culture," he admits to himself, "doesn't come from an academic point of view, but from a feeling that I am a part of it."

"As far as I'm concerned—to sit in New York and publish writers that people don't believe even exist, like Shoshannah Shababo (who died two years ago with barely any recognition in Israel), or Samir Naqqash (who lives in Petah Tiqva and writes in Arabic)—that means taking part in the creation of *mizrahi* Israeli culture."

Your family origins are from Yugoslavia. From a geographic vantage point, that's closer to central Europe—so where does this attraction to the East come from?

I wouldn't be too sure about the geographic allegiance. What's important is the cultural connection, and from that standpoint we're talking about Sephardic culture in a wider sense. My parents also spoke Ladino as kids and on the street where my father grew up there was a mosque next to the synagogue. In the final analysis, feelings determine this and I feel like a *mizrahi* Jew.

Is there some significance to the fact that you are doing this work in the United States? After all, you gather your materials here and your natural audience are readers of Hebrew.

It does sound somewhat ridiculous to publish Israeli writers abroad who are barely known in Israel. Part of the answer to your question has to do with the fact that you'd have a hard time finding an Israeli publisher who would publish them because it's not economical. The second part of your answer has to do with the fact that for American readers, Israeli literature means—at best—Oz, Applefeld, and Yehoshua. When Israeli literature is presented in the United States, there is always an emphasis on its being primarily a "Western" literature, something that draws on the sources of European culture. Something that can be easily identified with and understood. This fits in nicely with the rest of what comes from Israel: music that can easily be placed, and the politics of a "Western" country surrounded by "Eastern" enemies. What I've been attempting to do is to show that we are talking about a country that is fundamentally Middle Eastern, despite the political conflict. I teach Hebrew and non-Western literatures. When you read the writers in my anthology alongside Oz or Grossman, you really do feel that the connections are tenuous; but when you read them alongside Jabra Ibrahim Jabra, a Palestinian living in Iraq, or a Lebanese novelist like Hanan al-Shaykh, you immediately discover the connections: the concerns are identical—with language, politics, identity, with a sense of the writer's otherness.

A few months ago I was at a literary gathering organized by the Israeli Consulate in New York with Meir Shalev and Batya Gur. I asked them how they saw the relationship of Israeli culture to that of other cultures in the region, and Shalev said to me: "What? You want me to write in Arabic?" I said that I didn't think he would be able to but perhaps his children might choose to write in Arabic. After all, Anton Shammas chose to write in Hebrew in order to reach a certain audience. There's abolutely no reason why there can't be a reciprocal relationship. This is already happening in music, because that's an area where influences move much more quickly and naturally. There is absolutely no reason why such things shouldn't also happen in literature and other aspects of culture as well.

This approach easily corresponds to some tendencies of multiculturalism prevelant in American universities. To give preference to an anonymous Third World writer over a more well-known and established writer because it's politically correct.

I am adamantly opposed to that kind of approach. In my opinion, that only presents a formula to build more ghettos. To say that Toni Morrison is an important African-American writer or Erez Bitton is an important poet of Moroccan origin, such an approach is bogus multiculturalism. It is antidemocratic and looks at the "other" like someone with a disability while at the same time appearing to treat the other like an equal since it's fashionable and "correct" to do so. That's one of the reasons why I called the anthology "Israeli Writing" and not "Mizrahi Israeli Writing," for example. As far as I'm concerned, Morrison and Bitton are simply good writers. Period. Gender, skin color, and ethnic origins are irrelevant.

Even so, perhaps more readers prefer Oz and Shalev to Shababo and Naqqash simply because they think they're better writers? Perhaps some of those forgotten writers actually deserve to be forgotten.

Maybe, but maybe not. We're not talking about a horse race here, and actually determining what it means to be a good writer or a less good writer is practically impossible. What seems more important to me is the possibility of giving expression to voices that have no other opportunity to be heard. Many of the writers included in the anthology have simply said things that others before them haven't.

How did you find the writers gathered in the anthology? It almost seems like you exerted yourself to find long-forgotten names.

In order to find them, I simply had to search well. To inquire. It wasn't simple, but the fact is they exist, and if you seek you shall find. The anthology includes twenty-five writers. Some of them are truly unknown, like Tikva Levi (a poet who hasn't published any of her work in Hebrew); and there are others who are more well known, like Amira Hess or Erez Bitton. All in all, perhaps a third of the writers included knew another third of the writers included. They simply have no platform here. If they are referred to at all, it's usually as something folkloric or as a curiosity.

If that's the situation in Israel, who is interested in them in the United States? To whom in New York does the work of Nissim Rejwan or Lev Hakak speak to?

When I publish these writers there I bring them into a completely different context, one that might not necessarily have anything to do with Israelis or Jews, but one in which people are simply looking for interesting literature. For the average American reader, the name Hakak means as much or as little as the name Shalev so that they both begin with the same odds and what truly matters is the work itself.

Alcalay's interest in *mizrahi* culture doesn't stop at his efforts to retrieve forgotten writers from anonymity. As far as he is concerned, this is only part of a much more ambitious project dealing with the place of Jews in the Levant and an attempt to connect contemporary Israeli culture to a Mediterranean context whose roots go back to the establishment of Islam in the region during the ninth century, a period in which, for several hundred years—Jewish culture flourished in the Arabic language. In 1985, when Alcalay got a Fulbright Fellowship and returned to Israel for another period of several years, he worked on crystallizing this project in a book called *After Jews and Arabs*. During this period, as well, he was active in social movements like *East for Peace* and the *Oriental Front;* he also served as an observer at military trials for Amnesty International. The thesis expounded in *After Jews and Arabs* is presented as a blend of historical, literary, and sociological research, with innumerable quotes from diverse sources as well as personal reflections that bring each point home, according to one of the enthusiastic reviews. When it came out in 1993, the book was listed as one of the year's top twenty-five by the *Village Voice* and as one of the year's top choices by the London *Independent,* where it was characterized as having the "sense of a three-dimensional drawing."

"It's impossible to speak about Israeli culture in 1995 without think-ing about the Mediterranean context of the last 1000 years," Alcalay states as he tries to sum up over 300 pages in a few sentences. "In the field of womens' studies or the study of other minorities, intensive activ-ities are under way to reassess all the factors leading to the present state of affairs."

"This is not really happening in Jewish studies. I am investigating the relationship between Zionism, for example, and the rest of Jewish history; or the particular relationship between Zionism and the Jewish communities in the Arab world and, having done that, writing a differ-ent history. According to my way of looking at things, the Jews are an organic element in this part of the world. I am connected to this place."

The passage from such an assertion to a right-wing political stance seems pretty close to me.

The assertion that I am connected here cannot be the basis for any ter-ritorial claims, but part of an effort to represent Judaism as an element of Levantine culture. I am speaking of cultural allegiance, psychological and not necessarily political allegiance.

And what about those Jews whose cultural and ancestral roots reach back to Eastern or Western Europe? Do they connect to the Levant? How many of them actually even want to feel part of the region?

To be *mizrahi* is not a question of blood, but consciousness. An Ashkenazi can also be *mizrahi* if they have the right approach. The ques-tion as to whether someone who was born and raised in Europe or in Anglo culture *wants* to feel *mizrahi* is certainly a difficult one, but when you speak about the Israeli-born, there is less and less superficial differ-ence between *mizrahim* and those whose families arrived from Poland. In the past few years a culture has been created here that is much closer to Levantine than to European culture. You could say that Israelis have finally begun to acclimatize themselves to the Levant in all kinds of ways. This can be seen most conspicuously through things like food and music, but also in architecture, dress, and behavior.

Another area that Alcalay specializes in—quite apart from teaching con-temporary Hebrew literature as a professor at Queens College or his efforts to establish a Jewish connection to the Levant through rediscovering forgotten Israeli writers—has to do with increasing American awareness of the events taking place in the former Yugoslavia. His family background naturally aroused his interest in the situation. His command of the language, along with his gravitation toward literature in general, very quickly turned him into one of the most active translators in the field. During the four years in which the war has lasted in former Yugoslavia, Alcalay has managed to guest edit a special issue of the journal *Lusitania,* dedicated to the war; he has published translations by the Bosnian journalist Zlatko Dizdarević regularly in *Time* magazine (a collection of these translations appeared in the United States under the title *Sarajevo: A War Journal*); and he has found himself a much sought after speaker at events where the American public has decided to turn some of its attention to that distant war.

When the war in Yugoslavia is over and there is peace in the Middle East, you'll be left without work.

I would be very happy to find myself laid off and go back to American literature and my own writing. There are also more than a few other languages and cultures I'd be happy to get to know.

Translated from Hebrew by Ammiel Alcalay
1995

Interview with Ammiel Alcalay by Zlatko Dizdarević

In the United States, and particularly in New York, it is almost impossible to begin any kind of discussion on Bosnia these days—not to mention a discussion about Bosnian writers or journalists—without crossing the tracks of Ammiel Alcalay, an American of Sephardic origin whose family arrived in the environs of the former Yugoslavia back in the fifteenth century. Ammiel was born in Boston forty years ago, and after journeying long in various parts of the world, settled with his family in New York some ten years ago. He is a professor at Queens College in New York where he is chairman of the department of Classical, Middle Eastern, and Asian Languages and Cultures. Among his contemporaries, he is considered one of the most authoritative experts on the politics and culture of the Middle East.

In the new edition of Edward Said's already classic text *Orientalism*, Said writes the following about Alcalay's book *After Jews and Arabs*: "Long represented as a battle ground for Arabs and Jews, the Levant emerges in Alcalay's book as a Mediterranean culture common to both peoples."

Ammiel Alcalay found himself attacked from various quarters for quite some time regarding this thesis, particularly from those who were never ready to accept the possibility of long-term reconciliation between Israelis and Palestinians. Alcalay's conviction that the problems of the Middle East can be resolved through tracing and reaffirming the common historical background of the inhabitants of the region is more concretely confirmed as time passes.

Alcalay's exceptional interest in the events of Bosnia-Hercegovina is notable, but only at first; he has, in fact, carried through an immense effort at concrete engagement in the situation in order to provide the wider American public access to the work of Bosnian writers, journalists, and intellectuals. Countless are the number of texts by Bosnian writers that Alcalay translated through his own initiative and found outlets for in American newspapers, literary journals, and reviews. During the war, he translated four books by Bosnian writers that were published in the United States, and he is presently working on a fifth with Semezdin Mehmedinović. He edited a complete issue of the journal *Lusitania* in 1993 that was dedicated to Sarajevo. At the time, it was the first American publication to present material on Bosnia and the war through the eyes of Bosnians. Following this, Alcalay published dozens of articles, reviews, and commentaries on Bosnia. He also managed, something not very common in the United States, to write reviews of books that hadn't yet been translated into English: these included works by Ivan Lovrenović, Ivo Banac, Zdravko Grebo, and others. Alcalay also translated many pieces by Bosnian journalists. With all of this, one must also stress that the Alcalays' home is always open to Bosnians passing through on their way back home as well as to those who've left home to stay in America or travel even farther.

Where does this interest in Bosnia-Hercegovina and its culture come from, to the point that you've almost become a kind of representative or "promoter" of its culture?

I grew up with the very impressive story of the fate of Jews, of the Sephardic Jews of Spain and their culture, which was permeated by and intertwined with the rich Arabic and Spanish cultures of the period. I always had the feeling that this period of multicultural richness represented the true renaissance, prior to that period that we think of in classical terms as the European renaissance. From my first visit to Bosnia, I sensed that this richness of intertwined cultures and the very particular spirit engendered by it was still alive and well there. This was not simply connected to the place, but more within people themselves, even those Bosnians that I met far from Bosnia, like in Israel. Bosnians who had been living in Israel for forty years still held on to that special and particular spirit that had always attracted me.

As far as Yugoslavia is concerned, it had been clear to me for quite some time in which direction things were heading. I experienced my first confirmation of these suspicions in the 1980s in connection to the events in Kosovo. When the war already started and spread from Croatia to Bosnia, I thought about what I might concretely be able to do within the framework of my own possibilities. I was very aware of the enormous impact of the media in such situations. I had quite a bit of experience regarding this through my involvement in the Middle East. It became very clear to me that an effort had to be made to clear out some space in the American media for the "Bosnian voice" to come through. I put my efforts into engaging as many friends and acquaintances as possible in the media and literary circles to push in this direction.

Was it difficult at that time for the "Bosnian story" to penetrate the American media?

At first I not only thought that it was difficult, but practically impossible. Although various American stars revolved around Sarajevo, I already had prepared a lot of translated texts from *Oslobodjenje* and various other sources that I offered to magazines and journals here. I tried to see if I could get a regular column, for which I could supply texts weekly from Bosnian sources, but it was extremely difficult.

When did things change?

As you know, many journals—the *New Republic,* the *Village Voice, Time,* the *New York Times,* and others—eventually did open their pages to Bosnian writers. This began after the first book was published, following the lead of the excellent reviews it got. Eventually it got to the point that TV producers would try and find me to get in touch with Bosnian intellectuals. Actually, though, if one looks back, the issue of *Lusitania* that I edited received much wider attention than a journal of that sort usually gets because the famous rock critic Greil Marcus made an exception by putting the journal in his Top Ten list of 1993. The initial efforts paid off as Bosnia began to be seen not only through the eyes of

American journalists but through an increased presence of Bosnian voices in the media.

Do you think that the publication of books and various texts by Bosnian writers, at the beginning of 1993, might have had any effects on the formation of American policies in the former Yugoslavia?

Possibly but, unfortunately, not enough of an effect. Knowing Americans, however, and their general relationship to the world and foreign affairs, I actually found any interest surprising.

How do you interpret the fact that the struggle for a multicultural, multireligious Bosnia didn't have greater resonance in America, a country unsurpassed in its mixture and varieties of peoples?

Right from the beginning I maintained that the struggle for Bosnia was not simply a struggle for that state, but a struggle for principles that I believed in and for the affirmation of those principles throughout the world. It is a pity that many of the significant figures who were engaged in the Bosnian question didn't understand how important it was to translate this concept into the language of every ordinary American. I have a sense that there was much too much intellectualizing going on and that certain basic truths about what actually was at stake there were never formulated precisely enough. Because of this, ordinary citizens couldn't see through the fog to fundamental facts such as who started first and why, who is the victim and who the criminal, where it would all lead, etc. Bosnia revealed both the remarkable fragility of the international community as well as that of civil society itself, and the mutual lack of resolve to intervene in similar situations in the future, in some other place. Naturally, this "lack of resolve" is the result of concrete interests and the settling of various scores.

Do you think that American interest for Bosnia, even that level existing two years ago, has now receded completely?

America is in the phase now of clearing its conscience regarding Bosnia. I know that in historic situations like this, one of the great dangers is the loss of historical memory, the loss of crucial facts and feelings. That's why right from the start my intention was to contribute toward the establishment of some kind of self-styled base of facts about what took place in Bosnia, things that no one could come along and obliterate or negate. On a very concrete level, we are now in the process of instituting a program on Human Rights at Queens College and it is significant that through such a program I and others can present materials and texts firsthand, things about Bosnia written by Bosnians themselves.

You are quite familiar with the fate of many Bosnian writers, journalists, and cultural figures. What do you think is the best way to help these people and give them the possibility to continue their work and, in the process, best help themselves and the culture they form a part of?

Americans, as far as problems like this go, are quite practical and pragmatic. I was recently at the PEN American Center with Semezdin Mehmedinović and they posed the very same question to us. We said that to ensure the continuity of Sarajevo, for example, as a multicultural center, the most efficient means would be to simply support the return of intellectuals and artists who have fled but want to return in a concrete way. I hope that a project like this actually gets off the ground.

Let's go back to some general issues. After a period of some hope, it seems like the world has gone back into a cycle of violence, blood, and terror. Almost every day another battleground like Bosnia faces us. The Middle East, Chechnya, Liberia, Somalia, Rwanda, Haiti, and on and on. Do you see some connection between all of these events; are they the result of neglect on the part of the international community of some general principles that the world has finally decided to officially lay to rest?

When one speaks of hope, the following question immediately poses itself: hope for whom? As a Jew living after the Holocaust, I have absolutely no illusions about human rights, the international community, etc. I see the present state of affairs in the world as quite terrifying. States are withdrawing more and more and there is a general growth of global privatization and corporatization. On a practical level, civil institutions are hemmed in and under attack from all sides, regardless of whether that takes place through military or economic forms of aggression. There's no question that war still makes good, lucrative business sense and perpetuates certain global structures. We know that this has always been the case, but there is a greater concentration of capital now in fewer and fewer hands with no heed paid to any kind of borders or limits. The drama is being played out in every corner of the globe, just the momentum is different. In short, the tendencies seem quite similar in Chechnia, the Bronx, or Bosnia. This is one of the reasons why I felt the need to become involved and do whatever was in my power against this global momentum.

In this context, could you say something about the relationship between events in the Balkans and those in the Middle East? During the war we've all heard comparisons between Lebanon and Bosnia, Sarajevo and Beirut. Is there any basis to these parallels?

I showed a friend of mine from Beirut, Hanan al-Shaykh, the work of a Bosnian writer that I translated; she is one of the most well-known writers in the Arab world and her reaction was immediate—she said: "I have the feeling that I wrote this." Unfortunately, there are so many parallels that you don't know whether to laugh or cry. Just like in the Middle East, it's quite clear that things never had to go as far as they went. The question now is whether this will just continue for decades like it has there. The only solution, logical and natural but essential from the standpoint of its preservation, is for the international community to protect a single and unified Bosnia. In addition to the existing problems of relations between two big powers over Bosnian terrain, one other issue there represents a real torment to the whole world, and that is this: the example of a multiethnic community in the Bosnian fashion, including mixed marriages, tolerance, and mutual respect, might actually turn out to be contagious and pose a real threat to the sterility of dead ended politics, and the further concentration of power and capital. That's how it was once with Beirut, which broke free from its surroundings and had to be destroyed. This is just one of the parallels with Sarajevo now but also, let's not forget, with a city like Granada in the past. History is repeating itself in Bosnia in the most tragic ways possible. Despite this, I must say that I'm amazed by the strength and dignity of Bosnians as they resist the cataclysm. This human response is always the strongest form of resistance to programmatic evil. The world thought that the story of Bosnia ended with Dayton but apparently this story won't end just like that, after one conference. It will go on for a long time and there will be another thousand and one stories written about it.

Translated from Bosnian by Ammiel Alcalay
1996

On the Home Front:
For/Za Sarajevo

Under Siege

A *Paper House: The Ending of Yugoslavia,* by Mark
  Thompson. New York: Pantheon, 1992.

The Balkan Express, by Slavenka Drakulić. New York:
  Norton, 1993.

Journal de guerre: Chronique de Sarajevo assiegee, by
  Zlatko Dizdarević. Paris: Editions Spengler, 1992.

Although Somalia—despite U.S. intervention—failed to find a home in
American public discourse, the bloody wars in the former Yugoslavia, that
proverbial "heart of Europe," certainly have. Like American foreign policy
itself, the intellectual industry is finally starting to, if not fit pieces of the
puzzle together, at least put them on the table. The varied fates of *A Paper
House: The Ending of Yugoslavia* by Mark Thompson, *Balkan Express* by
Slavenka Drakulić, and *Journal de guerre: Chronique de Sarajevo assiegee*
(War Journal: A Chronicle of Sarajevo Under Siege) by Zlatko Dizdarević,
tell us a great deal about how this discourse is being shaped.

Originally published in London, *A Paper House* was, remarkably enough, picked up immediately for American distribution. Although it has been received well, it has not gotten the attention given, for example, to Robert Kaplan's regrettable *Journey Through the Balkans* or Misha Glenny's prescient but deeply flawed *The Fall of Yugoslavia*. Where Kaplan gratuitously moves his arguments along by relying on general assumptions about "the Balkans," Mark Thompson actually illuminates through specific examples. A young British journalist and London correspondent for the Slovenian magazine *Mladina*, Thompson has written an extremely ambitious book that combines erudition and humor with compassion. A personal, historic, and political travelogue, *Paper House* takes us through a different region of the former Yugoslavia in each chapter. From Slovenia, we go to Istria, Bosnia, Kosovo, Montenegro, Serbia, Vojvodina, Croatia, and Macedonia. In moving from place to place, Thompson travels through layers of memory and event: medieval fiefdoms and later kingdoms; the Austro-Hungarian and Ottoman Empires, the two world wars and, finally, the present wars in Croatia and Bosnia. Thompson categorically rejects the bloody, seductive theory of "eternal ethnic hatred" that lie perpetrated so blithely by Bosnian Serb leader Radovan Karadžić and the Milošević regime precisely because they understood how fully prepared most Western policymakers and pundits are to believe it:

> It is pernicious, because it disguises a consequence as a cause and mystifies the conflict as an orgiastic free-for-all, far removed from political calculation: a spontaneous Balkan combustion—an outbreak of Balkan violence, endemic and insensate, that must be left to burn itself out. . . . Mr. Karadžić never misses a chance to explain in his good English that ceasefires keep being broken because ethnic hatred runs so deep. He knows his audience, and the message is seductive: "Don't intervene! You can't do anything about an ethnic conflict except stand well back. Outsiders would be attacked by everyone, they'd never get out alive." All of which is secret music to the ears of the Europeans who don't want to intervene anyway.[1]

While the mix of history, anecdote, and political analysis becomes stilted at times—as if Thompson felt bound to use the same pattern for each region—*Paper House* is filled with perceptions and judgments that could only be made by someone steeped in the varied cultures and histories that made up former Yugoslavia. In his superb chapter on Kosovo, Thompson traces the roots of Serbian ambition and Yugoslav fragmentation. Here we learn, for example, that from 1981 to 1989, "584,373 Kosovars—half the adult population—were arrested, interrogated, interned or reprimanded."[2] The repressive and racist policies carried out in Kosovo and perpetuated in Serbia and Montenegro through "an official hysteria, disseminated by politicians, intellegentsia, and media,"[3] clearly paved the way for horrors that have reached genocidal proportions.

Although Thompson's optimism regarding Bosnia's ability to stay out of the wars waged by Serbia against Slovenia and Croatia was premature (the book was finished in March 1992), his "Epilogue: The Final Solution of Bosnia-Hercegovina and Other Matters of Concern," more than makes up for it. This chapter, filled with a righteous indignation that never crosses over into sloganeering, is essential for understanding how Western policy and opinion have accepted the terms of the conflict as laid down by the Serbian agressors and not the Bosnian victims:

> The West pretends that the established process of negotiation does not inherently favor the aggressor and that the parties to the Bosnian conflict are more or less equally responsible for perpetuating the violence, because none of them will "compromise"—as if the price of compromise were identical for both sides . . . one might almost agree with the conspiracy theory rife among Bosnians themselves that Western leaders are more discomfited by the Sarajevo government's stubborn *and unexpected* survival than by their own vacillation or the monstrousness of "ethnic cleansing." If Izetbegović were to capitulate, the whole ungodly mess would seem so much clearer: the EC and the UN would be free to do business with the real power-brokers in Belgrade and Zagreb, and the Muslims could be ushered into a canton of their own.[4]

In the current climate of a politics of identity, the implications of European and American acquiescence in the ethnic/religious cantonization of a democratically elected, multinational, and pluralistic state government are truly staggering. The viable alternative that Bosnia represents, in which "nations are fairly thoroughly mixed, almost like the colours in a painting by Jackson Pollock, as President Izetbegović recently remarked,"[5] has been deemed unimaginable. Restoring this possibility, as Mark Thompson so eloquently illustrates, is what the survival of Bosnia is all about.

What has been almost entirely absent in American media coverage of the war against Bosnia is the tenacious persistence of Bosnian civil life in the face of unspeakable brutality and outside indifference. Like the Almohad invasion of twelfth-century Andalusia, the sacking of Baghdad by the Mongols, or the destruction of Beirut, the war in Bosnia is also a war against everything Sarajevo represents: its unique amalgamation of peoples, cultures, faiths, and styles; in short, its urban civilization. One of Sarajevo's most uncompromising and singular voices has been Zlatko Dizdarević, a journalist for *Oslobodjenje*, the Sarajevo daily that, against all odds (including the total destruction of its buildings), has continued to come out. The recent French edition of Dizdarević's *Journal de guerre (War Journal)*, was originally serialized in the Croatian paper *Slobodna Dalmacija*, before the general erosion of journalistic freedom and standards there, not to mention the Croatian government's own duplicitous policies regarding Bosnia. The fact that this stunning book remains unavailable in English—attempts at magazine or serial publication have failed—is a dismal indictment of the American print world's tunnel vision. This indictment is only compounded by the media space given to war tourists, sojourners, and other voyeurs.

Dizdarević, however, is no one's tourist or voyeur. Given an award by the French group Journalists Without Borders, Dizdarević refused to leave Sarajevo. As he writes on December 5, 1992, the last entry in the journal:

> To put it plainly, I can't leave Sarajevo at any price today, except through deceit, by pinning my back right to the floor. Those who have something to tell this arrogant world are precisely those who can't leave.[6]

Dizdarević's dignity and irony, his sense of understatement and the human perspective of his vignettes from the civil orders of hell place this chronicle in the company of other great testimonies from the further side of the abyss: parts of Primo Levi's *Survival in Auschwitz* and Jean Said Makdisi's *Beirut Fragments* come to mind.

In the entry for August 10, 1992, Dizdarević writes:

> The world is very moved at the discovery of concentration camps in Bosnia-Hercegovina. Actually, people are troubled since "indi-

cations" of conditions in the camps might prove to be true. Since the west is empirical, it must seek confirmation of its data in black and white or, perhaps, red and white, so that the "indications" will become accepted as something palpable. In any case, there is quite a commotion.[7]

Dizdarević then goes on to point out that while various empiricists went in search of evidence at the camps, Elie Wiesel among them, they completely disregarded the fact that Sarajevo itself—and all the other besieged towns and cities—had themselves taken on the classical characteristics of concentration camps.

Recording everything from cat-and-mouse games played between residents and snipers to the system of food distribution, Dizdarević presents a city using all its wits to survive. In one of the book's most moving passages, he describes the exodus of Sarajevo's Jewish community:

The Jews will be back one day, of this I am certain. Meanwhile, their departure marks the initial realization of Karadžić's plan. If those who have lived in Sarajevo for five centures leave the city, it will never be the same. It is 500 years that the Sephardim have established themselves on this soil. Today, they must leave in order to survive. The circle closes, the message from one monster to another, Ćosić to Karadžić, has been delivered: "Keep going, as long as what was once impossible becomes possible."[8]

Many more passages deserve to be quoted: Dizdarević and his colleagues work in the basement of their ruined building, sleeping on cots. On June 11, after eight days underground, they emerge only to discover "new horizons," different landscapes and views of the mountains:

It has taken me all morning to understand why I can suddenly see certain parts of the city I've never been able to see from my window before. The answer is simple and stunning: buildings, walls, branches that were always part of my surrounding landscape have simply vanished.[9]

Although it is ultimately unfair to compare Dizdarević's book to Slavenka Drakulić's *Balkan Express,* it is impossible not to, given the limited space available for translations in this country. Although Drakulić has been a consistent oppositional voice in an increasingly repressive and nationalistic Croatia, the most acute parts of *Balkan Express* report on the inner front. She reveals the innocence and odd sense of privilege accorded people of her milieu who came of age in Yugoslavia in the late 1960s and 1970s. Fed by heroic imagery of Tito and the partisans, stable to the point of amnesia, and possessed with an urbane irony regarding "truths" of any kind, this generation grew up curiously uninformed by a political consciousness. It is almost as if only the pomp, ceremony, and cynical opportunism of the Nonaligned Movement, and none of its real hope for change had silted the ideological brainpan of an entire generation. Drakulić examines this terrain with a fine-tooth comb, often revealing great pain in the process, and here her writing resonates most fully. Yet, a number of the pieces in *Balkan Express* skirt a fine line between honest scrutiny and a sense of self-pity that, especially when compared to Dizdarević's clarity, is almost embarrasing. Unfortunately, this quality of ruminative sadness—available to a relatively privileged participant in events that have the taint of the exotic but can nevertheless touch our "common" humanity—is precisely what makes Drakulić so presentable to a certain kind of American audience. And this severely limits Drakulić's potential, so starkly displayed in the book's most powerful piece, "And the President is Drinking Coffee on Jelačić Square," a description of a small demonstration by survivors of Vukovar across the street from a cafe where Croatian president Tudjman studiously ignores them:

> Just as I arrived I saw a short woman dressed all in black with messy hair, maybe in her fifties, pass the bodyguard and stop by the President. She began to talk to him in what seemed a calm tone of voice. As the President turned his head in surprise two men rose from their chairs and grabbed the woman's arms. The situation was tense, some people stood up in confusion. Some left. But the woman just stood there talking (he obviously didn't order her out) as if she didn't care what happened to her. When the bodyguard let her free, she pointed several times at the mass of people whom he hadn't, or didn't want, to notice. He shook his head. . . . That was all he did: I never saw him once open his mouth and talk to her. The woman went out, her face racked with pain.[10]

Drakulić's chilling description of this incident delineates the relations of power now holding sway, relations in which the ethereal 1,000-year-old "dream" of Croatian independence is invested with more value and legitimacy than the victims upon whose corpses such folly has been erected. As the corpses pile up, the least we can do is arm ourselves with accurate information, particularly the kind offered by Dizdarević, as we imagine what it might be like to sit in the basement of *Oslobodjenje* and begin the entry for July 18, 1992, with these words: "It's two o'clock, and no one has been killed yet."[11]

1993

Bearing Witness

A Witness to Genocide by Roy Gutman. New York: Macmillan, 1993.

Why Bosnia? Writings on the Balkan War; Rabia Ali & Lawrence Lifschultz. Stony Creek, CT: The Pamphleteer's Press, 1993.

Most American discourse on the genocide in Bosnia has been framed by great lies justifying the world's inaction and supposed impotence. These include such racist but useful clichés as "ancient animosities," "tribal blood feud," and "religious war." After all, what can Western powers—so committed to such universal principles as freedom, democracy, and human rights—possibly accomplish in the face of such barbarity and lack of reason, if the "warring factions" insist on remaining so intractable? Many politicians, intellectuals, anti-interventionist liberals, and even some sympathetic, in principle, to the Bosnian "cause," have taken their cue from these tales of Balkan exoticism, this glimpse of the mysterious Orient in Europe's backyard, to assuage what little they have left of their

conscience. Both *A Witness to Genocide* and *Why Bosnia?* serve as powerful antidotes to these grotesque, all too pervasive distortions.

An award-winning correspondent for *Newsday,* Roy Gutman broke
the story of Serb-run death camps in Bosnia during the late summer of
1992. More recently, he has exposed corruption and collusion at the
highest levels of the UN forces in Bosnia, documenting involvement in
drug smuggling, rape, and "acquiescence" to the "favors" of Bosnian
women held captive in Serb-run brothels. *A Witness to Genocide* contains
Gutman's dispatches from Bosnia beginning in November 1991 and ending in late June 1993. The superb reporting, its deep indignation held in
check by Gutman's awareness of the outside world's willingness not to
believe, is complemented by a lengthy introduction and short epilogue.
Here, you can feel the sting of Gutman's outrage at the machinations
that went into creating the climate for nonintervention: he names
names, among them Lawrence Eagleberger and Brent Scowcroft (both
Serbo-Croatian speakers and members of Henry Kissinger Associates, a
company with extensive economic and political ties in Belgrade). Nor
does he shirk from calling genocide by its name, not only by invoking
the authority of Simon Wiesenthal, but even more importantly, by tracing the steps of political perception, interest, and complicity that
resulted in policies that have condoned and even abetted the slaughter.

While a collection of dispatches might seem to have a built-in
disadvantage, the cumulative effect of reading these accounts in their
chronological order is quite staggering. Gutman, also a speaker of
Serbo-Croatian, did not allow himself the dubious "luxury" of staying in
Sarajevo, but traveled, as he puts it, to "the interior." Perhaps more than
any other Western journalist, he has managed to convey the genocidal
nature of the Serbian project, depicting the massive destruction and des-
ecration of religious monuments and cultural institutions, the effects of
mass rape, calculated terrorism carried out against unarmed civilians,
and the wholesale liquidation of professional and political elites in
smaller Bosnian cities. This crucial aspect of the "war"—a term that
hardly applies in this case—is depicted with fierce precision in a dis-
patch from November 8, 1992:

> The Serb guards strode menacingly into the crowded basement
> room in the middle of the night and called out the names of seven
> men. It was a virtual *Who's Who* of leading Muslims and Croats
> from nearby Prijedor: Muhamed Čehajić, the elected lord mayor of

the city of 112,000; two gynecologists at the Prijedor hospital; the owner of a cafe and art gallery; a state prosecutor; and two others. Aside from one Croat, all were Muslims.

One by one, they rose from the corrugated cardboard and rags on which they slept in the administration building of the mine complex-turned-concentration camp. They were led away by the guards and never again seen alive. Several eyewitnesses reported seeing and identifying the corpses of the seven men in a nearby field the next day. . . . Over two days, July 26 and 27, the Serbs called about 50 people, according to witnesses, and they included judges, businessmen, teachers, surgeons, and civil servants.[1]

As the crimes perpetrated in Bosnia threaten to become a purely "humanitarian" or "cultural" issue, it is extremely timely and important to get the political perspectives offered by Gutman and, more densely and analytically, through the broad picture presented in Rabia Ali and Lawrence Lifschultz's superb *Why Bosnia? Writings on the Balkan War.* Divided into four parts, *Why Bosnia?* contains a finely tuned medley of voices, mostly ex-Yugoslavs (Bosnians, Croatians, Serbs, Montenegrans, Slovenians, and Albanians), as well as a number of non-Yugoslav scholars and journalists. The selections—ranging from first-person accounts by concentration camp survivors to detailed political and economic analyses of Yugoslavia's dissolution—are interspersed with Bosnian literary texts such as Nerkesi Muhammed's century-poem of praise for Sarajevo and Mak Dizdar's sparse and powerful century-lyrics. An extensive and brilliant introduction by the editors refute the great lies in fine, chronological detail, and should serve as a primer for anyone prepared to engage in concrete political activity. Although inevitably permeated by loss and mourning, *Why Bosnia?* strives to be put to use as an organizing tool for those becoming aware of, as Slavoj Žižek puts it, the "dialectical reversal in which something that, within a given set of circumstances, appeared as the most backward element, a remnant of the past, suddenly emerges as the premonition of what lies ahead."[2] What lies ahead is described in Enes Karić's remarkable "The Land of Inexhaustible Inspiration: Extract from a Sufi Chronicle of 2092," with all the bitter irony and magnanimous humor that a true Bosnian can muster:

In Bosnia people die by the unbearable lightness of the creativity of evil. . . . For Bosnia is the land of inexhaustible inspiration on the unbearable lightness of dying. You see, not long ago, even the theologians fell into a dark quandary over the question of how to bury a man who had been reduced to a greasy stain on the pavement after a direct hit by a piece of hot iron, 120 millimeter caliber, from the hills! Yes, yes, Bosnia is a theological inspiration as well, my friends. This is a theology of new elements and new definitions of death, the grave, the funeral. Some theologians already promise volume upon volume of learned answers. . . . It is said in a certain Islamic tradition that the dear God holds the human heart between his two fingers. When one strolls along the streets of Paris, New York, and Munich, one would do well to believe this, because in Bosnia, my friends, it is quite easy to believe. When you see so many places where molten rain falls down from the hills and you still stretch out in one piece in your skin, then you do know that the paths of the Lord are inscrutable. And you understand that Bosnia, the land of inexhaustible inspiration, is held in the palm of His hand.[3]

Both in its conception and the range of information it makes available, *Why Bosnia?* is the most accessible starting point for exploring the details and implications that lie in wait between the lines of Roy Gutman's eyewitness accounts. In "The Albanians of Kosovo: Self Determination Through Nonviolence," for example, Shkelzen Maliqi goes to the root of Serbia's move toward extreme nationalism and fascism. In "Separating History from Myth," an extensive interview done by the editors with the historian Ivo Banac, we are given acute political analysis tempered by a profound and deeply embedded sense of historical perspective. In a different vein, Thomas Harrison points to the relationship between policies on Bosnia "and the new Administration's systematic abandonment of the 'pro-democracy' foreign policy promised by Clinton during the electoral campaign—as seen in its reversals on Haiti and China."[4] Implied in these policy discussions are issues closer to home, closer to what Slavoj Žižek has brilliantly described as "postmodern" racism, a climate in which "Apartheid is legitimized as the ultimate form of anti-racism, as an endeavor to prevent racial tensions and conflicts."[5] Žižek goes on to say that:

In former Yugoslavia, we are lost not because of our primitive dreams and myths preventing us from speaking the enlightened language of Europe, but because we pay in flesh the price for being the stuff the Other's dreams are made of. . . . Far from being the Other of Europe, former Yugoslavia was rather Europe itself in its Otherness, the screen onto which Europe projected its own repressed reverse. . . . Against today's journalistic commonplace about the Balkans as the madhouse of thriving nationalisms where rational rules of behavior are suspended, one must point out again and again that the moves of every political agent in former Yugoslavia, reprehensible as they may be, are totally rational within the goals they want to attain—the only exception, the only truly irrational factor in it, is the gaze of the West, babbling about archaic ethnic passions." (238–39)[6]

We would do well to take heed of this gaze, as it bears down upon us too. *Why Bosnia?* and *A Witness to Genocide* are both essential sources, as well as excellent places to find at least some shelter, sustenance, and ammunition as the salvos defining the coming millennium, long since fired, find ever more victims.

1994

European Ghosts, Bosnian Corpses

Today it is difficult to say what is historically true and what is mythical about the Battle of Kosovo. But today it doesn't really matter.

SLOBODAN MILOŠEVIĆ, June 28, 1989

Sarajevo, Exodus of a City, by Dževad Karahasan. Translated by Slobodan Drakulić. New York: Kodansha, 1994.

Ex Tenebris: Sarajevski dnevnik, by Ivan Lourenović. Zagreb: AGM, 1994.

Cijena Bosna, by Ivo Banac. Zagreb: Europa Daras, 1994. Bosnia: A Short History, by Noel Makolm. New York University Press, 1994.

Slaughterhouse: Bosnia and the Failure of the West, by David Rieff. New York: Simon and Schuster, 1995.

Twilight of the Idols, by Aleš Debeljak. Translated by Michael Biggin. Fredonia, New York: White Pine Press, 1994.

At the end of *The Thousand and One Nights: Sarajevo Stories,* a collection of short texts by Sarajevans and visitors there is a calendar that begins on April 4, 1992, and ends on January 1, 1995. Sarajevans came to think of this date, a thousand and one days after the attack on Sarajevo began, as the day the siege would end. Like in *The Arabian Nights* (when Shaharazad kept herself alive by telling stories), the Bosnians, having all but given up telling the world its stories, continued telling stories to themselves, as a way of staying alive. The crowning irony is that even this fantastic tale of one thousand and one days has been usurped by the Serbs in the form of a "cease-fire" signed on the thousandth day of what—to begin with—wasn't a war but a slaughter.

As Bosnians endure a third winter under siege by Serbian fascists and Christian fundamentalists diligently carrying out genocide by fire and diplomacy, the truth of Milošević's words is undeniable. The urgency that Bosnia supposedly represented to a "concerned" world as little as a year ago has been transformed, strangely deflated, as if Bosnia and what it stands for truly *doesn't* matter any more. What is allowed to matter now is the "war," and the Serbs have dictated all of its terms. The Serbs have dictated these terms not, as too many otherwise able minded people have come to think, because they pulled the collective wool over the eyes of well-intentioned Western politicians, but because they understand only too well the interests of those very politicians. So many truisms have come to be accepted by now that references to actual history and its consequences seem like wild deviations from the script.

In the face of such events, the assertion of Dževad Karahasan—novelist, playwright, and former dean of the Academy of Theatrical Arts at the University of Sarajevo, now living in exile in Austria—that a certain kind of literature is responsible for the destruction of his country might seem far-fetched. In "Literature and War," he writes: "It is responsible indirectly, by transgressing against the fundamental rules of its craft and its integrity, and thus contributing—as much as it could, and that was a lot—to the spreading of general indifference in an indifferent world. For, let us not fool ourselves: the world is written first—the holy books say that it was created in words—and all that happens in it, happens in language first."[1]

With the growing list of books on Bosnia appearing in this country, Karahasan's haunting and eliptical *Sarajevo, Exodus of a City* is only one of a handful actually written by a Bosnian. Long overdue in translation, Karahasan's work includes the prescient *Of Language and Fear* (1987) in which he grappled with the djinn fighting their way out of various bottles in the collective postcommunist restructuring of Yugoslavia's past, and *Eastern Diwan* (1989) an ambitious and exquisitely wrought novel that reenacted a more distant but no less relevant past, that of early Islam. Despite an awkward translation that too often loses Karahasan's tone of subdued dignity, *Exodus of a City* is powerful not just for what it reveals to readers but for what it has revealed to and about its author. Realizing that former colleagues have become the enemy, Karahasan questions his own responsibility: "I am not interested in their personal guilt (God will surely judge them, and perhaps even honorable people before that), but in the culpability of my craft, the craft I cannot practice anymore, before answering some questions. We persistently avoid those questions, acting like Sleeping Beauties who dream about pure form, the beauty of the beyond and similar esoteric inventions, believing that we will never be awakened by a prince red with children's blood."[2] Being jolted out of the illusions of his former self becomes more than a metaphor as Karahasan realizes he has become exiled from a past he has no desire to return to.

This past is not only impossible to reconcile with the present, but even helped bring it about. He is also unable to return because he has become exiled from his city. It is this exile from what he loved most about Sarajevo that is so painful: the sustained interplay of inside and outside, whether in the movements between private and public space or in the rich passages from internal, personal allegiances to external identities in the form of diverse faiths, cultures, and commitments. Karahasan's Sarajevo had many such cosmopolitan passageways. Now, the city is almost entirely outside, so to speak, and its residents live only in a disastrous public sphere—forever exposed to danger.

The free interplay of inner and outer space that Karahasan describes so eloquently has proved, like his own openness toward those who would betray the city, to be Sarajevo's downfall. Discussing the "right to a view" so characteristic of Sarajevo's architecture, where the gradation of every street and house allowed people to see some of the city's panorama, Ivan Lovrenović writes: "When the army of the former Yugoslavia stationed itself all around the city, stockpiling shells, digging heavy artillery in and setting up machine gun and sniper nests, and when the Serbs started using all these murderous means on a daily basis, for the first time in half a millenium, Sarajevo unveiled its beauty only to find that beauty to be a punishment and a nightmare. This is a city that is impossible to defend. It is its own fatal trap."[3]

Lovrenović, another Bosnian now in exile in Croatia, has not seen his work translated into English; editor of *Svjetlost,* one of Europe's best publishing houses before the war, Lovrenović is also a poet, novelist, and essayist. His uncompromising work seems almost antithetical to what generally passes for "informed" intellectual discourse in North America: fiercely local, his erudition goes to the deepest roots of language's connection to place while conveying the sense that no culture is "foreign." Lovrenović's political intelligence and acute historical readings of human motivation make him less concerned with the role of the outside world. Once an open city containing many worlds, Sarajevo now has to recognize another place that never loomed so large before the siege, a place defined as "the outside world." Lovrenović, for one, doesn't think too highly of it:

> Moral accommodation—this is the mark of modern Europe and the world, perhaps the highest achievement (why not even the goal?) of technologically conceived western consumer civilization at the end of the 20th c., going into the 21st. When you think, even in a quick panoramic scan, of what Europe has gone through in only the last 2000 years, or even the last 200 years—from the guillotines of Paris, the French-Austrian-German-Russian-Turkish slaughter, bloody revolutions, world wars, Hitlerism and Stalinism, Auschwitz and the Gulag—then you see that it's only now, in the last couple of years, that she's had a historical second to doze off a bit, to take a breather from these awful goings on and the even more awful need to be *morally awake*. What a terrible strain—to remain morally alert, to always have your uneasy conscience plugged in! So just as Europe finally succumbed to sweet indulgence, to the idyl of prosperity and affluence, the fairy-tale of democracy—boom: the Balkan slaughterhouse! You can just imagine how much they hate us in European parliaments—each and every one of them, and all of them together (no kidding). Irretrievably, mercilessly, with wanton irresponsibility, their whole dream has been ruined . . . Let me go further, to the verge of what is bearable, and ask: isn't there perhaps in this hatred just a nuance more rage vented on the victims than the murderers (even without taking into account the fact that everyone knows precisely who is who)! I mean, what the hell did you have to get us into all this for anyways? And once you started, why weren't your reflexes on the alert, the reflexes of potential victims, instead of naively and sheepishly peeking your half-wailing half- accusing gaze over here at us, at a world that's gotten out of the

throat-cutting business. . . . And besides, what the hell do we need this whole bloody, morbid circus for anyways? War criminals, victims, mass graves, camps, hunger, sickness, rivers of people carrying things, hysterical children. . . . What's in it for us if we identify with the victims and try the murderers?[4]

One senses that this raging noise of too-real metaphors—idylls of prosperity and slaughterhouses, whole dreams, victims and murderers—is a trap in which everything has to stand for something else in order to be recognized as having universal significance. The Serbs' offensive has to be a rerun of Kosovo, Bosnian Muslims have to be fundamentalists, the UN has to be the outside world, murderers must be irrational, or not. Anything which cannot fit into this rationalizing semantic scheme, this displaced warfare, becomes *merely* Bosnian, or merely Balkan. Lovrenović wants to flee this universalist trap, screaming; to claim the local without being buried in it; to fight on the home front.

These concerns, particularly in historical terms, also characterize the essential work of Ivo Banac. Like Lovrenović, Banac is Croatian; both have worked to reimagine and rewrite a Croatian history whose only version most people know is the one filtered through Yugoslav communism. This history is inseparable from Bosnia, just as is the awareness (so clear in Karahasan) that the use of language has consequences. A prominent voice of opposition to the Croatian nationalist regime of Franjo Tudjman, Banac—now a history professor at Yale—has been particularly vocal over Bosnia. *The Price of Bosnia* collects articles, interviews, and public statements from 1992 and 1993. Well aware that he is stepping through a minefield of contested "truths," Banac does not mince words. When even some Bosnians have questioned "independence," he comments: "The war began because Milošević's Serbia wanted to take over those parts of Croatia and Bosnia-Hercegovina that "Greater Serbs" assumed to be part of the Serbian national space. This is the actual and fundamental cause of the war. Actually, when the European community recognized Croatia, Serbia had already captured and occupied a third of its territory. Those opposing recognition would probably agree with most of this but then claim that the recognition of Bosnia-Hercegovina made the conflict inevitable. If by this they mean that Serbia was uncompromising in not accepting Bosnia's independence, they would be entirely correct. But isn't this simply blaming the victim? Why was she walking through the park at night? If she had stayed home, they wouldn't have raped her. If Izetbegović had surrendered to Milošević and given his consent for Bosnia-Hercegovina to remain in a rump Yugoslavia under Serb domination, none of this would have happened. Bosnia's "sin" is its "unreasonable" wish to be free and independent."[5] In this light, Banac's investigations into the ways history has been manipulated in ex-Yugoslavia are keys to grasping the present situation; the precision of his method, always politically informed, has been emulated by too few historians of the region.

Nevertheless, despite the compression of events and the reigning misconceptions about the "Balkans," Noel Malcolm has managed to write a superb primer, *Bosnia: A Short History.* Although Malcolm has a tendency to sum up complex events and processes with a little too much certainty, it is a risk he takes in order to convey a cohesive and highly inclusive narrative, one that at least tries to take into account differing versions of key events. Regarding the "historical truths" and "myths" of the Battle of Kosovo in 1389, for instance, we learn that the Bosnians and Serbs were actually *allies* against the invading Ottomans. Regarding the status of Orthodox Serbs under Ottoman rule, we learn that: "In terms of Church organization, the Serbian Orthodox Church remains virtually invisible on the territory of modern Bosnia proper in the pre-Ottoman period. After the arrival of the Turks, however, the picture begins to change quite rapidly. From the 1480s onwards, Orthodox priests and believers are mentioned in many parts of Bosnia where they were never mentioned before. . . . Although the Orthodox suffered a fair share of indignities and oppressions, it is no exaggeration to say that the Orthodox Church was favored by the Ottoman regime."[6] While Malcolm's premodern sections sometimes suffer from an infusion of nation-state assumptions, his synthesis of sources and events is masterful.

In the modern period, Malcolm is highly sensitive to some of the issues that, in retrospect, are most important. Speaking of the revival of Serb nationalism in the 1980s, for example, he refers back to Tito's Yugoslavia and party stranglehold on versions of the World War II and its aftermath: "The regime would have reason to regret its long-lasting suppression of objective historical studies of the war."[7] Cutting through the usual mumbo-jumbo about Islamic fundamentalism, he notes that one of the primary charges against Bosnia's current president, Alija Izetbegović, in his 1983 trial (he and twelve others were accused of "hostile and counter-revolutionary acts derived from Muslim nationalism"), concerned Izetbegović's unequivocal support of "Western-style parliamentary democracy."[8] Malcolm concisely presents facts that remain astonishing. When he states that "the federal army and its paramilitary adjuncts carved out within the first five to six weeks an area of conquest covering more than 60 per cent of the entire Bosnian territory";[9] we realize that the war has been at a virtual standstill ever since, despite the obscene imbalance of power. Yet, he occasionally falls into the trap of thinking that the "paralysis" of the West was not self-induced but came about through some lack of understanding.

This same fault runs through sections of David Rieff's long-awaited *Slaughterhouse: Bosnia and the Failure of the West,* but much more deeply. The title itself assumes an enormous amount: what precisely, for example is the West? And if it has failed now, when did it last succeed? Such a fault is odd given that Rieff's indictment, not only of the United Nations but of the political policies that made it act the way it did, is complete and quite damning. In fact, it is the most consistent and detailed account of the utter bankruptcy of these policies yet to appear in this country. Thus, it seems bizarre when he writes, for example: "What the Serbs wanted was victory. That was what the United Nations and the European Community, Vance and Owen, and the rest could never face up to. It is an old problem besetting liberals faced by totalitarians, this inability to believe that what the murderers said to their domestic audiences reflected what they planned to do better than what they said around the conference table."[10] This almost contradicts Rieff's earlier position that Bosnia-Hercegovina, "a state formally recognized by the European Community and the United States on April 7, 1992, and by the United Nations on May 22, 1992, was allowed to be destroyed. . . . And this was not, as so many pretended, the result of some grim, ineluctible law of history, but rather a testimony to specific choices made by those who governed the rich world and by the civil servants who administered the international system that they had created."[11] Vance and Owen may be liberal dupes or realpolitik schemers but, at Rieff's chosen level of generalization, they can't be both.

As one of the faithful, someone who kept going back to what Sarajevans had come to call a "safari" to the "zoo," Rieff has to face the issue of voyeurism. His narrative voice in *Slaughterhouse* blends the informed visitor, the less-informed visitor coming of age, the comrade showing solidarity, and the foreign affairs expert. One would hope this mélange is a strategy designed to deflect some readers and invite others rather than a sign of confusion. Nevertheless, the question of precisely whom this book is addressed to remains crucial. Given Rieff's media prominence on Bosnia, there is little doubt that—despite his insistence that Bosnia is a lost cause—the book is still an attempt to testify to a certain truth. In effect, Rieff allies himself at the beginning of the book to the hopes and naïveté of Bosnians who believed themselves European, part of the "civilized" world, while at the end he laments: "What is certain is that a lot of dreams have died in Bosnia during the past two and a half years; the dream that the world has a conscience; the dream that Europe is a civilized place; the dream that there is justice for the weak as well as the strong."[12]

These are precisely some of the illusions that Karahasan, for example, watches explode within and outside of himself. On the other hand, they are illusions that Ivan Lovrenović, Ivo Banac, and others never subscribed to in the first place. In his all too brief *Twilight of the Idols,* the Slovenian poet Aleš Debeljak manages to maintain the latter group's political alertness while still identifying his losses: not of conscience, justice or unified Yugoslavia but of the interplay of specific cultures and peoples he grew up with. When he writes that "we will have to learn to live with new values and ideals in the coming century, for our century died in Sarajevo,"[13] his tone may be distinguished from Rieff's. Debeljak's irony is couched in the fact that he now lives in another country, even though his physical residence remains the same. This country is a place where the rock "singers and poets" whose names "remained unpronounceable anywhere in Western Europe" but who "embodied the flickering light in a tunnel of political obscurantism for an entire generation, can no longer listen to each other."[14] These shattered dreams have nothing to do with the "great" issues but with the unyielding facts and pain of local life and knowledge. Debeljak escapes the trap of universalizing rationality, where war is displaced into language, because poetry and the country he loves can only survive outside that trap.

Which brings up a major but seldom discussed issue. It would be naive not to think that the kind of human and political motives that put Bosnia where it is today are not also at work elsewhere. Take publishing, for example. *Slaughterhouse,* with the machinery of a major publisher behind it, must be set in relief against many of the other books on Bosnia, some published by small presses or universities, others not even translated. This is not to deny the power or possible use of a book like Rieff's but simply to present a context for examining the hierarchies that exist here, among ourselves and in our language. Who gets to speak, and for how long? On whom do we rely for accurate local knowledge? If we insist on everything signifying something else—Bosnia as a metaphor for the failure of the West—we will never gauge the true implications of the slaughter. As Karadžić and Milošević gleefully prepare themselves to become visiting dignitaries in Washington, these do not seem like idle issues. Shattered dreams alone and the placement of Bosnia as a footnote to universal history will simply not suffice.

1995

For/Za Sarajevo

In the name of God, the Compassionate, the Merciful, I call upon as witness the ink and the pen, and that which the pen inscribes; I call upon as witness the uncertain darkness of twilight, and the night and everything it brings to life; I call upon as witness the waning moon and the whitening sun; I call upon as witness the Day of Judgement, and the soul that chastises only itself; I call upon as witness Time, the beginning and the end of everything—that every person is always at a loss.

The Quran

I begin this, my story, for naught—with no benefit to myself nor to others, from a need that is stronger than profit or reason, that my record remain, written in anguished colloquy with myself, with the faint hope that someone will find a solution when the accounts are settled, if ever, when I leave a trail of ink on this paper that lies in wait for me like a challenge. I don't know what will be written, but something of what transpired within me will remain in the hooks of the letters, for it will no longer fade in the billowing fog, as if it had never been, or as I no longer know what was. This way, I will be able to see myself as I am, that stranger I do not even know, yet it seems stranger still to me that I haven't always been what I am now. I am aware that my writing is entangled, my hand shakes because of the disentangling that awaits me, because of the trial that I am beginning, a trial at which I am everything, judge, witness, and defendant. I will be as honest as I can, as anyone can, since I am beginning to doubt that sincerity and honesty are the same, sincerity being the belief that we speak the truth (and who can be convinced of that?), and of honesty there is plenty, and they do not sit well among themselves.

My name is Ahmed Nuruddin; it was given to me and I took it as offered, with pride, and now I think of it, after a long sequence of years that grew on me like skin, with amazement and sometimes even mockery, for the light of faith sheds arrogance that I didn't yet feel, though now I am somewhat ashamed of it. How am I a light?

By what am I illuminated? Knowledge? Higher morals? A pure
heart? The true path? Certainty? Everything comes into question,
and now I am only Ahmed, neither sheikh nor Nuruddin.
Everything falls from me, like a skirt, like an armor, and what
remains is that which was before: a naked skin and a naked man.

Meša Selimović, *Death and the Dervish*[1]

Like the prayer that precedes Selimović's astonishing work, his
words make the primordial and implicit distinctions between things that
turn chaos into structure, even if that structure can never be quantified:
names and what they are not, the act of testimony and its twists through
time and the imprint of other eyes, the powers of inscription and its
attendant risks. These risks included being left open (as letters are) to
breaks in its transmission, left waiting to be read defiantly (against the
grain), or worse, simply being forgotten. The novel was written as an
allegory of the circumstances surrounding the death of his brother in
Tito's Yugoslavia; but the horrors of another war demand that we take
up the burdens of transmission, that we reread this work and place it in
Bosnia, for Sarajevo, the truest capital, in the present, of a residence, a
steadfastness that cuts to the bloody bone of any world that can proceed
from here on in.

Such an unfashionable word as *residence,* with all it implies (and
which could just as well be rendered as *presence*), also cuts to the bone
of many of the debates that often seem so frivolous and removed from
the concrete effects of representation and violence: the rights to land
and bread, neighborhoods and villages, vaccinations and literacy, control over what the earth and the mines and the hands and the minds and
tired upright backs produce. In "The Race for Theory," Barbara Christian
writes:

> Now I am being told that philosophers are the ones who write lit-
> erature, the authors are dead, irrelevant, mere vessels through
> which their narratives ooze, that they do not work nor have the
> faintest idea what they are doing; rather they produce texts as dis-
> embodied as angels. . . . I can only speak for myself. But what I
> write and how I write is done in order to save my own life. And I
> mean that literally. For me literature is a way of knowing that I am
> not hallucinating, that whatever I feel/know is. It is an affirmation

that sensuality is intelligence, that sensual language is language
that makes sense.[2]

Although we do not presume to speak for anyone, least of all citizens under siege, we can bring information to bear upon a place that finds itself, as one citizen of Sarajevo writes, in an "information quarantine," cut off from any contact with the outside world. In an age obsessed with news "coverage" (sometimes with good reason), we must combat the tyranny of choice representatives, of a new ghetto that leaves the structures of dominance in place while fighting tooth and nail to get in for a sound bite. The disparate voices gathered here—and there are voices behind these texts, disembodied as some of them might be—infect each other with antibodies emerging from deep within the pool of unfulfilled desires, relentlessly to combat the media's global reach, to categorize and colonize our very memories. As Fanon put it so cogently:

> Colonialism is not satisfied merely with holding a people in its grip and emptying the native's brain of all form and content. By a kind of perverted logic, it turns to the past of the oppressed people, and distorts, disfigures and destroys it.[3]

Nor do we intend, in this gathering, to erect monuments to an idealized past, to seek solace in times that might seem better than these, as tempting as that often is. Rather, we would join in an exhilarating chorus to pump up the volume of the late Audre Lord's courageous lines: "When you impale me / upon your lances of narrow blackness / before you hear my heart speak / mourn your own borrowed blood / your own borrowed visions . . . for we are all children of Eshu / god of chance and the unpredictable / and we each wear many changes / inside of our skin . . . if we do not stop killing / the other / in ourselves / the self that we hate / in others / soon we shall all lie / in the same direction . . ."[4] Blackness, in this case, like any people's source of power, is not at issue here, but just the straight and narrow of it.

As the grappling over versions and events fervently continues, we must at least record the changing qualities of lives, relationships, and peoples—with the sensitivity of a seismograph—to disrupt patterns of thought, imagery, and action that simplify and obliterate the complexities and possibilities of pasts and presents as they are being made into memories of our future. The works woven together here span an enormous range and intensity of sensual knowledge, knowledge and sense, the keys to release those memories from their chambers. Each piece adumbrates the resounding pain and clarity of letters from hell, the accounts of ethnic cleansing, the scenes envisioned and lived before the conflagration in the former Yugoslavia.

With good faith but more than a minor sense of misgiving at the betrayals involved in speaking from such a distance, this is, finally, a message in a bottle. The more obvious course it can take is toward there, away from us, but the assumptions involved in such a journey do, indeed, border on sheer arrogance. In the case of Sarajevo, the equation can never be so simple; for like any place steeped in the banal details of its inherited wisdom, the city and its citizens have always held the new-fangled and the imported at bay through a variety of smokescreens and subterfuges. As the Bosnian writer Aleksandar Hemon writes: "There is always time, you just have to know how to lose it. A true *haji* knows that life is not determined by the amount of time, just as wealth is not determined by the amount of money. Life is laid out in quickly passing moments, so there has to be time for each moment. . . . Everyone in Sarajevo is well aware that, despite everything, there's no help to be had, that history's whore will come for its own, that it will carry some mortal disease, that once a bullet will strike from some hob-nailed boor just down off the mountain. . . . But at least they'll know that they lost their own time, of their own free will and fully conscious. . . ."[5]

In at least a gesture of solidarity, we should remember that our time is only ours to lose.

1993

"All the time in the world . . ."

I find that I have less and less to say about anything these days so I do more and more translating, to at least let others be heard. Ceding one's voice, giving up authority, is also very much a part of living in the city, a place where others can be a conduit through which parts of yourself are expressed, just as buildings and our use of them internalize their diverse histories, styles, and statements about our relationship to space and time. Partly because I know the language, and read the press in Bosnian, Croatian, and Serbian, because I have friends who are there and friends from there who are here, I can say that I am somewhat informed, that, actually, I might have a better idea of what is going on there than many who have gone to visit and even report or write books about their experiences. This kind of knowledge is barely comprehensible here, and occasionally even considered superfluous or an obstacle to the packaging of personalities, the simulation of the real that touring or voyeurism can claim as personal narrative, as the eyewitness learning as they go, learning more about what they didn't know, as they go. This naïveté, this ahistorical and uninformed voice has characterized much of the discourse about Bosnia in this country.

At the risk of appearing to be on the wrong side of a debate, of a struggle that is now taking place in Bosnia-Hercegovina—as it inevitably had to—I would begin from a very different premise than is usually invoked. At the risk of lapsing into a reliance on the very essences that I have spent so much energy fighting against, I would say that the creation of the independent state of Bosnia-Hercegovina as a multiethnic, multinational, secular democratic country with a clearly Muslim president, in the person of the former political prisoner Alijia Izetbegović, presented a grave threat—as absurd as this may sound—to Western Europe, Russia, and many Arab states. This is why the media has consistently turned the Bosnians into Muslims, why the army of Bosnia-Hercegovina is referred to as the Muslim-led army while nowhere do we hear of the Milošević regime as a Christian fundamentalist regime or the army of Karadžić as a Christian led army. Such concerns may seem out of place when the issue is fascism but fascism and purity go hand in hand and I am convinced that while the French are prepared to award the Prix Goncourt to a Moroccan writer like Tahar Ben Jelloun, they are clearly unprepared to allow Tahar Ben Jelloun's daughter or son to become the prime minister of France. Although the English may be prepared to protect Salman Rushdie, they are also quite unprepared to allow the son or daughter of a Jamaican or Pakistani immigrant to rule their government. European countries are fundamentally Christian, that is, when push comes to shove, they can also be considered Christian fundamentalists whose history of intolerance and inquisitions is a model for modernity and the technological methods of killing and control perfected in the twentieth century. When we speak, for instance, of the civilization of Andalusia, of the millennial presence of Islamic and Jewish culture in Europe, we do not speak of European Muslims and European Jews: they remain a category apart, ethnically cleansed from the imperial curriculum. Like the assault on Bosnia's unequivocally mixed and symbiotic culture, even the historical presence of such examples represent a retreat to people afraid of giving up control of their very shadows to the sun. After the *fatwa* was issued against Salman Rushdie, otherwise reasonable and politically correct postcolonial people invoked Voltaire as a voice of enlightenment. Yet Voltaire's dying thought was to cleanse Europe of the Turks: "It is not enough to humiliate them," he said, "they should be destroyed. Beat the Turks and I will die content."[1]

Although friends in the Middle East find much of this self-evident, I have never encountered anyone here that speaks of such issues. As far as Arab regimes are concerned, we should not forget that progressive movements have been ruthlessly suppressed since the turn of the century, either by colonial powers, through the interests of local rule, or both. We should not forget that many social reformers including Muslim brothers, feminists, socialists, communists, democrats, and artists still rot in the cells of Morocco, Egypt, Iraq, Kuwait, Saudi Arabia, and many other countries. In the eyes of such regimes, the independent state of Bosnia-Hercegovina would not represent, by any means, a good example to such prisoners of hope, nor to the people in whose name such prisoners forfeited their freedom. The PLO itself, in collusion with Israel, has now turned itself into a classically repressive modern Middle Eastern regime: Palestinian leftists share cells with Muslim brothers. It would bring a smile of recognition on the face of Sadat. Nor, for that matter, should we forget that Israel, a tacit and sometimes not so tacit supporter of the Milošević regime, is absolutely unprepared to have someone named Muhammad or Leyla—citizen or not—rule the Jewish state.

So the question of Sarajevo, like the fall of Granada that signified a new world order in which East became East and West became West without the twain ever meeting, is not by any means a simple question having to do with the purported betrayal of some mythical European civilizational values that never existed in the first place. It is, rather, part of a new crusade of power and purity in which Saudi and Gulf money generated by gas-guzzling Americans and Europeans is invested in the bastardization of Islam in order to foment unrest based on very real popular economic and political disenfranchisement; this, in turn, justifies continuing Western support of these repressive regimes. A Bosnia-Hercegovina ruled by the mullahs would be more than a self-fulfilling prophecy fueled by the West, it would be a perfect, even, I daresay, a happy ending for Europeans, Russians, and even Americans only too ready to materialize their racist assumptions. Such a state could be even more isolated, scorned, and controlled than it is now, under siege. Oil or not, a way could always be found to provide assistance to a government willing to repress its own population, a population hell-bent, apparently to the point of suicide, on celebrating their impurity, their stubborn unwillingness to divorce their spouses and disown their half-, quarter- and eighth-breed offspring. We are nowhere near this state of wild abandon, of common life and love that knows no bounds. But the future is ahead of us, we have all the time in the world.   1995

Notes

Local Politics: The Background as Foreword

1. Aleš Debeljak, *Reluctant Modernity* (Lanham, Maryland: Rowman and Littlefield, 1998; p. x.
2. Jack Spicer, from "After Lorca" in *The Collected Books of Jack Spicer,* edited by Robin Blaser (Los Angeles: Black Sparrow, 1975), p. 25.
3. Adonis, *An Introduction to Arab Poetics,* translated by Catherine Cobham (London: Saqi Books, 1990); pp. 73, 82, 97.

Preludes: An Opening

"weighing the losses, like stones in your hand"

1. Quotation from Min Sun Min, a Burmese writer and student leader who gained asylum in the United States; from "Burmese Rebel Recalls Days of Violence," by Chris Hedges; *New York Times;* August 9, 1990; p. B4, column 3.
2. The photograph described appears as number 3 in the series of photos between pages 164 and 165 of *Freedom From Fear and Other Writings* by Aung San Suu Kyi (New York: Penguin, 1991); the text is from p. 3.
3. Robert Frank, 1993; it appeared as a text in his exhibit at the Whitney Museum in 1996.
4. *The Compact Edition of the Oxford English Dictionary* (Oxford University Press, 1971); p. 772.
5. Ibn al-Athir; in Francesco Gabrieli's *Arab Historians of the Crusades* (New York: Dorset Press, 1989); pp. 182–83.
6. *The Aeneid of Virgil;* Book IV, 182–86; translation by Allen Mandelbaum (New York: Bantam, 1972), pp. 85–86.
7. Mahmoud Darwish; *Memory for Forgetfulness: August, Beirut, 1982* (Berkeley: University of California, 1995); translated by Ibrahim Muhawi; this is a collage of quotes from pp. 47–48 and 14–15.
8. Ibid., pp. 87–9.
9. Aïcha Ben Abed Ben Khader and David Soren, *Carthage: A Mosaic of Ancient Tunisia* (New York: The American Museum of Natural History and W. W. Norton, 1987); pp. 41–42.
10. As above; p.108.
11. For a synopsis of these sources, see John Maxwell O'Brien, *Alexander the Great: The Invisible Enemy* (New York: Routledge, 1994); pp. 82–97.
12. M. Beer, *The General History of Socialism and Social Struggles* (New York: Russell and Russell, 1957); Vol. One, p. 135.
13. Ibid., p. 136.
14. Ibid., p. 117.
15. Jayce Salloum; among texts displayed in "Kan Ya Ma Kan / There Was and There Was Not," an exhibit at American Fine Arts in New York from June 20 to July 13, 1996.

16. *The Random House Children's Encyclopedia* (New York: Random House, 1991); pp. 412 and 25.

17. This text, known as The Carthage Tariff, is one of many of fragments found in Carthage over a number of years beginning in 1858; in *The Ancient Near East: An Anthology of Texts and Pictures,* edited by James B. Pritchard (Princeton University Press, 1958), pp. 223–4.

18. A fragment from Isidorus the Gnostic, first and second century A.D.; it appears in G. S. Kirk and J. E. Raven, *The Presocratic Philosophers* (Cambridge: Cambridge University Press, 1957); p. 62.

19. *The Aeneid of Virgil* (New York: Bantam, 1972); translation by Allen Mandelbaum; Book I, 798–800; p. 20.

Of Books and Cities / The Journey

My Mediterranean

1. This excerpt from Yitzhak Gormezano Goren's as yet untranslated novel *An Alexandrian Summer* (Tel Aviv: 'Am 'Oved, 1979), appears in my translation in *Keys to the Garden* (San Francisco: City Lights, 1996), p. 169.

2. George Seferis, *Poems,* translated from Greek by Rex Warner (Boston: Little, Brown, 1964), p. 83.

3. Assia Djebar, "A Forbidden Glimpse, a Broken Sound," in *Women and Family in the Middle East,* edited by Elizabeth Warnock Fernea and translated from French by J. M. McDougal (Austin: University of Texas, 1985), p. 350.

4. Mahmoud Darwish, "When the Martyrs Go to Sleep, in *Modern Poetry of the Arab World,* edited and translated by Abdullah al-Udhari (Hammondsworth: Penguin, 1986), p. 139.

The Quill's Embroidery: Untangling a Tradition

1. Shem Tov Ardutiel, from Sanford Shepard's *Shem Tov: His World and His Words* (Ediciones Universal: Miami, 1978), p. 84.

2. From "Theodosia" and Section XII of "Armenia," in Osip Mandelstam, *Selected Poems,* translated by David McDuff (New York: Farrar, Strauss and Giroux, 1975), pp. 61, 109.

3. *Ethical Writings of Maimonides,* edited by Raymond L. Weiss with Charles E. Butterworth (New York: Dover, 1983), p. 62.

4. Elie Kedourie, "Mr. Memmi on Jewishness and the Jews," in *Arabic Political Memoirs and Other Studies* (London: Cass, 1974), p. 102.

5. S. D. Goitein, *Studies in Islamic History and Institutions* (Leiden: Brill, 1966), pp. 246–47.

6. Shmuel Trigano, *La nouvelle question juive* (Paris: Gallimard, 1979), p. 208 [my translation].

7. See Maurice Blanchot's essays on Kafka in *The Sirens' Song,* edited by Gabriel Josipovici and translated from French by Sacha Rabinovitch (Bloomington: Indiana University, 1982), particularly "Kafka or the demands of literature," pp. 121–44.

8. *The Scorpion,* Albert Memmi, translated by Eleanor Levieux; Chicago: J. Philip O'Hara, 1971; pp. 97–98.

9. For more on this, see "Freedom, Language, and Negativity," in José Faur's *Golden Doves with Silver Dots: Semiotics and Textuality in Rabbinic Tradition* (Bloomington: Indiana University, 1986), pp. 59–83.

10. Susan A. Handelman, *The Slayers of Moses: The Emergence of Rabbinic Interpretation in Modern Literary Theory* (Albany: SUNY Press, 1982), pp. 37, 32.

11. The Rev. Benjamin Artom, *Sermons Preached in Several Synagogues* (London: Trubner and Co., 1873), pp. 136–37.

12. Edmond Jabès, *The Book of Questions: Return to the Book* (Vol. 3), translated by Rosemarie Waldrop (Middletown: Wesleyan University Press, 1972–1987), p. 145.

13. Jacques Derrida, *Writing and Difference,* translated by Alan Bass (University of Chicago Press, 1978), p. 9.

14. My translation from Hebrew appears in Haim Schirmann, *Hebrew Poetry in Spain and Provence* (Jerusalem: Bialik Institute, 1979) [Hebrew], vol. 2, p. 512.

15. Jacques Derrida, *Writing and Difference,* pp. 76–77.

16. *Babylonian Talmud,* Tractate Shabbat, 11a.

17. From "Providence: A Conversation with Edmond Jabès," in Paul Auster's *The Art of Hunger* (New York: Penguin, 1993), p. 161. The interview was conducted in French and translated by Auster; it appeared originally in *Montemora* 6, New York, 1979.

The Quill's Embroidery: Poetry, Tradition, and the "Postmodern"

1. Ammiel Alcalay, "The Quill's Embroidery," *Parnassus: Poetry in Review,* Vol. 11, No. 1, 1983; p. 102.

2. In R. Hayyim Raphael Shoshannah, *I Shall Arise at Dawn* (Beersheba, 1986) [Hebrew].

3. Foreword to *I Shall Arise at Dawn* (see note 2).

4. R. Hayyim Raphael Shoshannah, *I Shall Arise at Dawn,* p. 22. Vol. 1 [my translations from Hebrew].

Paris/New York/Jerusalem: The Unscheduled Flight of Edmond Jabès and Jacques Derrida

1. Stephen Jay Gould, *The Mismeasure of Man* (New York: Penguin, 1984), p. 16.

2. From *Bereshit Rabbah* (On Genesis) in *Midrash Rabbah,* Genesis, edited by H. Freeman and M. Simon, vol. 1 (London: Soncino, 1939).

3. Jacques Derrida, *Writing and Difference,* translated from French by Alan Bass (University of Chicago, 1978), pp. 76–77.

4. Jacques Derrida, *Margins of Philosophy,* translated by Alan Bass (University of Chicago, 1982), p. 271. The final quote is from the *Book of Exodus* 28, verses 15–19.

Perplexity Index: On Golden Gloves with Silver Dots

1. Unpublished paper by David Shasha.

2. José Faur, *Golden Doves with Silver Dots* (Bloomington: University of Indiana, 1986), p. 62.

3. James Joyce, *Finnegans Wake* (New York: Penguin, 1976). p. 103.

4. José Faur, *Golden Doves with Silver Dots*, p. 121.
5. Theodor Adorno, *Minima Moralia*, translated from German by E.F.N. Jephcott (London: Verso, 1978), p. 15.

Desert Solitaire: On Edmond Jabès

1. Edmond Jabès, *The Book of Margins*, translated from French by Rosemarie Waldrop (University of Chicago, 1993), p. 173.
2. Ibid., p. 171.
3. Ibid., p. 125.
4. Ibid., p. 43.
5. Edmond Jabès, *A Foreigner Carrying in the Crook of His Arm A Tiny Book*, translated from French by Rosemarie Waldrop (Hanover and London: Wesleyan University Press, 1993), P. 50.
6. Ibid., p. 9.
7. Ibid., p. 79.
8. Ibid., p. 68.
9. Edmond Jabès, *The Book of Margins*, p. 90.
10. Edmond Jabès, *A Foreigner Carrying in the Crook of His Arm A Tiny Book*, p. 111.

Behind the Scenes: Before After Jews and Arabs

1. William Carlos Williams, *Pictures from Breughel and other poems* (New York: New Directions, 1962), p. 120.
2. Mahmoud Darwish, *The Music of Human Flesh*, translated by Denys Johnson-Davies (London and Washington: Heinemann and Three Continents, 1980), p. 10.
3. Ammiel Alcalay, *After Jews and Arabs* (Minneapolis: University of Minnesota Press, 1993), p. 27.

Forbidden Territories, Promised Lands

On Arabesques

1. Yael Lotan's article first appeared in the Hebrew daily *al-Hamishmar*, July 4, 1986; it was later published in English by the Palestinian weekly *Al-Fajr*, August 14, 1986, p. 10, and also in *Modern Hebrew Literature*, Vol. 13, Nos. 1–2, Fall/Winter 1987, pp. 41–44.
2. Gilbert Sorrentino, "Language—Lying and Treacherous," in the *New York Times Book Review*, May 25, 1986, p. 23.
3. Jamal Eddine Ben Cheikh, "Ecriture et ideologie (la littérature algérienne horizon 2000)," in *Les Temps Modernes* (Paris: October, 1977), p. 377.

After the Last Sky

1. *After the Last Sky*, Edward W. Said, with photographs by Jean Mohr (London and Boston: Faber and Faber, 1986), p. 61.
2. Raja Shehadeh, *Samed: Journal of a West Bank Palestinian* (New York: Adama Books, 1984), p. 89.

3. *After the Last Sky,* pp. 146, 150.
4. Ibid., pp. 140–41.
5. *Samed: Journal of a West Bank Palestinian,* p. 64.

Who's Afraid of Mahmoud Darwish?

1. All of the material quoted here appeared in the Hebrew press in various forms during the weeks following publication of Darwish's poem. The most accessible source available referring to the controversy surrounding the poem can be found in *Palestine mon pays: l'affaire du poème,* edited by Simone Bitton (Paris: Editions de Minuit, 1988).
2. Mahmoud Darwish, "We Travel, Like Other People," in *Modern Poetry of the Arab World,* edited and translated by Abdullah al-Udhari (Hammondsworth: Penguin, 1986), p. 142.
3. *Deuteronomy* 7:1–3.
4. Jamal Eddine Ben Cheikh, "Ecriture et ideologie (la littérature algérienne horizon 2000)," in *Les Temps Modernes* (Paris: October, 1977), p. 377.

Israel and the Levant: "Wounded Kinship's Last Resort"

1. Ilan Halevi, *A History of the Jews,* translated from French by A. M. Berrett (London: Zed, 1987), p. 210.
2. Ibid., p. 210.
3. In *Keys to the Garden* (San Francisco: City Lights, 1996), p. 294; translated from Hebrew by Yaffa Berkovitz.
4. The phrase is actually Victor Zuckerkandl's and is quoted by Mackey in his "Sound and Sentiment, Sound and Symbol." It originally appears in Zuckerkandl's *Sound and Symbol: Music and the External World* (Princeton University Press, 1956), p. 371. The Mackey essay can be found in *The Politics of Poetic Form: Poetry and Public Policy,* edited by Charles Bernstein (New York: Roof Books, 1990).

Forbidden Territory, Promised Land

1. Ilan Halevi, *A History of the Jews,* p. 228.
2. Shlomo Swirski, *Israel: The Oriental Majority,* translated by Barbara Swirski (London: Zed, 1989), p. 49.
3. Ibid., p. 34.
4. Ibid., p. 53.
5. Ibid., p. 54–55.
6. Ella Shohat, *Israeli Cinema: East/West and the Politics of Representation* (Austin: University of Texas, 1989), p. 61.
7. *Israeli Cinema: East/West and the Politics of Representation,* pp. 272–73.

In True Colors

1. Kamal Boullata, *Faithful Witness,* p. 9.
2. Ibid, p. 42.
3. Ibid, p. 105.

The State of the Gulf

1. "Social Change in Munif's *Cities of Salt*," paper delivered by Issa Boullata at the Center for Contemporary Arab Studies, Georgetown University, March 22, 1991.
2. John Updike's piece, "Satan's Work and Silted Cisterns," appeared in the *New Yorker*, October 18, 1988, pp. 117–19.
3. Abdelrahman Munif, *Cities of Salt,* translated from Arabic by Peter Theroux (New York: Vintage, 1989), p. 1.
4. Ibid., p. 18.
5. Ibid., p. 31.
6. Ibid., p. 595.
7. Hanan al-Shaykh, *Women of Sand and Myrrh,* translated from Arabic by Catherine Cobham (New York: Anchor, 1992), p. 12.
8. Ibid., pp. 114–15.
9. Ibid., pp. 235–36.

Our Memory Has No Future

1. Etel Adnan, *Paris, When It's Naked* (Sausalito: Post-Apollo Press, 1993), pp. 7–8.
2. Ibid., p. 101.
3. Ibid., p. 59.
4. Etel Adnan, *Of Cities & Women (Letters to Fawwaz)* (Sausalito: Post-Apollo Press, 1993), p. 37.
5. Ibid., p. 22.
6. Ibid., p. 23.
7. Ibid., pp. 24, 26–27.
8. Ibid., p. 42.
9. Ibid., p. 56.
10. Ibid., p. 82.
11. Ibid., p. 112.

"The war was ending, the diasporas beginning"

1. Interview from Ferid Boudjedir's 1987 film *Camera Arabe.*
2. Juan Goytisolo, *Disidencias* (Barcelona: Seix Barral, 1978); pp. 308–9 [my translation].
3. Ibid., pp. 306–7 [my translation].
4. Ibid., pp. 316 [my translation].
5. Ibid., pp. 296 [my translation].
6. Wilson Harris, from "Profiles of Myth and the New World," in *Nationalism vs. Internationalism: (Inter)National Dimensions of Literatures in English*; Wolfgang Zach, Ken L. Goodwin, eds. (Sonderdruck: Stauffenberg Verlag); p. 85 [no date].
7. Jed Rasula, "Notes on Genre," in *The L=A=N=G=U=A=G=E Book,* edited by Bruce Andrews and Charles Berstein (Carbondale: Southern Illinois University, 1984), p. 103.
8. Wilson Harris, "Quetzalcoatl and the Smoking Mirror: Reflections on Originality & Tradition," *Review: Latin American Literature and Arts* 50 (Spring 1995), pp. 78, 80.

9. Juan Goytisolo; *Disidencias* (Barcelona: Seix Barral, 1978); pp. 316 [my translation].

10. Wilson Harris, "Quetzalcoatl," pp. 82–83.

11. Goytisolo, *Quarantine,* p. 83.

Dispatches

A Stitch in Time

1. For more on Antebbi, see my *After Jews and Arabs: Remaking Levantine Culture* (Minneapolis: University of Minnesota, 1993), pp. 52–55.
2. The interview with Vanunu appeared in *News from Within* (Vol. IV, No. 7, July 10, 1988, published by the Alternative Information Center in Jerusalem.
3. Moise Ventura, *Soupirs et espoirs: Echos de la Guerre 1939–1945* (Paris: Librairie Durlacher, 1948), pp. 76, 88; [my translation from French].
4. *Soupirs et espoirs: Echos de la Guerre 1939–1945,* p. 99.

Ushering in the New Order

1. On this phenomenon, see Robert I. Friedman's piece "War Now" in the *Village Voice,* February 26, 1991; pp. 27–29.
2. The quotes that follow appeared in a story by Einat Berkovitz in the Israeli daily *Hadashot,* February 2, 1991; pp. 6–7, [my translation from Hebrew].

Reflections at the End of 1992

1. John Burns followed the fate of the Džirlo family in dispatches from June 1992 until the end of the year; the story about Mirta Kamhi is from the *New York Times,* December 25, 1992; pp. A1 and A20.
2. From *Keys to the Garden* (San Francisco: City Lights, 1996), pp. 306–7, [my translation from Hebrew].

Why Israel?

1. Eliyahu Eliachar, *Life Is with the Palestinians* (Jerusalem: Council of the Sephardic Communities, 1975), pp. 277, 236; [my translation from Hebrew]. For more on Eliachar, see my *After Jews and Arabs,* pp. 10, 32, 40–42, 55, 212–13, 221.

The Return: Variations on a Theme

Understanding Revolution

1. Jean Genet, "Four Hours in Shatila," *Red Bass* 12, p. 52.
2. Nazim Hikmet, *Selected Poetry.* New York: Persea, 1986, p. 97.
3. From *War Generation: Beirut,* a film by Mai Masri and Jean Chamoun, 1988.
4. Jean Genet, *Red Bass* 12, p. 52.
5. Charles Bernstein, "The Dollar Value of Poetry," in *The L=A=N=G=U=A=G=E Book,* edited by Bruce Andrews and Charles Bernstein, (Carbondale: Southern Illinois University Press, 1984), p. 139.
6. Bernard Noel, "The Outrage Against Words," as above, p. 190.

7. Local news opinion poll on Noriega and the invasion of Panama.

8. Jerry Estrin, *in motion speaking* (San Francisco: Chance Editions, 1986), p. 49.

9. From Ghassan Kanafani's "The Land of Sad Oranges" in *Men in the Sun* (London: Heinemann, 1982), p. 61.

10. A letter from prison reprinted in *News from Within* (Vol. III, Nos. 11–12; September 10, 1987), an invaluable source of information on Israel / Palestine published by the Alternative Information Center; POB 24278 / Jerusalem, Israel. The director of the center, Michael Warschawski, then faced a twenty-month prison term for providing printing services (a handbook on how to resist arrest) to a "hostile organization." In a mission for PEN, Allen Ginsberg collected information on Warschawski (an Israeli Jew residing and working in West Jerusalem) along with cases of Palestinian journalists from the occupied territories. Attempts to make strong statements on these matters were either significantly qualified or fully suppressed by a faction in PEN led by Cynthia Ozick.

11. From "Vanunu's Abduction," *Sunday Times* (London), August 9, 1987.

12. Prison from Mordekhai Vanunu to his brother Meir; *News from Within* (Vol. III, Nos. 5–6; March 31, 1987). Meir Vanunu, by leading an international campaign on behalf of his imprisoned brother (including a petition signed by twenty-seven Nobel Prize winners), also faces imprisonment should he return to Israel.

13. These quotes are from a taped interview with Mordekhai Vanunu done in the context of a project I headed from 1985 to 1986 on the political attitudes of Jews from Arab countries. Very little appeared on this project in the English or Hebrew press although considerable attention was paid to it in French and Arabic; the study itself appeared in *Perspectives Judeo-Arabes* (no. 7, August 1987). The full interview with Vanunu appeared in my English translation in *News from Within* (Vol. IV, No. 7; July, 10, 1988). For more current information on Vanunu, contact U.S. Campaign to Free Mordekhai Vanunu; 2006 Fox Avenue, Madison, WI 53711; phone/fax (608) 257-4764.

14. Saida Hamad, from "Minors Tell Stories of Torture while in Detention," in *Al-Fajr*, an English language Palestinian weekly (Vol. VIII, No. 382; September 13, 1987).

15. The information on Naila Ayesh's case was culled from a number of sources: "Woman Miscarries During Interrogation," by Dina Lawrence and Kameel Nasr, in *Al-Fajr* weekly (Vol. VIII, No. 357; March 20, 1987); the Hebrew press (my translations), and the invaluable bulletins of The Database Project on Palestinian Human Rights, 1 Quincy Court, Suite 1308, Chicago, IL 60604. The text of her husband, Jamal Zaqout's letter (appearing in caps), is from the Database Project.

16. "Cartoonist Naji Ali Dies in London," obituary appearing in *Al-Fajr* weekly (September 6, 1987).

17. "'No beating for beating's sake'—Rabin," by Asher Wallfish (*Jerusalem Post*, no date). Above this is "Rabin inspects wall of bloody beatings," by Joel Greenberg, one of the uprising's most vigilant reporters; and above that is a photograph of then Defense Minister Rabin "at the blood-stained wall in Ramallah."

18. Transcript of Faisal Husseini's trial in Jerusalem District Court that I made for Amnesty International, March 29, 1987.

19. From *State Terrorism at Sea*, available from the Committee Against State Terrorism at Sea, POB 20479, Jerusalem, Israel.

20. From "Appeal No. 12;" at the beginning of the uprising, a concerted effort to gather and circulate these remarkable documents in English was made by the Palestinian Center for the Study of Non-Violence; POB 20317; Occupied Jerusalem, via Israel.
21. Some of the most striking eyewitness reports of the devastating camps war in Lebanon came from Dr. Pauline Cutting, a British surgeon; "10,000 quit Rashidiyeh as siege ends," (*Jerusalem Post;* Monday, February 16, 1987); and "What Else Is Left To Eat?" (*AL-AWDAH* English Weekly; February 15, 1987).
22. Raja Shehade, *The Third Way.* London: Quartet, 1982.
23. Mahmoud Darwish, from: "Fragments from a Diary of Everyday Sadness."
24. Abu al-Ghazali, the eleventh-century Islamic theologian and mystic.
25. Abdellatif Laabi, *Rue du Retour.* (London: Readers' International, 1989), pp. 99–100.
26. Quoted from Erica Hunt in a talk given on the panel "Poetry for the Next Society: Design For Continuing Investigation," at the St. Mark's Poetry Project; May 7, 1989.
27. Tina Darragh, "Error Message," in *Poetics Journal* 5, p. 120;
28. Andrée Chedid, *The Sixth Day* (London: Serpent's Tail, 1987), pp. 141–142.
29. Michael Camber, "No Refuge," *Z Magazine* (December 1989), p. 71.
30. Interview with John Stockwell, *Z Magazine* (December 1989), p. 34.
31. This description of Cairo appears in Yitzhak Shami's "The Vengeance of the Fathers," in *8 Great Hebrew Short Novels,* edited by Alan Lelchuk and Gershon Shaked (New York: New American Library, 1983), p. 126.
32. Bernadette Mayer, *Eruditio ex Memoria* (Lenox: Angel Hair Books, 1977), unpaginated.

Exploding Identities

1. Edmond Jabès, *From the Desert to the Book: Dialogues with Marcel Cohen,* translated by Pierre Joris (Tarrytown, N.Y: Station Hill, 1990), p. 40.
2. See Mark R. Cohen's "The Neo-Lachrymose Conception of Jewish-Arab History" followed by Norman A. Stillman's "Myth, Countermyth, and Distortion" in *Tikkun,* Vol. 6, No. 3 (pp. 55–64). There is also an exchange of letters in the following issue, Vol. 6, No. 4 (pp. 96–97), entitled "Revisionist Jewish-Arab History: An Exchange."
3. Jane S. Gerber, *The Jews of Spain* (New York: Free Press, 1992), p. 279.
4. Haim Chertok, *We Are All Close: Conversations with Israeli Writers* (New York: Fordham University Press, 1989), pp. 4–5.
5. Warren Bargad and Stanley F. Chyet, *Israeli Poetry: A Contemporary Anthology* (Bloomington: Indiana University Press, 1986), p. 3.
6. Gershon Shaked, "Struggling Against the Ashkenazi Establishment," in *Modern Hebrew Literature* 10; New Series (Spring / Summer 1993), pp. 4–5.
7. Ibid., p. 6.
8. Ibid., p. 7.
9. "Rehabilitation or Libel: A Conversation Between Ya'akov Besser and Shimon Ballas," *Davar;* October 23, 1992; p. 25 [my translation].
10. Benjamin Harshav, *Language in Time of Revolution* (Berkeley: University of California Press, 1993), p. 15.

11. Ibid., p. 81.
12. Ibid., p. 82.
13. Ibid., p. 84.
14. Ibid., p. 110.
15. Ibid., p. 85.
16. Ibid., p. 166.
17. Robert Alter, *Hebrew & Modernity* (Bloomington: Indiana University Press, 1994), p. 7.
18. Ibid., pp. 42–43.
19. Shmuel Trigano, *La nouvelle question juive* (Paris: Gallimard, 1979), p. 208 [my translation].
20. Ibid., p. ix.
21. Ivan Lovrenović, *Ex tenebris: sarajevski dnevnik* (Zagreb: AGM, 1994), p. 43.
22. Ibid., p. 44. [My translation, as above].
23. See above, note 9; p. 129.
24. Erica Hunt, "Notes Towards an Oppositional Poetics," in *The Politics of Poetic Form: Poetry and Public Policy,* Charles Bernstein, ed. (New York: Roof Books, 1990), p. 200.

Speaking with Forked Tongues, or Parables of Equilibrium

1. Langston Hughes, "The Negro Speaks of Rivers," in *Selected Poems* (New York: Vintage, 1974), p. 4.
2. Yosef Ibn Chikitilla, *Gates of Light* (Jerusalem: Mossad Bialik, no date); edited by Yosef Ben Shlomo [Hebrew; 2 volumes; my translation], p. 54.
3. Linda Hayward, *Hello, House* (New York: Random House, 1988), p. 32.
4. Etel Adnan, "In the Heart of the Heart of Another Country," *Mundus Artium,* Volume 10, No. 1, 1977, p. 31.
5. Fadwa Tuqan, *A Mountainous Journey: A Poet's Autobiography* (St. Paul: Graywolf, 1990), p. 231. Translated from Arabic by Naomi Shihab Nye.
6. Assia Djebar, "A Forbidden Glimpse, A Broken Sound," translated by J. M. McDougal, in *Women and Family in the Middle East: New Voices of Change,* edited by Elizabeth Warnock Fernea (Austin: University of Texas, 1985), p. 350. Originally in Assia Djebar, *Femmes d'Alger dans leur appartement* (Paris: des femmes, 1980), pp. 167–89.
7. Fanny Howe, "The Contemporary Logos," in *Code of Signals: Recent Writings in Poetics,* edited by Michael Palmer (Berkeley: North Atlantic Books, 1983), p. 54.

Diasporas/Exiles

1. This line appears in a poem by Mony de Boully called "Beyond Memory," translated from Serbo-Croatian by Aleksander Nejgebauer in *Voices Within the Ark,* edited by Howard Schwartz and Anthony Rudolf (New York: Avon, 1980), p. 1129.
2. Albert Swissa, *The Bound* (Tel Aviv: Siman Kriya, 1990), p. 19; [my translation from Hebrew].
3. Edward Said, *After the Last Sky* (London and Boston: Faber and Faber), p. 33.
4. Mahmoud Darwish, *Memory for Forgetfulness,* translated from Arabic by Ibrahim Muhawi (Berkeley: University of California, 1995), pp. 86–87.

5. Adonis, "The Other Body," my translation from Arabic, with Kamal Boullata, in *Lusitania: For/Za Sarajevo* 5, Fall 1993 (New York), p. 95.
6. Nazim Hikmet, "Things I Didn't Know I Loved," in *Poems of Nazim Hikmet*, translated from Turkish by Randy Blasing and Mutlu Konuk (New York: Persea, 1994), p. 234.
7. This appears in Dževad Karahasan's *Sarajevo, Exodus of a City*, translated from Serbo-Croatian-Bosnian [sic] by Slobodan Drakulić (New York: Kodansha, 1994), pp. 96–97. The passage above is my translation from the original *Dnevnik Selidbe* (Zagreb: Durieux, 1993).

On the Home Front: For / Za Sarajevo

Under Siege

1. Mark Thompson, *A Paper House: The Ending of Yugoslavia* (New York: Pantheon, 1992), pp. 326–27.
2. Ibid., p. 128.
3. Ibid., p. 129.
4. Ibid., p. 330–31.
5. Ibid., p. 320.
6. Zlatko Dizdarević, *Sarajevo: A War Journal*, translated from French by Anselm Hollo, edited from the original Serbo-Croatian by Ammiel Alcalay (New York: Henry Holt, 1994), p. 167.
7. Ibid., p. 127.
8. Ibid., p. 137.
9. Ibid., p. 39.
10. Slavenka Drakulić, *The Balkan Express* (New York: Norton, 1993), p. 109.
11. *Sarajevo: A War Journal*, p. 110.

Bearing Witness

1. Roy Gutman, *A Witness to Genocide* (New York: Macmillan, 1993), p. 109.
2. Slavoj Žižek, "Caught in Another's Dream in Bosnia," in *Why Bosnia? Writings on the Balkan War*, edited by Rabia Ali and Lawrence Lifschultz (Stony Creek, CT: Pamphleteer's Press, 1993), p. 234.
3. Enes Karić, in ibid., pp. 125–26.
4. Ibid., p. 186.
5. Ibid., p. 234.
6. Ibid., p. 238–39.

European Ghosts, Bosnian Corpses

1. Dževad Karahasan, *Sarajevo, Exodus of a City*, translated from Serbo-Croatian-Bosnian [sic] by Slobodan Drakulić (New York: Kodansha, 1994), p. 75.
2. Ibid., p. 85.
3. Ivan Lovrenović, *Ex Tenebris: Sarajevski Dnevnik* (Zagreb: AGM, 1994), p. 103, [my translation from Bosnian].
4. Ibid., p. 37.

5. Ivo Banac, *Cijena Bosna* (Zagreb: Europa Danas, 1994), p. 122–23, [my translation from Croatian].
6. Noel Malcolm, *Bosnia: A Short History* (New York University Press, 1994), p. 71.
7. Ibid., p. 206.
8. Ibid., p. 208.
9. Ibid., p. 238.
10. David Rieff, *Slaughterhouse: Bosnia and the Failure of the West* (New York: Simon and Schuster, 1995), p. 182.
11. Ibid., p. 23.
12. Ibid., p. 225.
13. Aleš Debeljak, *Twilight of the Idols,* translated from Slovenian by Michael Biggins (Fredonia, New York: White Pine Press, 1994), p. 25.
14. Ibid., p. 54.

For/Za Sarajevo

1. Since this was written, Selimović's book has appeared as *Death and the Dervish,* translated by Bogdan Rakić and Stephen M. Dickey (Evanston: Northwestern University, 1996); the translation above is mine, from the original *Derviš i smrt* (Zagreb: Školska Knjiga, 1974), pp. 23–24.
2. Barbara Christian, "The Race for Theory," in *Making Face, Making Soul,* edited by Gloria Anzaldua (San Francisco: Aunt Lute, 1990), pp. 339, 343.
3. Frantz Fanon, *The Wretched of the Earth,* translated from French by Constance Farrington (New York: Grove Press, 1968), p. 210.
4. Audre Lorde, *The Black Unicorn* (New York: Norton, 1978), pp. 113–14.
5. In *Lusitania: For/Za Sarajevo* 5, Fall 1993 (New York), p. 13.

"All the time in the world . . ."

1. Quoted in Tomaž Maštnak's "A Journal of the Plague Years: Notes on European Anti-Nationalism," in *Lusitania: For/Za Sarajevo* 5, Fall 1993 (New York), p. 90.

CITY LIGHTS PUBLICATIONS